FIRST IN
THE FIELD

GAULT OF THE PATRICIAS

by

Jeffery Williams

Vanwell Publishing Limited
St. Catharines, Ontario

First published in the United Kingdom in 1995

This edition first published in Canada in 1995 by
Vanwell Publishing Ltd
1 Northrup Crescent
PO Box 2131 Stn. B
St Catharines
Ont. L2M 6P5

Canadian Cataloguing in Publication Data
Williams, Jeffery
First in the field
Includes bibliographical references and index.
ISBN 1-55068-055-2
1. Gault, A. Hamilton (Andrew Hamilton), 1882–1958.
2. Canada. Canadian Army. Princess Patricia's
Canadian Light Infantry.   3. Canada. Canadian
Army – Officers – Biography.   I. Title
FC543.G3W55   1995   356'.189'092   C95-931417-2
F1028.G3W55   1995

ISBN 1 55068 055 2

Printed in England by Redwood Books.

Ja Cotten
BGEN

2001.

FIRST IN THE FIELD

By the same author:

Princess Patricia's Canadian Light Infantry, Leo Cooper, 1972
Byng of Vimy, Leo Cooper, 1983
The Long Left Flank, Leo Cooper, 1988

TO
ANNE NATION

Anne did more than anyone to keep Hamilton Gault's
memory bright. She knew that this book was dedicated to her,
but, tragically, she died before it was published.

CONTENTS

LIST OF MAPS

Chapter 1

EARLY LIFE

In Montreal there are the poor, the rich and the Gaults

Canadian saying.

In the late summer of 1954, aboard an RCAF aircraft waiting at Montreal were veterans of Princess Patricia's Canadian Light Infantry, bound for a regimental reunion in Calgary. Most had fought in the First World War; many were decorated but none so lavishly as one of their number, George Pearkes, with his VC, DSO, MC and bar. As civilians, they had done well – bankers, politicians, industrialists and a judge. Guy Simonds, the Chief of the General Staff, had joined them as a guest.

Their Colonel-in-Chief, Lady Patricia Ramsay, was already aboard when the Founder, on two sticks but with grin unchanged, stumped through the door. Someone shouted, 'It's Hammie.'

In an instant all were on their feet and cheering, united once more under the sway of his remarkable personality.

His old Patricias knew him as a soldier – of his wounds, his legendary bravery and open-handed generosity – but little of the part he played in British politics, of his flying, his discovery of the embryonic *Luftwaffe* in the early years of Hitler's power, his work to expand the pre-war RAF, his adventures in Africa and the Canadian bush. They had heard rumours of scandal in his private life but nothing at all of its tragedies. And they had no inkling of what next he intended to do for his country.

Andrew Hamilton Gault was born into a family of 'Ulster Scots' who, like many others, escaped from economic convulsions in Ireland by emigrating to Canada. That he was brought up in a position of privilege and wealth speaks for their industry and resilience. That he became a soldier, a philanthropist and a romantic idealist is due, in some measure, to their example and the traditions of his forbears. Some of these may have been French.

1

In the sixteenth century the Gaults were one of the most influential families of the province of Tours.[1] Two sons of the family, Eustache and Jean-Baptiste, successively became bishops of Marseilles. After his death, the relics of the latter were credited with miraculous cures and there was a move to have him beatified. This tenuous link with France was, later, to grow in importance in the eyes of the Gaults of Montreal.

In 1842 Leslie Gault of Strabane saw the last edifice of his commercial empire crumble. The first to fail had been his timber business, ruined by the opening of the British market to cheaper wood from the Baltic. Plummeting prices crushed his grain trade. Then disaster struck his ships – three lost in a single storm and the cargoes of five others thrown onto a depressed market. The bank which he had opened failed and his savings vanished.

Ominously, one of the ships which foundered off the Orkneys was the *Leslie Gault*. Financed by him and built by his brothers, Archie and Henry, in St John, New Brunswick, to carry immigrants there from Londonderry, she had been the pride of his fleet. Did the loss of the ship that bore his name augur more than commercial disaster?

The canal along which his lighters had borne grain to Derry now lay empty and silent below the manicured grounds of his house. His barns bulged with unsold corn. Once the principal businessman of three counties – Tyrone, Londonderry and Donegal – and 'having filled every office of honour his fellow townsmen could confer upon him',[2] he faced a bleak future which promised little for his children, let alone the possibility of recovering even a part of his fortune.

He called on David Baird of Londonderry, one of his oldest friends, for one last favour – a passage for himself, his wife Mary and ten of their children to Canada in the barque *Marchioness of Abercorn*. Its master and mate had sailed the *Leslie Gault* and 'the family felt that the voyage would be more agreeable under their care.'[3] They sailed as summer ended.

Leslie's wife, Mary, was taken ill on the autumn day they landed at Quebec. At her insistence they went on to Montreal where they intended to spend the winter before travelling further west. Throughout the long, cold winter she showed no improvement. Spring brought hope and a lightening of spirits but no change to her condition. As summer came, the prospects of moving west diminished with each day. Then in August, 1843, disaster struck again. Leslie Gault came down with cholera and, within three days, was dead.

Her health broken, Mary Gault was ordered back to Ireland by her doctor, leaving 21-year-old Mathew in charge of the family in Montreal. Henry and John, his older brothers, were to remain in New Brunswick to become solidly established in shipbuilding at St John.

The outlook was bleak but not disastrous. Two of Mathew's sisters, Mary Anne and Catherine, were aged nineteen and sixteen, old enough to manage the household and care for the younger children. A small amount of capital remained and they still owned a 32-year leasehold on the house in Strabane.

But tragedy continued to plague the family. In 1844 Henry, the oldest brother, was drowned at sea. Less than a year later, came the news that John, too, had died.

Years later, Mathew's oldest son dryly summarized the first few years in Montreal:

> After trying for a situation without success, Mathew Hamilton commenced business and the family practised strict economy. But even that would have been insufficient if money had not arrived from the sale of property in Ireland. Then the Montreal Savings Bank failed, in which he had placed money, and he decided to purchase a farm, which could not run away.[4]

Far from robust, Mathew Hamilton Gault was not suited to the life of a farmer. At fifteen, he had been thrown from a horse, severely injuring his spine and had spent a year 'confined to a sofa'. He never completely recovered his health.[5] The immediate result was predictable: after three years hard work, the farm was abandoned as unprofitable.

Mathew began to look elsewhere for a livelihood. In 1851 he obtained the agencies of the Insurance Companies of British America and of Mutual Life of New York which soon began to prosper. Later he founded and became President of the Exchange Bank of Canada, Director of the Montreal Mortgage and Loan Company, Director of the Richelieu and Ontario Navigation Company and Managing Director of the Sun Mutual Life Insurance Company.[6]

In politics he was a Conservative, a friend of both Sir John A. Macdonald and Sir George Etienne Cartier who had played leading roles in Canadian Confederation. In 1878 he was elected to Parliament for the riding of Montreal West and remained its member until his death in 1887.

While his fortunes fluctuated, Mathew was guardian to his younger brother, Andrew Frederick, only nine when their father died. He oversaw his education at the Montreal High School and, when he was 16, found a place for him in Walter McFarlane's dry goods firm.

3

Four years later, in 1853, Andrew launched his own wholesale dry goods business, being joined later by his older brother Robert. Within a few years Gault Brothers and Company were the largest cotton wholesalers in the country. During the American Civil War they profited both by supplying the Union Armies and by trading in the world cotton markets.

In the 1870s A.F. Gault bought his first cotton mill. Eventually he owned seventeen, one being the largest in North America. He became known as the 'Cotton King of Canada' and one of the most generous benefactors of the Church of England in Canada.

His mills were typical of the time, dark and forbidding. In them he employed thousands of children; yet the sight of a beggar child in rags could move him to tears. There was no hypocrisy in this. The employment of children was universal in the textile industry and the large families of the urban poor would have starved but for the wages their children brought home.[7] Gault treated his employees well and provided them with schools, both for general education and trades training.

During one of his frequent visits to England, he met Louisa Harman who lived in Annerley, one of London's southern suburbs. In 1864 they were married.

Large families were regarded as normal at that time. A.F. Gault's parents had thirteen children, his older brother Mathew, fifteen, his sister Emily, seven. But much as he and Louisa wanted children, there were difficulties. Their first four sons were still-born, followed by another who lived for barely a month. Then Lillian, their first daughter, arrived. She was followed fifteen months later by a son who survived for only half a day. A little more than two years later Louisa miscarried a second daughter.[8]

It was no secret that Andrew Frederick longed for an heir. There is a Montreal legend that, after Gault's wife became pregnant in 1881, he prayed for a son and promised the Bishop of Montreal that if the child were a boy, he would build a theological college for the Diocese.

He and Louisa were determined that everything possible would be done to ensure a safe delivery. At the time, the most eminent gynaecologists were practising in England and it was there that 'A.F.' sent Louisa to be with her mother for the duration of her pregnancy.

There, at Margate in Kent on 18 August, 1882, a son was born and 'A.F.' kept his promise to God and his bishop. In his gratitude, he built and endowed the splendid Montreal Diocesan Theological College which stands near McGill University.

So it was that Andrew Hamilton Gault came to be born in England.

Called 'Hamilton' by his parents and family, he was 'Hammie' to his friends.

Little is known of his childhood. One photograph survives, a formal family group taken in 1890, in which Notman, that most skilled of photographers, caught something of their personalities. Hamilton at seven, dark-haired, eyes gleaming, in knickerbocker suit, Eton collar and patent leather shoes sits on a tricycle, impatient to escape.

Montreal was then the financial and commercial capital of Canada and home to a remarkable group of entrepreneurs. Their wealth was reflected in splendid mansions and the quality of their social life. Their children were educated at private schools. They travelled widely but, during most summers, evaded the smothering humidity and heat of the city by escaping to their 'cottages' on the cool lakes and rivers of Quebec. Music, the theatre and opera flourished, as did sailing, racing, polo and the hunt. With few exceptions, these magnates were of British descent. Most believed that the Québecois argot of their servants was to Parisian French as Cockney to educated English and they disdained to learn it.

In building 'Rokeby', his impressive house on Sherbrooke Street, A.F. Gault had lightened the heavy gray stone of the typical Montreal mansion with large windows and topped its roof with two fanciful crenellated towers complete with machicolations and a flagpole. From its west side, a large conservatory opened onto the gardens. A circular carriage drive surrounded the lawn and flower beds which lay between house and street. A journalist of the time wrote, 'There is a geniality – almost a vivacity – about it and a frank challenge to the taste and admiration of the passer-by. One feels instinctively that a companionable man dwells within, and warms toward him.'[9] Modern critics would be less generous.

There is no record of how the house came by its name or of any connection between the Gaults and Rokeby Park in Yorkshire.

Compared to the flexible standards of conduct of sophisticated society in London and Paris, those of Montrealers were unbending. In this milieu and under the daily influence of his deeply religious parents, young Hamilton absorbed the ideals and graces of a Victorian gentleman. He accompanied his parents to Europe and New York, and began to develop a lifetime love of travel, literature and music. He learned to ride, shoot and sail under the ablest of instructors.

But best of all for him, each July the disciplines of Rokeby were put aside when the family moved for two months to a lakeside 'cottage'. In its unspoiled woods was born Gault's love of the wilderness that was often to become a yearning which could only be assuaged by the freedom of lonely places. It was there that he learned to handle a canoe like an Indian, to swim, stalk and shoot game and to fend for himself in the woods.

When he was thirteen, in 1895, Gault entered Bishop's College School at Lennoxville, Quebec. Founded in 1836 and patterned on an English public school, the aim of BCS was to prepare young men for university. Cricket, rugby and hockey were compulsory, as was membership of the Cadet Corps. Formed during the American Civil War in 1861 as the Volunteer Rifle Company, it was (and remains) the oldest cadet corps in Canada. It has the rare distinction of having been called out on active service during the Fenian Raids of 1866.

(Little is known of Hammie's experience at Bishop's. The School's records of his attendance were lost in a fire. After A.F. Gault's death in 1903, his widow moved to England taking the family papers with her. These were inherited in due course by Hammie's nephew, Clive Benson. When he died, his widow Judith destroyed them all, depriving us of information about Hamilton's childhood and youth.)

The Cadet Corps provided Gault's first military experience and helped fire his ambition to be a soldier. Most boys at BCS were fascinated by Britain's colonial wars but usually confined their reading to newspaper and magazine accounts of dramatic events like the Jameson raid and battles in the Sudan. By the time he was fifteen Gault had read Field Marshal Lord Roberts' *41 Years in India* and books on Wellington's Peninsular campaigns. With them began a lifetime interest in the profession of arms and in international relations.

Gault had been brought up in the faith of the Anglican Church and on 16 April, 1899, after he had left BCS, he was confirmed by the Bishop of Montreal at St. George's, the family church. The following September he entered the science faculty at McGill but left at the end of the academic year to study for entrance to Oxford.

The Boer War had begun in 1899. Soon after returning to Montreal from BCS, when he was eighteen, he obtained a commission in the 5th Royal Scots, the city's most fashionable militia regiment, in which two of his cousins were already serving. Newspapers were full of the war, it was the major subject of conversation in the officers' mess, and Gault followed its progress day by day.

His father had purchased Glenbrook, a summer home 100 miles east of Montreal on the shore of Lake Memphrémagog, and a steam yacht, the *Actaea*, in which to cruise its waters.

About that time Hammie suffered an attack of typhoid fever and was

joined at Glenbrook during his convalescence by his boyhood friend
Percival Campbell. Some six years later he wrote to Campbell who was
recovering from the same disease in Paris.

Do you remember the time we were together at Glenbrook just
after my attack of typhoid? Do you know I count those days as
some of the happiest in my life. The morning we sailed around
Long Island with a light stern breeze, the boom almost scraping
the perpendicular cliffs, when the sun shone brightly in a clear
azure sky, and the foliage harmonized with everything, ranging
from deepest green to palest yellow and blood red, was especially
beautiful. Well I wish we could be there now for your convalescence. . . . Undoubtedly Europe is glorious but for gaining health
and being able to forget the worries of this life of varied vicissitudes,
give me a month at the lake with nothing near you but soul
invigorating nature.[10]

At eighteen he was an inch over six feet in height, large-boned and
lithe. Already little humour wrinkles were appearing at the corners of
his intelligent grey eyes. With dark hair and aquiline features, he was
becoming handsome – decidedly so when he appeared in the full-dress
scarlet and kilt of the Scots. Eager though he became in the early
months of 1901, there seemed little possibility of his taking part in the
distant war in Africa.

His social life was not confined to the militia. He had a circle of
friends with whom he had grown up, closest of whom was Percival
Campbell whose family owned a huge seigneury centred on an impressive *manoir* on the south shore of the St Lawrence. Amongst their other
interests was a thriving hotel business, the jewel being the Windsor in
Montreal of which A.F. Gault was a director. Hammie and his friends
often met there in the evening to play cards, talk over a drink or attend
its fashionable supper dances.

One of the social events of that year was the wedding of his sister
Lillian, now 23, to Percival Benson. Her parents were not enthusiastic
about the match – there is no record of what Hammie thought – but
when it became obvious that Lillian would not change her mind, they
went to extraordinary lengths to secure her future. The results were to
have a significant influence on Hammie's life.

Benson had been born in Australia and, as a child, had been brought
to live in England by his widowed mother. He had little if any money
of his own and was about to become a junior diplomat in the British
Foreign Service. A.F. Gault feared that, far from leading a glamorous

life in the world's major capitals, his daughter was more likely to spend years in squalid Balkan or Oriental towns. He gave his consent to the marriage on the condition that Benson give up his diplomatic career for the life of a country gentleman which he was prepared to finance. Benson agreed.

After their wedding, Lillian and Percival Benson took a lease on an estate near Taunton in Somerset and resigned themselves to a life free from financial worries, centred on their mutual love of horses.[11]

Chapter 2

THE BOER WAR

When war broke out in South Africa in 1899 sentiment among Canadians was divided along fairly predictable lines. Those of French descent were unenthusiastic about supporting a war of only indirect interest to Canada. Their views were shared by some of British ancestry but not by the majority. There was a strong imperial sentiment in the country and, particularly in the West, a feeling of kinship to the British colonists on the veldt.

Uncertain of the country's mood, the Government responded reluctantly to a British request for help by raising and despatching an infantry battalion to the Cape. When popular support for the war became more apparent, they offered a further two mounted regiments and three batteries of artillery at Canadian expense.

Other units were formed in Canada. Lord Strathcona's Horse, raised entirely in the West, was financed by the former Donald Smith, one of the builders of the CPR. Early in 1901 twelve squadrons of the South African Constabulary, recruited in Canada at British expense, sailed from Halifax.

In the following autumn a proposal by Major W. Hamilton Merritt of Toronto to recruit a further mounted regiment at British expense found its way to London and was accepted. It was to be a 'temporary corps' of the British Army, organized as an Imperial Yeomanry Regiment of four squadrons. A field hospital was also to be formed. Recruiting began across the country on 9 December, 1901.

On the following day a telegram from London informed the Canadian government that two transports were proceeding to Halifax to carry the new regiment and the 10th Field Hospital to South Africa. As they could carry 1,002 officers and men and 1,096 horses, the regiment was increased by a further two squadrons to a total of 901 officers and men.

Militia regiments were asked to nominate officers. From the 5th Royal Scots three were selected, one of them 2nd Lieutenant A.H. Gault.

Hamilton's was not an obvious name for Lt- Colonel G.W. Cameron, his commanding officer, to put forward. That he was enthusiastic, strong and fit, a good shot and a bold rider was beyond question but he had only the slightest of military qualifications and was barely nineteen. Fortunately for Gault's military ambitions, Cameron had recently returned from a year's service in South Africa where he had won a DSO for gallantry.[1] Not only was he capable of assessing the young officer's potential for active service but his recommendation carried the authority of experience.

The embryonic squadrons of the 2nd Regiment, Canadian Mounted Rifles, as the new unit was to be known, moved late in December from their recruiting areas across Canada to barracks in Halifax. There they came under the command of Lt-Colonel. T.B.D. Evans, an experienced regular officer. Major Hamilton Merritt became his energetic and outwardly loyal second-in-command. What Evans did not realize was that Merritt was burning with resentment. His was the idea of raising the regiment, he had recruited and organized several of its squadrons and considered himself not only qualified to lead them in the field but entitled to do so.

If young Gault had any illusions about the realities of military life and the limitations of his knowledge, he was soon to lose them. On 29 December he wrote to his friend, Percival Campbell:

They have placed me in E squadron with No. 3 troop. Elmsley is capt., Carruthers, senior subaltern, Marshall next; Clarkeson next; and your Uncle Bill junior sub. . . . On Thurs Clarkeson and I had to take our troops out for Rifle practice. When we had got to the station on our return journey we sent the troops off to Barracks under the senior NCO as we wanted to get back to the Hotel – we had been on duty for 10 hours. Of course the Colonel has to meet the troops without any officers and we got particular damnation from the Adjutant.

Next day, Friday, I had to march my troop to the Armoury for Kit. I managed to get there and back somehow without any breaks – the Lord be praised. On Sat. there was a Muster Parade and I poor devil had to march my troop off in front of the Colonel. Fortunately I managed it alright. You see I generally get my sergeant to do the drilling, as I'm a bit green. To-day I'm the poor devil of an Orderly Officer, all alone up here by myself, and responsible for 900 horses and 700 men. My first duties commenced this morning – I had to see that the fodder and oats were all right. Then I had to see that the 900 horses were properly watered and fed. Then I had to inspect the Canteen and men's dinner. Then the sentries and guard. Then I had to place the new picquet and guard and dismount the old one. I will soon have to attend Tattoo and again inspect the sentries, guard and prisoners and tomorrow morning I again have Stables, inspect the Huts and wash houses and also the Latrines. Then I'm off duty and have only the responsibility of my troop. So you see I am pretty busy, – a damn sight busier than I've ever been in my life before. All the officers are first class chaps especially those in our squadron, and luckily I pull well with all.

The conditions of service set out in the recruiting posters required only that men be able to ride and to shoot, adding that 'Preference would be given to men who had previous service in South Africa and to single men'. Fortunately several veterans joined, but, despite the mandatory qualifications required of a recruit, many in the ranks had barely been astride a horse before.[2] Compared to them, Gault was an experienced soldier and, tall and strong in his well-cut uniform, looked it.

There was little time for training in the two weeks before they were to board ship. Men had barely been issued with their uniforms, rifles and equipment before the horses arrived. The weather was foul – rain followed by a two-foot fall of snow. Hammie Gault was having his problems:

> Well, old socks, your uncle Bill is off on Tues. for Cape Town with about 500 men and horses. The Major [Merritt] is going with us in command.
>
> We have all been busy as H- for the last week or so, in fact since we got down. There has been nothing else for the last week but mounted parades morning and afternoon, rain or shine, and it rains here the whole time. We get up at 6 a.m. have breakfast and are in the saddle at 8 am for an officer's ride. Then at 9.15 comes the first mounted parade and it lasts until 11.45. Then we have to get our horses dry, watered, fed, bedded, and own saddlery cleaned by 12.30. Then a rush for lunch and in the saddle again at 2.15 until 4.30, and we have to be through 'Stables' by 5.30. So you see we have not much time to ourselves and we are kept hard at it for our pay.
>
> This aft. we had a mounted parade through the City of Halifax. I'm sure I did not see more than one pretty girl the whole time. Dashed if its worth it. It ought to have been in Montreal ...
>
> The other day the C.O., Adjutant and Major came up when I was drilling my troop. God knows how I did it, but I wasn't called

down. You see I get called down nearly every day by that bloody Adjutant, damn him. Fortunately I'm not the only one though, as all the subalterns get it right in the neck from him.[3]

Unfortunately for future harmony in the regiment, it was to sail to South Africa in two ships. Merritt, as second-in-command, was in charge of the squadrons carried by the transport *Manhattan*. They sailed on 14 January, 1902, into the teeth of a North Atlantic gale.

Gault told of their experiences in a letter written four weeks later:

It was rough as H- for three days after we left Halifax and my G—! My G—! how those horse lines smelt. . . . At intervals of five minutes I had to make a rush for deck and then I would cat and cat and reach and reach and rubber out to sea. Then back to Stables and then again up for another rubber. However I did not miss any duties and after a few days, when we got into the Gulf Stream, the atmosphere became warmer and the sea calmer and ever since the weather has been beautiful. I have been well and have enjoyed myself immensely.[4]

Other entertainments were organized – boxing and wrestling matches and concerts under the stars. There was plenty of time for reading and playing cards, for sitting in the sun and for simply watching the glistening sea. The main military preoccupation was caring for the horses. While their stalls were being cleaned, they were exercised by walking them around the decks which had been covered with coconut matting.

So far we have lost six horses: most of them died of colic. One horse in particular suffered awful agonies. I watched him dying for about an hour. He started by jumping out of his stall (if you have not seen the stalls you can't imagine what an impossible feat it is) and putting things generally on the rough, so that they had to chloroform him. They then put him back into his stall and strapped him up, toppled him over and practically put him in a network of ropes. Even then when he came to, he broke the ropes, and how that animal strained in his agony; it was most pitiable to see.

The next day I being Orderly Officer had to witness the post mortem. Good Lord! when the Vet ripped him open, I nearly had a fit. Several of the Tommies catted, and I nearly did, at the stench. It was found that the poor animal had died of acute peritonitis so you can imagine how he suffered.

Between you and me, although it is rank insubordination, the Major [Merritt] is a damned old fool. Honestly I never saw such an idiot. He is most impracticable, besides being cranky. All of us swear that we won't go into action under him and I hope to 'Gaud' I won't be compelled to serve much longer under him.

. . . Old McNicholl, the Govt. agent looking after the horses says that my lot are in the best condition on board, consequently I have developed a swelled head, but I feel fully repaid, as I have taken rather a lot of trouble on the nags. I have not lost a horse yet and don't think I will as they all seem very fit.[5]

The *Manhattan* called at Cape Town to take on stores and land some sick but no one was allowed ashore. She then rounded the Cape of Good Hope for Durban. Porpoises kept pace with the ship, arching through the waves, while schools of flying fish glistened fleetingly in the sunlight. After more than thirty days at sea, the troops watched silently as they passed the almost unbearably beautiful distant white houses, trees and green grass of East London and Port Elizabeth.

On 18 February they arrived at Durban where, in the heat of summer, they were greeted by a horde of small boys selling pineapples and bananas. Soon Merritt's three squadrons were aboard a ramshackle train, bound for a camp near Newcastle in the north of Natal.

A week later Colonel Evans and the remainder of the Regiment joined them, but were quarantined because of an outbreak of smallpox. Gault was delighted to discover that with them was Lt-Colonel Cameron of the 5th Royal Scots, who had joined 2nd CMR as a major after the *Manhattan* had sailed.[6]

During this time Merritt's detachment carried out the Regiment's first operational task. A squadron was sent to hold Botha's Pass whilst other units conducted a sweep to round up a Boer commando.

Merritt saw in this insignificant operation a chance to achieve his long-smouldering ambition. He proposed to the Commander-in-Chief that, since his half of the 2nd Canadian Mounted Rifles was operational and the other was not, his should become a separate regiment with him promoted to command. Lord Kitchener did not agree; Colonel Evans was furious. Later he reported that Kitchener had inspected the Regiment on 1 March and had 'found everything satisfactory'.[7]

Such politicking was of no direct concern to Gault but it confirmed his opinion of Major Merritt.

Last Fri 150 of us were ordered out to hold a pass: of course with my usual luck I couldn't go and old 'Beef' Clarkeson went. It did not matter much for the Boers broke through the block-houses and got away into another division. The only thing our boys did was to shoot at a couple of poor Kaffirs and kill a Government mule. The rest of us were ordered on trek last Mon. – heavy marching order – everybody was wild, as we were sure we were off. However we only got as far as Newcastle and the General sent us back. However, we may go any minute now and everything is in readiness.

. . . Merritt is getting madder every day. I hope to God we are not sent off under him but I suppose we will have to bow to the inevitable, as the Colonel and other half of the regiment is in quarantine.[8]

E Squadron was kept busy during the two weeks at Newcastle escorting convoys of wagons. Hauled by up to ten span of oxen or mules, these were slow-moving and awkward to handle in rough country. Gault had taken to writing joint letters to Campbell and another close friend, Douglas Mackedie:

You are both damn swine, I haven't heard from either of you for God knows how long. . . .I suppose you chaps are and have been having the Devil of a good time – tobogganing, skating, dances and everything else. Many a time I think of you two fuckers, as the Tommy would say, sitting in that old scoundrel's rooms in the Windsor sipping your Scotchs.

Last night I pictured you in the old way, lounging about with your pipes, while I, your Uncle Bill, was huddled up under my rubber sheet (7x7) with the rain pouring down, and running in little rivulets around my Wolseley bed. We have been very busy since last Mon trekking; today is Sunday. 12 o'clock Mon, orders came for us . . . to move off by 1 p.m. Well you can bet we had to hustle, but we got away in time. We trekked over to Umbana. . . . We there found out that we had to do some convoy work over some bad country, where 10 days before some Lancers had been cut up.

Next morning Reveille went at 1.30 a.m. and we were off at 2.30 – I being Advance Guard. Of course it was pitch dark and you can't imagine how difficult it was to keep the road. Half the time we were off our horses hunting for the right track. About dawn we reached our destination, Kweek Spruit, and your Uncle with his usual brilliance took up a position a mile and half beyond. No

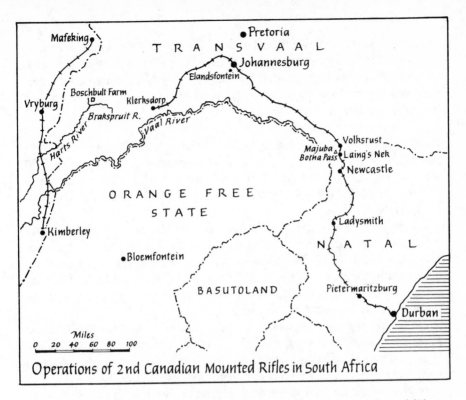

Operations of 2nd Canadian Mounted Rifles in South Africa

enemy appeared and about 2 hours afterwards the empties which we were expecting came in.

The next day we had the same work, the only exciting part of the day was when we were coming in (my troop being rear guard) some Boers hung on my right flank just out of range.[9]

While at Newcastle, the 2nd CMR learned that they were to join the division commanded by Major-General Walter Kitchener, brother of the Commander-in-Chief, which was beginning active operations in the western Transvaal. On 14 March they began a two-day ride to Volksrust via Laing's Nek and Majuba, scene of the British disaster of 1881.

Mon Dieu! but what a place for an enemy. If they had been there with a couple of guns they would have cut us all up. . . . Old 'Beef' Clarkeson, who was flank guard to the column, got fired at by mistake by one of the blockhouses; one of his men got shot through the pants. . . . We are off to Clerksdorp (sic) tonight by train. . . . They say 60,000 troops will be mobilized there to go after De la Rey. He's a damn clever chap, but I hope this time we'll get him by the pants.[10]

From Volksrust the Regiment moved by rail to Klerksdorp, 90 miles southwest of Johannesburg where Walter Kitchener assigned them to a group of columns commanded by Colonel Cookson. Three days later, serious campaigning began. Gault wrote no more letters from South Africa to his friends.

Beginning in 1899, the opening phase of the South African conflict had resembled a European war in that it was conducted by opposing field armies, organized along conventional lines. It ended with the destruction of the Boer army in October, 1900. Its character then changed completely.

Living off the country, the Boers now fought as guerrillas, raiding deeply into country which the British thought was secure. Under such resourceful leaders as Christiaan de Wet, Jan Smuts and de la Rey, their commandos struck where least expected, then vanished. For the remainder of the war, the British strove to hunt them down and separate them from their sources of food and supplies.

On taking control of operations at the end of November, 1900, Lord Kitchener organized his forces into mobile 'columns' as agile as the enemy. Their size varied but usually consisted of one or more mounted regiments with one or two pieces of artillery or machine guns.

In the following year the British began to quarter the country with lines of fortified posts connected by barbed wire fences against which the mobile columns attempted to herd the Boers. Gradually they succeeded and in March, 1902, only a few commandos remained under the resourceful General de la Rey. Klerksdorp, where the 2nd CMR were bivouacked, was at the apex of a V of two such fence lines.

As darkness fell on 23 March the Regiment left camp to meet the enemy for the first time. Gault, with his troop of E Squadron, was in the left wing of the Regiment, which, to his relief, was no longer commanded by Merritt but by his old CO, Major Cameron.

They travelled light, no greatcoats, no wagons, no ambulances. Each horse carried 6 pounds of oats, each man a half day's ration of biscuit and tinned meat and 180 rounds of ammunition. Their orders were to ride 45 miles west through enemy-frequented country and be in position on Witpoort Ridge by daybreak. There they would join other columns in a return sweep to the east.

The night was clear and moonlit as Gault's squadron moved due west at a fast trot, occasionally breaking into a gallop. The country was rolling, broken by ridges and partly covered by scrub bush. The pace was dangerous, appallingly so to men accustomed only to the risks of the hunting field. Ant holes and rabbit burrows felled several horses;

weak animals broke down. No effort was made to pick up either fallen men or horses. This was cavalry at war. They arrived on Witpoort Ridge at 3am.

Two hours later the drive to the east began, four mounted regiments in line moving at the trot. Gault saw little of the enemy; a few small groups of Boers were encountered by his regiment of which they killed or wounded four and took three prisoners with a collection of wagons, Cape carts, cattle and ponies. They had lost one man wounded and thirty horses left injured or exhausted on the road. They had ridden 80 miles in 23 hours.[11]

The action was typical of that stage of the war and, despite the small returns for the effort involved, the army reported the results as satisfactory.

A week later 2nd CMR marched with the main body of Colonel Cookson's column in a reconnaissance toward the junction of the Brakspruit and the Hart's River. The left wing under Major Cameron was escort to the baggage convoy. Hammie was acting as regimental orderly officer and rode with Colonel Evans.

About 10 am Lieutenant Casey Callaghan, commanding the Regiment's scouts, picked up the trail of some 500 men and two guns who were only a few miles ahead. The column changed direction to follow Callaghan who soon sighted the enemy. Cookson ordered Evans to hold back the CMR until Cameron came up with the convoy, while he led the rest of the column forward at the gallop. When the vanguard of sixty men caught up with the scouts, they raced to capture the guns but were stopped by a determined enemy rearguard. Beyond them the main force of Boers, 2,500 strong, were deploying to attack.

Simultaneously, to the rear, the baggage convoy came in sight, not following the road but moving across country in line abreast, with squadrons of 2nd CMR to its front and flanks. All that could be seen of it were the escorting cavalry followed by immense clouds of dust. Faced by what appeared to be a very large mounted force, the Boers held back. The delay was enough to give the outnumbered British time to prepare to meet the attack at Boschbult Farm.

As the wagons of the convoy joined them, men rushed to haul them into a laager, wired them together and began digging trenches. 200 mounted infantry were posted with two machine guns and a pom-pom 600 yards in rear of the farm. Lieutenant Bruce Carruthers with the 3rd and 4th Troops of E Squadron (the latter, Gault's troop, temporarily under command of its sergeant) had formed the rearguard of the convoy and remained near the mounted infantry as an observation post for the regiment.

The defences were far from ready when the enemy guns opened fire and dismounted riflemen began closing in on three sides of the force. For three hours the Boers concentrated a heavy fire on the British and Canadians, many of whom were hit. Their rifle fire was deadly but fortunately few of their artillery shells exploded. Several times they attempted to approach, only to be driven back by the defenders' fire.

At the height of this action Carruthers moved his men to two positions close to a detachment of 75 mounted infantry. Suddenly several hundred Boers swept down, stampeding the mounted infantry through the Canadian line. In the confusion Carruthers, assisted by his NCOs, kept control of the 20 men who were with him, dismounted them and formed a curved line to face the Boers. With no cover of any kind, they held their position until their ammunition was exhausted and 17 out of the 21 were killed or wounded.

At about 5 pm, the Boers had had enough and began to withdraw. Firing died away and during the night, the enemy vanished.[12]

There is no record of Gault's part in the battle or of his reaction when he learned of the gallantry of his men under Carruthers' command. Probably he cursed his luck in not being with them. He never forgot their example.

The Battle of Hart's River, as members of the Regiment called it (or of Boschbult Farm, to give it its official name) was the most costly fought by the Canadians in South Africa. The 2nd CMR lost 57 men, or 9% of their strength, in an action which history has forgotten. Compared to the organized slaughter of the following decade, these figures seem slight but for the men who were there they were grim enough.

By then the war in South Africa was in its final, least glamorous phase. People were tired of it. No flags and holidays marked the defensive success of the 2nd CMR at Hart's River.

For a month, beginning ten days later, Gault took part in a series of drives which finally brought the war to an end. Short of food and water and seldom resting, he and his troop formed a small segment of the line of British columns which relentlessly swept the parched countryside from Hart's River toward the Mafeking – Kimberley railway.

Ahead they could see knots of Boers on the skyline, watching for an opening through which to break. As the end came near the sweeping searchlights of armoured trains along the railway silhouetted them at night. There were no holes in the British line, no escape. On 23 May, near Vryburg, most of the commandos surrendered. The war was over.

During the next month 2nd CMR moved by stages to Elandsfontein, then to Durban where they embarked in the S.S. *Winifredian*. They arrived in Halifax on 22 July, a month before Gault's twentieth birthday.

By then Hammie, bronzed and toughened by hard campaigning, had seen enough of war to confirm his military ambitions. Colonel Evans thought enough of his performance in action to recommend him for a commission in the British regular army. Scarcely had he set foot in Montreal than he boarded ship for England where his father, having accepted that his son had no wish to enter his business, was already lobbying the War Office.

Chapter 3

THE GOOD LIFE

Andrew Frederick Gault's campaign to obtain a commission for his son in the British army reveals much about both men and their position in life. His first shot was an approach through Lord Strathcona early in July, 1902, which drew a negative response from the War Office. He then enlisted the support of Lady Aberdeen, the formidable 'governess-general' of Canada in the 1890s and Sir Charles Tupper, the former prime minister, both of whom were friends of Lord Roberts, the Commander-in-Chief of the British Army. To Lady Aberdeen, he gave a proud father's opinion of his son.

> He is a very excellent young fellow, full of military enthusiasm, is an exceptionally strong character. He is 6ft. 2 in.[sic], is a splendid horseman, very affable and agreeable, has had a good education and will, if the opportunity offers, make a splendid officer.[1]

Both wrote to Roberts[2] and 'A.F.'followed with a letter of his own:

> My old friend Sir Charles Tupper informed me that he had made application to you for a commission for my son A. Hamilton Gault. . . .
>
> He is now on his way to this country for the purpose, if possible, of securing a commission in one of the Lancer Regiments. He is a young man of excellent ability, strong and active, great will power and I think is sure to succeed in anything he undertakes. He is fired with military enthusiasm from his earliest youth and has declined an interest in my business that would in all probability give him twenty thousand dollars a year. I think he got his final convictions of military life from reading your *41 Years in India* four or five years ago.

Time would attest to the accuracy of A.F. Gault's assessment. Lord Roberts replied:

Owing to the end of the war there are a large number of officers who have been employed away from their regiments to be absorbed. . . . No more direct commissions to the cavalry can be considered.[3]

Hamilton arrived in England to be told by his father that at present he had little chance of becoming a professional soldier. There is no record of how he reacted to this shattering of his military ambitions or of what alternatives he considered. The prospect of life in the head office of a major corporation certainly held little appeal for a young man so fond of physical challenge and outdoor life.

One thing is clear, he had no intention of giving up his military interests. On returning to Montreal, he re-joined the 5th Royal Scots where he had become imbued with the colonial tradition that a gentleman's military obligation to the country was not limited to his person but extended to his purse and possessions as well.

The Canadian Militia, of which the Scots were a part, traced its origins to the formation of the French and English colonies in North America. At that time survival of a settlement could well depend on its ability to defend itself. Every man was armed and was expected to fight whenever the colony was attacked. Under the Militia Act of 1868 every able-bodied male between the ages of eighteen and sixty was a member of the militia and liable to be called out on service in an emergency. It was a provision which was never exercised but it underlay the ethos of militia service which has served the country so well in war.

Some militia units were never more than social clubs, but the 5th Royal Scots took their soldiering seriously. It was as well that they did so, for in the period when Hammie first knew and then joined them, they were twice called out in aid of the civil power. The first occasion was in October, 1900, when the regiment restored order in Valleyfield where a strike by labourers employed by a contractor on a new mill being built for 'A.F.'s' Montreal Cotton Company degenerated into a riot.

Gault joined the Royal Scots soon after, when the operation was still being re-hashed within the regiment. He soon learned that membership of the militia, with its pleasant society and obligation to defend the country, involved also a serious commitment to law and order.

On the next occasion when the Scots supported the civil power, Gault was with them. At the opening of navigation on the St. Lawrence on 28 April, 1903, troops were summoned to deal with serious rioting in the Montreal docks. Next day the 5th Royal Scots were called. The regimental history recounts that, under the command of Lieutenant-Colonel Carson, the regiment took up a position on Commissioners Street from the foot of Berri Street eastward. Here, protecting a mile and a half of the waterfront, 'the Regiment had much disagreeable duty to perform. The first day Lieut.-Colonel Carson had to advance his line several times to force the crowd back.' For two long weeks the work of guarding the area which included the CPR freight sheds and elevators continued until the difficulties between employers and men were settled.[4]

After he and Hamilton returned from England, 'A.F.' began to lose his customary vibrant energy. Within a few months, doctors diagnosed Bright's disease (acute glomerulo-nephritis). With the onset of the steaming heat of the Montreal summer, Hammie helped his mother take him to Glenbrook, their much-loved summer home on Lake Memphrémagog. There, on the evening of 6 July, 1903, he died.

In his will A.F. Gault provided generously for his wife. He had already established a trust for Hamilton and his sister Lillian by a gift of shares and securities through which they received an annual allowance. The trustee was authorized to deliver these to the children when he and Mrs Gault thought fit, those to Hamilton, 'only when he shall have attained the age of twenty-one or more.' (He was six weeks short of his majority when his father died.) In addition, Hamilton received Rokeby, Mrs Gault, Glenbrook.

The balance of the estate was placed in the hands of trustees in equal shares for Hamilton and Lillian. From it each was to be paid an allowance of $5,000 per year. Once Hamilton reached the age of thirty, the trustees might divide the full net income of the estate, less the allowance for his wife, between the children and might then deliver the capital to them, if they saw fit to do so – a provision fraught with potential problems.

A.F. Gault signed his will on 11 June, 1902, shortly before he left for England. The trustee named to control Hamilton's shares was James Rodger, the chief executive of the Gault Brothers Company, one of 'A.F.'s' oldest associates. To give him, with Hamilton's mother, control of Hamilton's allowance and the discretion as to when he should turn over control of the capital which was its source, implied that, before doing so, he would need to be convinced that the young man was capable of managing his affairs.

Hamilton Gault had inherited not only wealth but the obligations imposed by his considerable shareholdings in his father's business, about which he knew little. Any thoughts which he may have harboured about becoming a professional soldier were replaced by the need to establish himself in the world of commerce, textiles and finance and, in particular, in the eyes of James Rodger.

The weeks which followed his father's death brought a host of problems about which decisions needed to be made. In particular, would his mother move to England to be close to Lillian and her own sisters? Where would he live? What would he do?

A hint of a new interest was revealed in a letter written from Glenbrook in August, 1903, to Percy Campbell: 'Marguerite Stephens, a friend of my mother's is with us now, so that I have to help amuse her most of the time – awful bore!'

He cannot have been serious. Graceful, tall and slender, her dark hair framing wide-set eyes and full lips in an oval face, Marguerite was strikingly attractive. (Every year, she and her mother, each as elegant as the other, visited Paris and London to renew their wardrobes.) And she was good company. Noted for her vivacity and charm, she was one of the most popular young women in Montreal. Like Hammie, she loved the wilderness of Quebec and she rode beautifully. Her father was the Hon. G.W. Stephens, a wealthy former minister of the Quebec government; an older sister was married in England and two half-brothers by his first marriage were in Montreal.

In the autumn, Hammie entered The Gault Brothers Company and began to learn the business as his father had done, by selling goods in a dry goods shop. After a few months, he moved into the office as an invoice clerk. He retained his commission in the 5th Royal Scots and went out with the Montreal Hunt whenever he had the chance. But his main interest that winter was Marguerite Claire Stephens.

Within seven months of their first meeting, on 16 March, 1904, they were married, less than a year after Hammie's father's death. The wedding took place in the Stephens' ornate, flower-filled drawing room, where two white kneeling cushions had been placed beneath a floral bell suspended from an arch of roses. Only the immediate families attended. Mae Wedderburn-Wilson, Marguerite's sister, was matron of honour and George Stephens, her brother, was best man. After a short honeymoon in England the young Gaults moved into Rokeby.[5]

Hammie by now was regarded as one of the Royal Scots most able young officers. He had attended a militia staff course at Kingston[6] and in June was assigned to the staff of Colonel Gordon, the regular officer in command of the annual militia training camp as a 'galloper' or liaison officer. Khaki had not yet been adopted by the Militia which still wore the brilliant uniforms of Queen Victoria's army. Gault now gave up the kilt, the scarlet doublet and feather bonnet of the Scots for a staff officer's blue frock coat and black cocked hat.

By his presence during the week-long camp, Lord Dundonald, the controversial British general who commanded Canada's Militia, contributed no little tension to the usual relaxed and friendly atmosphere. An officer who was there suggested that Gault's military service nearly ended in anger and frustration.

He [Dundonald] was a gallant soldier but like all the Cochranes, very hasty and hot-tempered and most over-bearing to his subordinate officers. We had a big field day towards the end of the camp, and being on the staff, I was very near to the General. As he had no staff of his own with him, he naturally used Colonel Gordon's gallopers. . . .

During the course of the manoeuvres, Dundonald told Gault to instruct the Cavalry Brigadier to bring the men past at the trot. Gault duly carried the message, and the cavalry duly carried it out. But as soon as the General saw them coming at the trot he turned and yelled at Gault, ' What do you mean Sir? Did I not tell you the gallop?'

'No, Sir,' said Gault, 'you told me the trot.'

'Silence, Sir!' said the General, 'I will not have you contradict me!'

On this Colonel Gordon, who did not like to have his pet galloper reprimanded for nothing, said to the General, 'I am perfectly certain that you said the trot, Sir.'

This so put Dundonald out that he fairly sputtered with wrath. He still insisted that he had said gallop and was exceedingly rude about it. . . . Gault had brought his two best horses from Montreal at his own expense, and had gone to a good deal of trouble to help make the camp a success. He did not at all like the way in which the English commander thought it necessary to impress his importance on the Canadians.[7]

Undoubtedly Hammie was annoyed, but, having been in South Africa, he knew that 'Dundoodle' was regarded as a figure of fun by the 3rd Mounted Brigade which he commanded. Even as the incident took place, the General was involved in a row with the government which resulted in his dismissal a few days later.

Gault was not finding office work at the Excelsior Woollen Mills in Montreal much to his taste, as he told Percival Campbell:

Things have been damned slow, absolutely nothing for me to do, but come down to this B—— office and grind or sit round on my bottom and do nothing. I have only been out twice with hounds this year, which is pretty poor for me after my fourteen days of last season, but such is life.

Reg Gault has been in town for the past couple of weeks, so last Thurs a few of us went out and dined at the Kennels and had a little game. First we played 'Petit chevaux' and then poker. Mac was out and won all the money, I never saw such luck – three times on Boulter, and I the Bank. At poker Mac still kept his lead and was very much to the good until after we left the Club. Someone, less sober than the rest started breaking hats, and then it was rough house for about ten minutes. Reg came out of the melee nil hat. Then Mac and Allan Law started tossing for a new hat and continued all the way in in the car, until old Mac had lost almost all his earnings. He however finished about $10.00 to the good so it wasn't so bad. The next morning every one swore they were out anything from $5.00 to $100.00, which if true made Mac out a most horrible liar.[8]

Two months later, he wrote again:

So you are going to winter at the Riviera – you lucky swine. How I envy you in those sunny and balmy climes! I've never liked our Canadian winters very much, and as I have been shivering and cold for the past month you can imagine how your letters tantalize me. I can just see you, you dog, reclining at midday with the beautiful hot sun shining down upon you, and a little fountain playing near at hand, while the enchanting strains of a Bohemian band come softly over the balmy air, and above all to have that old and trusty friend - a Loewe – between your teeth. . . .

Do you remember the plaza at Interlaken with the band playing all morning and all the lovely women about. Didn't we have a good time there?

My thoughts of you, far away, surrounded by palm trees and beautiful scenery, has been rudely awakened by the rude crash of my telephone three inches from my head. Imagine the change; I had almost warmed myself by the thought of sunny climes conjured up in my brain by you, and to find myself shut up within the four hideous walls of my office looking out upon a yard with shouting swearing carters, and the rasping metallic sound of St. Marie punching the typewriter in the outer office ——— You talk about

Bastilles, St. Lazares, Charentons, and the old Bailey, but tell me friend, what could be more torture than the scene I have just depicted, or more of a prison than from 9 a.m. to 5 p.m. bounded by St. Helen & Recollet Sts?[9]

Six months later he was working unenthusiastically in the head office of The Gault Brothers Company. His envy of Campbell's travels was unabated. He wrote to him in London:

So you are thinking of taking the Norway trip, how delightful it will be to sail up the fjords by moonlight and watch the ever-changing landscape with its beetling crags and mantelled summits. That G— D— custom's clerk has just placed a bunch of invoices, a foot deep, at my elbow, thereby interrupting the idealistic train of my mind, and bringing me with great force from the sublime promontories and capes of the North to the always ridiculous varnish of my office desk, the various pigeon holes in front of me labelled with small insertions of cardboard, and the two ink stands, one containing black and the other red ink. Is not the jolt to say nothing of the fact, sufficient to make any man forget his self possession and make use of divers expressions to allay the burning fever? Surely, oh my countrymen, man was made not to sit within four walls, with musty papers and scribbling scribes to be his close companions, but rather to go out and battle with the world of elements![10]

In May,1906, he had news to impart. Not only had they had a royal visitor, Prince Arthur of Connaught, but Marguerite was expecting a child.

Well, we've had the Prince with us, and a very favourable impression H.R.H. has left behind him especially in the hearts of some of our fair ones. We had a dinner at St. James, which was really a pippin. . . . Personally if I had not had to attend Lady Allan's reception I would have been delighted to have remained. . . . However I remained sober and later took Marguerite and Miss Orian and Louise Hays up to Ravenscrag – what a jolly little girl Miss Louise is! Lord! I don't think I ever was in such a 'Free for all' except perhaps a public dance, but I must admit they made a brilliant affair of it – the decorations were gorgeous, and they had American Beauties [roses] all over the place (Fortu-

26

nately for Montague [Allan] they are not now at $24.00 per doz). . . .

We left rather early, as M was pretty tired and did not stop for the dances. Little Jeanne Taschereau was having the time of her life with His Royal Niblets: her big eyes were simply bubbling over with excitement and mischief. Trust a French girl for vivaciousness.

Marguerite really did not intend to go out at all before next autumn, but there was not much sense in going to one thing and not to another, so we have been taking the Horse Show in regularly thanks to our friends, as I did not get a box for this season. It is really an awfully nice and easy way of entertaining especially if you are interested in horse flesh, but it plays H— with your insides – Champagne started last Tuesday with the Prince and it has continued ever since with sundry rich dishes thrown in between the glasses. . . .

I shall be glad to have a week at the Lake to recuperate.

Gault at nearly twenty-four was learning that fast footwork was sometimes necessary in managing his investments.

The market went to pieces the beginning of last week. I woke up one morning to find myself about $5000 to the bad and a falling market with no chance to sell a block. My broker came down on me to take the stock off his hands as a favour – the brokers could hardly get money – and your little Uncle did some tall sprinting for cash. However, I got all I wanted and today I am only about $1500 to the bad and the market is strong.

His reading showed his continuing interest in military history and international affairs. He recommended that Campbell read Lord Roberts' *41 Years in India* and Wellington's Peninsular Campaigns. He commented that Henry Norman's *All the Russias* is 'most instructive'.[11]

Later that year, Hammie and Marguerite suffered the loss of their child, probably through a miscarriage for there is no record of its birth. Nor do we know if there were subsequent miscarriages but, later in their lives, there was ample evidence of their desire for children. Hamilton was never to have one of his own.

One of his few personal possessions which has survived from that time is a small cloth-bound telephone book, never used, probably a Christmas present from a child. In it are preserved eight letters in childish hands from Clive and Doris Benson, his sister's children, the earliest written about 1906.

Chapter 4

THE WILDERNESS

In the early years of the twentieth century much of Canada remained unknown to anyone but her native peoples. Unlike the medieval cartographer's 'Here be dragons', blank areas of the map offered no hint of the hazards and challenges which awaited those who might venture into uncharted wilderness.

At school Gault had studied the great explorers, Radisson, La Vérendrye, LaSalle, MacKenzie and Simon Fraser, who ranged through rivers and forests to the great plains, the mountains and the oceans beyond. Montreal had been their base and that of the fur traders and the *coureurs-de-bois* whose exploits on the trail had become legends. Like other boys of his generation, he had been absorbed by stories of the early settlers and of the Indians, the great hunters, with their mystical affinity with rivers and trees and with the birds and animals which lived in the forest. He longed to learn their bush craft and to travel their trails far from the comforts of civilization.

By 1907 his fascination with the wilderness had developed through experience, from the romantic notions of his boyhood into a love of its solitude and beauty and an almost primitive urge to meet its challenges. Marguerite, who had spent months of her childhood at the Stephens' summer home at Lac à l'Eau Claire, was almost as at home in the bush as he was. In July they set out on a month's expedition into the untamed country of central Quebec by canoe. The account of their journey which follows was based on Gault's meticulous log which he kept in a pocket note book.

From Montreal they planned to go by train to Roberval, thence by wagon to Saint-Félicien where they would pick up guides, canoes and supplies, thence to Doré where they would take to the water. Their objective was the area around Lac Mistassini, 500 kilometres north of the city of Quebec, a land of lakes and rivers, low hills and swamps, covered with spruce, poplar, birch and scrub bush. Their route would follow the Chicoubiche and Nicabau Rivers and a chain of lakes to the rough little settlement of Chibougamau, thence by Lac Wagonichi to their objective. They would return by a more easterly route via Lac File Axe, the Rivières des Canots and Chef then down the Chamouchouane to La Doré for a total distance by canoe of some 700 kilometres.

A night at a poor hotel in Roberval with the hire of rigs to carry them to St. Félicien cost Hammie what he thought was an exorbitant $21.00. On their arrival they learned that their guides had not arrived and there was no news of them.

Next day there was no message from Kurtness, the head guide, but someone opined that he might have gone down to Quebec for a few days. Hammie, 'spent the day in much uncertainty and exasperation caused by the non-appearance of the guides. Ordered paddles, poles and tump lines, so as to make a quick start as soon as the guides arrive.'

He then finished buying provisions and supplies for the trip, about 650 pounds of food of the simplest kind – beans, rolled oats, flour, tinned milk, coffee, biscuit, bacon, pork, onions, dried potatoes, prunes, figs, tea, flour, sugar and maple syrup as well as cooking gear, two tents, blankets, axes and other camp equipment. He had brought a .22 pistol, a 30.30 rifle and fishing rods and nets with which to supplement their diet.

While all this could be carried in the two canoes, when it was necessary to portage around difficult stretches of their route, some 900 pounds of gear plus the canoes would have to be carried on their backs. The guides could manage loads of up to 150 pounds each, Marguerite very little. Hammie was not sure of his capacity.

The guides finally arrived about noon next day. Gault was relieved and pleased by what he saw.

Joe Kurtness full blooded (Cree) Indian, thick set and wiry about 5 foot 9, rather full in frame and fine straight brown eyes as chief guide. Ambroise full blooded (Montagnard) Indian, typical type, thick set and full in frame, as cook. Baptiste (Montagnard), his brother in law, young man 5 foot 10, lanky build. And Joseph, Joe's brother in law, young man, mostly French blood, tall & lanky with frank straight face.

Finished buying provisions, loaded waggons and at 3 p.m. started on our way. Very heavy roads owing to last night's rain. Arrived Doré about 6 p.m. where we had a first class meal and found everything most comfortable and clean at Mac Valmorin's: contrast from Hotel Chibougamau at St. Félicien.

Found on inspection that both canoes had been slightly damaged. Pretty big load of provisions.

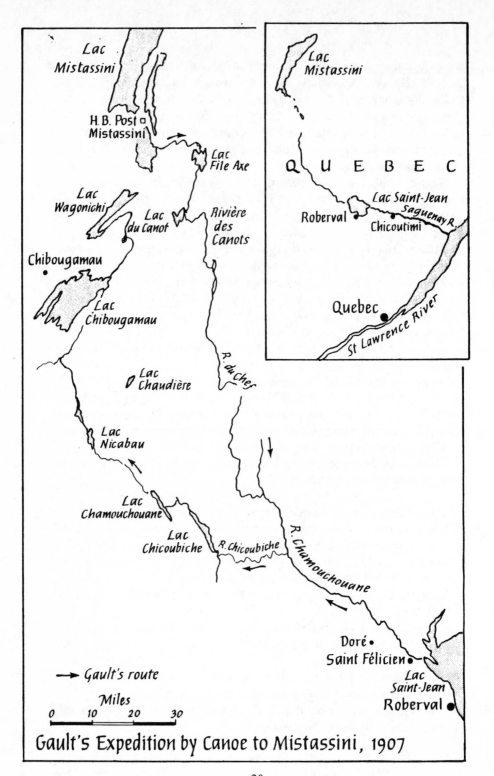

Gault's Expedition by Canoe to Mistassini, 1907

On 24 July they drove four miles, much of it very bad going through bogs and woods to Rivière Beau Trembles, where they left the rigs and took to their canoes to paddle the three miles to the Chamouchouane.

Lunched just above junction where Joe got some gum as both canoes take in water. Then proceeded up the Chamouchouane about 8 miles where we made camp on an ideal little plateau 20 ft above river. On the way up we caught 2 Doré & 1 pike which we had for supper together with bacon, bread & butter.

It rained hard the last 3 miles on the river and while we were making camp, the result being that we are all soaked. It is too bad for we have not yet got things straightened up and it would have been a great help to us to have had the first day out a fine one.

One can picture the scene – Hammie and the guides cutting birch saplings for tent poles and stripping them of their dripping branches, pitching the two simple 'A' tents, the larger for the guides, and getting their gear under cover. There were no camp beds, no sleeping bags. Hammie and Marguerite slept on the ground in wool blankets on a waterproof sheet; when it was dry, on a cushion of pine boughs. Ambroise would have started a fire which smoked and sputtered as he prepared supper.

The flies are fairly bad and like all woods flies so unsophisticated that you can kill them by the score. But why kill one poor victim when there are 20,000 ready to take his place.

Margie is in the blue canoe with Joe and Ambroise and I am in the red with Joseph & Baptiste. The guides are always joking whether it is fine or bad weather – we might take a leaf out of their book.

Last night was perfect Hades . . . You could cover up your head and even then you would find about 2000 mosquitoes to the square inch. Even Joe the head guide said they could not have been worse, and that the guides had not slept.

They were up at 5 a.m. and climbed into their wet clothes, but an hour in the warm sun dried them. That morning they tackled their first white water.

On my honour I don't see how it is possible for canoes to ascend but our fellows did it, nearly busting themselves in their efforts. Part of the way we walked along banks to lighten the load where a slip meant a sharp tumble into the river where one would probably be taken down a mile or so. The canoes have to be just so poised against the current that they hold up stream. Once our bow got turned and we were taken down a hundred yards before we could stop. Reached here [Rapide Pas de Foud] at 11 a.m.

. . . very hard going up Pas de Foud: You come to a tough bit in the rapide, the men strain at their poles, the canoe seems to stop with the force of the current, & the waters boil on each side of you so that you wonder that the canoe is not swept to Kingdom Come, the men put every effort into their poling, they encourage each other crying 'pousse, pousse la', the canoe moves an inch, two inches, three & before you realize it the difficulty is overcome and you find yourself on an elevation, a foot higher than you were a moment ago. It took us about 3 hours to get to Rivière au Crau where we caught our first ouananiche, two beauties, the fish leaping high in the air. . . .

Rain commenced shortly after leaving & within an hour we were soaked to the skin. We made camp here about 1 p.m. & there appears to be very little chance of our getting dry before to-morrow's sun. The rain is still coming down hard. I have just emptied about 4 inches of water out of my boots. Margy is as wet as the rest of us despite the waterproof which is useless in this sort of work: She is as cheery as possible – a regular brick.

July 27th Saturday. Rapide des Epinettes Blanche: Got up at 5.30 after a bad night with mosquitos to find it still raining. Managed to dry out clothes slightly before putting them on but they were still very damp. Rain let up a bit at 10 so we started on our way. Literally fought our way up the Epinettes Blanche, having to make one portage and two double loads. Lunched at Portage and almost immediately afterwards the rain started again & kept up in showers till time of writing.

Got to this place about 4 p.m. where we met Sullivan's party going south. Party has been north for past 6 or 8 months, went up in winter, received their first mail in six months last week from Johnson's outfit going north. It was one of the most picturesque sights imaginable to see the 5 canoes (about 20 men) coming down the lovely river. When we met they all landed and we had a pow-wow. They have had rain almost constantly since June 1st and have not had a chance to get dry since Monday last. The Voyageurs were garbed in coloured sweaters, scarfs & tams, faded into perfect harmony through much wear & constant exposure to the weather. When we parted we watched them round the bend in the rapid:

they made a weird spectacle in the fading light and disappeared from view in a few moments.

Our course today was between high & steep mountains with the ever swirling waters about us, and one could see the river (which is comparatively straight) winding from the hill far ahead, and the rapide breaking steeply downward. It would have made a perfect picture, though a sceptic would not have believed the detail. Margy thought a rabbit was a bear most of last night – it kept jumping up onto the tent.

July 29th Monday, Chaudière Falls: Today was my first try at packing, got on pretty well with 80 lbs at 1st portage & about a 100 lbs afterwards. It is splitting work however & after the first quarter of a mile you think you are going to die. You struggle on however, the perspiration streaming from you at every step and a hundred little devils running up the muscles of the small of your back & back of your neck. The big climb of Chaudière Portage was a bit killing.

After a week in which they had only had two fine days, frequent rapids barred their way, most of them too dangerous to be negotiated by poling the canoes upstream. Hammie now shared the heavy loads which had to be portaged around them, carrying either a canoe or a pack. On the Chicoubiche River their first portage was about half a mile up and down hill, followed by another of a mile and a quarter through swamp. At every step Hammie sank almost to his knees. By comparison, he found it almost relaxing to paddle the heavily laden canoes up the winding river through low swampland with water lilies and purple flags along its banks.

For the next four days, rain, mosquitoes, swampy portages and cold nights added discomfort to the arduous work of making their way upstream. On Lac Chamouchouane they rigged pieces of canvas on poles and sailed up the lake at four or five miles per hour. On 3 August they camped at Lac Joudains. It was cold and there were no flies to disturb their sleep.

Next morning, when Hammie put his head out of the tent, he had a shock:

Crawling across the ashes of last night's fire, 4 feet from the tent, was a snake fully four feet long and as thick as your wrist. I was too late to kill him, but after breakfast we killed 3 similar snakes of smaller size within a few feet of our tent. Apparently we were sleeping almost on top of a snake nest! Thank Heavens none of the beastly things got in our blankets. The first really fine day we have so far had – may it continue. . . .

That night, they camped beside a portage.

This morning's rising sun about 5:30 a.m. shone down the portage like a golden arrow, flanked by the black spruce, and makes the forest look like a great cathedral.

Aug. 6th. This evening I presented the guides with a cigar apiece. Joe, Joseph & Baptiste took it with as much manner as if they had been in a London dining-room, but old Ambroise, who was smoking his pipe, took up the cigar, looked at it, expectorated, threw his pipe far into the bushes, took an axe, chopped the end of it off & put the wrong end into his mouth, lit it & smoked away as happy as a king, reclining on some rocks with his head on a duffle bag & spitting away as fast as he could collect the wherewithal.

They had camped at Copper Point, a beautiful site below Paint Mountain. There they remained for the next day and paid a visit to a nearby gold claim while the guides baked bread on an old stove found at the camp and re-packed their provisions.

This evening is glorious, the birds singing in the forests, the sun's rays still on the mountains of the Divide and on Sorcier just opposite, and scarcely a breath stirring. In the far west the lake dips behind the horizon, its line only broken by a few islands. Very few mosquitoes or black flies.

Delightful as the camp was, the cold that night was so intense that they could not sleep. In the morning, while passing through some narrows, they saw a lynx swimming across the river and tried to head him off, but were too slow. 'He wagged his 3 inch stump at us a couple of times & disappeared in the forest.'

Among the lesser-known hazards for the inexperienced were the biscuits and baking powder bread produced by the guides: they were too much for Marguerite. As they left Waconichi for Lac Mistassini, she was suffering severely from indigestion. It was a gloomy day. The heights of Waconichi were wreathed in mists and they could see little of the beautiful lake, with its sheer cliffs rising from the water and its mountains at the west end. Hammie caught four toulege and shot a duck with his pistol – no mean feat.

Most impressed with Lac Mistassini which, although we are still in one of its smaller bays, gives you the idea of vastness. A good many islands on way to this point on which our camp is pitched. Tonight's sunset was weird, filling the northern heavens with an orange glow.

By the morning of 10 August Marguerite had recovered and was in better spirits. They arose at 4.30 and paddled nine miles up the lake to the Hudson's Bay Company post at the northern end. It was not a romantic sight.

Half a dozen unpainted wooden shacks and a few tents were clustered near the shore on which lay three or four canoes. Behind on a rise was the Factor's white-painted house, not much larger than one of the Indian shacks. Above it flew a red ensign with the letters HBC on the fly.

At the water's edge the entire tribe of Indians whose hovels surrounded the Post had gathered to meet them. At their head was their chief, Johnnie Bosin, wearing a white crepe band with an emerald green ribbon around his hat; Hammie thought he looked like an Irishman. After pitching their tents, they walked up to the Post to pay a formal call on the Factor, Jacob Izaroff, a Scot who, they discovered, was away fetching provisions. They left an order with his wife for some Indian work to be forwarded to them next spring.

Hammie was surprised to find that the Indians were Anglicans. A missionary from Moose Factory visited them once a year and the language spoken, other than Indian, was English, not French, as he had expected.

The Indians were short of provisions and were anxiously awaiting a shipment: Hammie and Marguerite decided to leave what food they could with them when they left in the morning. In the meantime, they gave a dozen or so children some chocolate and as a result were followed everywhere. At the Post they found Ambroise's dog, left there the previous spring, and, as there was room in the canoes, decided to take him with them.

That night, after they retired, most of the tribe came into their camp. The children circled about the Gaults' tent, whispering and keeping them awake until after 11 o'clock: the guides kept up a pow-wow with the Indians until much later. Hammie found it difficult to get them moving in the morning. They left in pouring rain, vowing never again to camp near H.B. Post Mistassini.

Their route now took them across the lake for about nine miles, followed by a series of portages as they made for File Axe Lake. All day it rained or drizzled. They camped on a narrow site by the ninth portage, their two tents being pitched within six feet of each other.

After having supper in the big tent we returned to our own to find that good old taciturn Ambroise had built a glowing fire at our tent's door, had driven in some stakes for us to dry our clothes on & had piled a huge stack of firewood within arm's reach, so that we are now seated just inside the tent enjoying the fire's warmth – good thoughtful old Ambroise.

Aug 12th. At the end of Upper Lac Du Canot, we landed at a small brule & had a great lunch of flapjacks, bacon & blueberries which Margy industriously picked. At the spot we found at least 16 bears' skulls left on stakes by the Indians. . . .Jack the dog was very good on the whole but required sundry bats on the head to keep him at the bottom of the canoe.

Aug. 13th Tuesday, Portage south of Du Canot: Drizzle off and on all day, no sun. Got up at 4 am, broke camp 5 am. Route: Down Du Canot river to Lac Bonhomme with two portages. At Lac Bonhomme, which is just a widening of the river, we stopped to visit the grave of an Indian, 'Mataba' who died some 30 years ago and who has since been styled 'Le Bonhomme' from his many good acts during his lifetime. Here we sprinkled the grave with tobacco according to Indian superstition. . . .

Today we had our first taste of running rapids. At first they were very small, but as the river grew in size they became larger and more tumultuous causing our guides to take more care (& work harder). It is most exciting & exhilarating but this is only the beginning: we are looking forward keenly to the really big rapids & Joe seems to think the Chamouchouane will be pretty bad in places on account of the unusual height of the water. Before this afternoon was over we were looking forward to the white water, the ordinary river paddling being far too tame.

Their journey now was almost entirely downstream and on the 14th, despite nine portages, they covered nearly 40 miles. Next day, after they ran into the Chamouchouane, was one of easy paddling interspersed with difficult portages and the thrill of running a succession of increasingly dangerous white water rapids.

The Horse Shoe is a bad rapide, impossible to jump, & even after the portage, pretty tough to navigate. In one place we were a little slow in crossing in front of a series of waves, which seemed to tower above us & shipped a little water. . . . The Deux Rapide is one of the prettiest spots we have so far seen. We lunched in a beautiful little sandy bay with two big rocky horns & the water tumbling in a multitude of waves just beyond.

We had a very exciting time at the Chaudière rapide, which although short is very fierce. At the end of the island within 60 feet is the whirlpool & the canoes have to turn in from the rapide into the back water between the whirlpool & the island. The waves appeared to be mountains high, and in places we could only see the heads of those in the canoe in front.

Joseph was so anxious to make the turn that he almost upset the canoe by shoving his helm hard down. Margy said his face, which is rather long, was a study, and we all had a great laugh at his expense.

After the whirlpool was passed I asked Joe what would have happened had we got into it. His answer was characteristic – 'Oh, we would all just be at the bottom, canoes and all.' But these men never make mistakes. It is the most exhilarating thing in the world this rapide jumping and Margy enjoys it immensely.

On Friday, 16 August, they raced down the river, making three portages during which Hammie carried 150 pounds on his back. Soon they were passing the occasional camp. Then the wilderness began to give way to farms and the fine agricultural land of the St John valley. By early afternoon they had reached their journey's end.

At Roberval they said goodbye to their guides and took the train to Chicoutimi. Next morning, clothed in conventional garb, they sailed down the Saguenay and arrived at Murray Bay in time for dinner.

We were glad to meet Miss Dorwin, Mabel, Muriel, Mrs. Bell & Miss Arubon, who were staying at the Hotel. After dinner the women all sat around & gossiped, Margy being right in her element after four weeks of isolation from the 'News' of the world.

By the age of twenty-seven, Gault had achieved a position of unusual prominence in business and society in Montreal, which then was Canada's main commercial and financial centre. In May, 1909, the Swedish government appointed him their Consul-General for all of British North America with the exception of British Columbia.

Disinterested opinions of his qualities are to be found in letters of Swedish officials to the Minister for Foreign Affairs in Stockholm. Magnus Clarholm, the Consul-General in New York, wrote that he had obtained Gault's agreement to accept the post only after assuring him that he would be assisted by a fully qualified consular officer to take charge of 'current matters' of the office. He added:

> Mr Gault is a member of one of Canada's richest and most distinguished families and has extensive and prominent commercial and political connections. Among others, the French, Italian, German and Norwegian consuls in Montreal, who are personally acquainted with him, have given him the very best recommendation, and I was assured that Sweden, in Mr Gault would find a most worthy representative.
>
> As Mr Gault, besides all the already mentioned advantages, gives me the impression of being an extraordinary educated, experienced and representative man and he has also promised that without any office subsidy from Sweden to provide and support worthy and suitable premises for the Consulate in some other place than where his business is located. I permit myself respectfully to recommend him as Swedish Consul General in Montreal.[1]

Most European countries which had trading links with Canada or who had supplied her with significant numbers of immigrants found they needed consular representation in the country. An inexpensive solution was to find a substantial local citizen or consul of another country to act for them in an honorary capacity. Previously the position in Montreal had been filled by the consul-general for France, M. de Loynes, under the general supervision of the Swedish consul-general in New York. On being informed of Gault's selection for the post, he commented:

> The choice of the Royal Government could not have devolved upon a more worthy person to fulfil the functions of the post. The owner of a large fortune and a beautiful residence in Montreal, M. Hamilton Gault belongs to the best society in which the distinction and charm of his manners place him in a rank of his own. Known to advantage in official circles, he is also, thanks to the importance of his business, in a position to give valuable service to Swedish interests and to impart accurate information to the Government about Canadian commerce and industry.[2]

Gault found himself responsible for duties ranging from the promotion of Sweden's trade to caring for the interests of its immigrants in Canada. Every year brought some two thousand of these through ocean ports, in addition to the seven to eight thousand people of Swedish descent who crossed the border annually from the north-western United States to take up land in the West. By 1912 their numbers reached 70,000. Particularly vulnerable and in need of protection were the six thousand labourers employed on railway construction across the country.

At the time of his appointment, Gault warned that he would be unable to hold it for more than two years and in November, 1911, he resigned. His final report, revealed the conflicting loyalties which the post entailed.

An important fact to bear in mind when Sweden's interests in this country are reviewed should be the general character of Canada, the natural resources of this country being in many respects the same as those of Sweden. Canada's enormous supply of timber, of minerals and water power, clearly indicate an industrial development analogous to that of Sweden. Canada is undoubtedly bound to become one of the leading pulp and paper manufacturing countries of the world, and everything seems to justify the great expectations entertained in connection with the full and rational exploitation of our mineral resources.

In view of the fact that the Canadian Government is anxious to promote trade with both European and Transatlantic markets, where Sweden has already interests to look after, it seems apparent that conditions here will require the Swedish Representative closely to watch the industrial development and to follow the commercial policy of expansion, reporting upon steps tending to create competition with Sweden in classes of goods abundantly produced by both Countries.

Pointing to an enormous increase in the business of the consulate during the preceding five years, he recommended that he be replaced by a full-time official of the Swedish consular service.[3]

The Swedish authorities appeared to value the work he did on their behalf but, by an oversight, he received no official thanks. A note 'Concerning a mark of favour to Consul General A. Hamilton Gault' on his file in the Foreign Office read:

Mr. Gault has ... without remuneration, in a very meritorious way taken care of the Consulate's affairs and has shown a great interest in Swedish affairs and interests in Canada. Owing to his influential position he has been able to serve our interests in many ways, and it would be very desirable to be able to count on Mr. Gault's valuable and kind support of our consular matters in the future.

At the time of his resignation, the question of a decoration for Mr. Gault came up and it was understood that one would be awarded. For some reason it appears to have been overlooked

An appropriate award would be the Knight's grade of the Royal Order of the North Star.[4]

There is no indication on the file of any action being taken, nor is there a record of an award being made. It would not be the only time that his public services went unrewarded.

During the autumn each year Gault turned from polo to hunting and racing 'over the sticks'. In 1909, while steeplechasing, he was badly injured when he and his horse fell. Only after his doctor had pronounced him fit in the new year was he able to turn toward a yet more arduous challenge.

By 1910 most of the world had been explored by European man. The only major land mass which remained unchallenged was the Antarctic. In London a syndicate had been formed to launch an expedition to the South Pole under the command of Captain Robert Falcon Scott of the Royal Navy. It would establish a base on the continent, following which its 'southern party' would cross the unforgiving terrain to the Pole.

On 21 February Gault cabled Scott, c/o The Royal Geographical Society, London: 'Very desirous to join southern party of Antarctic expedition. If application likely acceptable would leave immediately to see you.'

Four days later came a cable from Scott asking for his full particulars by mail. Gault's letter was already on the way. After outlining his education, service in South Africa and his experience in 'roughing it', in 'both winter & summer conditions in the northern parts of Canada', he ended with,

In my cable I especially mentioned that my application had reference to the southern party of the Antarctic Expedition, as I should hardly feel justified in absenting myself from my present responsibilities for so long a period unless there was a reasonable chance of my being selected to form what would to me be the great attraction of the expedition. Needless to say, however, I should be the last to press my point were it considered advisable for the success of the party that another should fill my place at the last moment.

Gault's letter was forwarded by mistake to Scott in Norway. No reply having come by 12 March, Gault cabled again, 'would be glad to run over to see you if you consider it desirable.'

Scott asked for a copy of the letter, which Gault forwarded with a covering note which reflected his eagerness. He had an important meeting in Vancouver at the end of April but could, 'run over to see you at the end of this month. The *Lusitania* sails from New York on the 30th & is due Fishguard 4th April. I could sail on the above date, have four days in London & return on the same vessel leaving Liverpool 9th proximo.

'This programme would give us an opportunity of fully discussing the matter under consideration and would leave me ample time to get to British Columbia by the end of next month.'

Gault's experience in the Canadian wilderness was extensive. He had travelled arduously in northern Quebec, hunted moose in the winter, shot Big Horn sheep in the Rockies and had learned to live by gun, snare and line as Canada's early explorers had done. What he did not appreciate was that physical and moral strengths alone were insufficient qualifications to take part in what was primarily a scientific expedition, as Scott's reply, which he received on 1 April, made plain.

As you can no doubt imagine it is necessary in selecting members for our Expedition to have regard for very special qualifications. I am afraid that your letter does not shew me that you have the necessary qualification for any of the few important positions which still remain to be filled.

With great regret. Believe me. Yours very truly, R. Scott Captain RN.

Gault turned from his disappointment over the Antarctic expedition to a project closer to home. On the south shore of the St Lawrence, east of Montreal, lay the great Seigneury Rouville, granted in 1694 to Jean-Baptiste Hertel by le Comte de Pallau et de Frontenac, Governor of New France. With the erection of a stone house in the 1750s, it became known as the Manoir Rouville.

In 1844 the fifth seigneur sold the estate to Major Thomas Edmund Campbell who renamed the Manoir after his family, of which Hammie's friend Percival was a descendant. On it he built a splendid Scottish/Elizabethan-style mansion and developed a model farm to inspire improvements in the agriculture of the region. He lived in considerable style and entertained a stream of international guests including the Prince of Wales (later King Edward VII).

In 1892 Hammie's father bought a large tract of the Campbell land, including part of Mont Saint-Hilaire, on which to build a country house. Unfortunately his daughter Lillian suffered so severely from hay fever whenever she visited Mont Saint-Hilaire that Gault sold it and built on Lake Memphrémagog.

Hamilton had known the mountain, its lake and surrounding woods since his boyhood explorations with Percival Campbell: in 1910 he learned that it might be sold. The opportunity of possessing such a wilderness so close to civilization, of being able to restore and protect it, would probably never come again. Owning it, whenever civilization gripped too tightly, an escape would be close at hand, and would be within reach of the polo, the hunt and the sailing he loved. He made an offer which, to his delight, was accepted.

Chapter 5

AFRICA

Almost every year since they were children Hammie and Marguerite had visited relatives in England, followed by extensive travels in Europe. In 1910 they spent the Christmas season with their respective mothers and sisters near Taunton and Chester, then set out for a five-month tour of Egypt and the Sudan.

The recent history of the Nile held an almost mystic fascination for Hammie. Pointing to the heart of Africa, within their lifetime it had been the route of explorers and armies. Fascinating and mysterious archeological discoveries were being made along its banks. He was familiar with Wolseley's and Kitchener's campaigns and with the history of ancient Egypt. It was not to be missed.

No record of Gault's impressions of their travels has survived, only an album of photographs without a single caption. Hardships were not apparent.

The first was taken at Gibraltar – the band of a British line regiment marching up the Rock. Then come deck games on board ship; Marguerite smoking a cigarette; a souk at Alexandria; a mosque at Cairo; the Pyramids; Marguerite, relaxed and assured, sidesaddle on a camel; the Sphinx; river boats and dhows on the Nile; Carnac; Hamilton beside a gun at Khartoum; Dervishes; the famous statue of 'Chinese' Gordon; Hammie playing polo; Marguerite, elegant in riding habit, sidesaddle on a pony; the Valley of the Kings; smiling Egyptian boys; an archaeological dig; Marguerite, graceful in flowing coat and enormous veiled hat, sidesaddle on a donkey; more deck games, then Capri.

June's heat had already begun when they returned to Montreal.

But there was another, harsher Africa, the land of the hunter, and it was to it that Gault turned for his next challenge. On 27 November, 1912, he and Marguerite left London with Percival Campbell for a big game safari in Kenya.

Next morning they arrived in Marseilles and visited the Church of St Theodore where the body of Jean-Baptiste Gault (1595–1643) lay buried, one of the two brothers who were Bishops of Marseilles and whose connection with the Gaults of Ulster was not clearly established. Hammie now owned his father's scarlet and gilt bound copy of Jean-Baptiste's biography, written in 1864 by l'Abbé Antoine Ricard. On the endpapers, unimpressed, Lillian Gault as a child had practised her signature.

Sailing on the German East African steamer *Bürgermeister*, via the Suez Canal and the Red Sea, they reached Aden at midnight on 10 December.

> Notwithstanding the hour, all went ashore to see the cable news. RPC [Percival Campbell] insisted on doing Nijinskies all the way down the Main St. & was ably assisted by MCG [Marguerite].[1]
> Before reaching Aden we held some highly successful deck sports . . . I won the cock fighting contest & got a couple of seconds. RPC & I should have carried off the wheelbarrow event together had not RPC dropped me on the deck & taken up his position on top of me which effectively put us out of the running.

Arriving at Kilindini on the 16th, they visited the old fort at Mombasa before boarding the train to Nairobi. At first impression, their compartment with its open sides and sunshade roof seemed primitive, but it rode surprisingly smoothly. For the first hour their route lay through the lush tropical vegetation of the coastal belt from which it ascended slowly into dry country covered with scrub. Though it reminded Gault of the veldt, it was a new world. At wayside stations they bought mangoes, pineapples, bananas and coconuts which they demolished at some risk to their digestions. An Indian tried to persuade them to buy two clawing, snarling lion cubs for 400 rupees.

They awoke next morning in semi-mountainous country surrounded by a park-like land literally covered with game. Crossing the Kapiti and Abbi plains, they saw thousands of hartebeest, wildebeeste, Grant's and Thompson's gazelles, impala, duiker, giraffe, monkeys and ostriches.

At Nairobi they were met by Captain O'Brien, a 'white hunter' of considerable repute, their safari manager. That evening they dined with the Cresswell-Williams to whom they had introductions from friends in Calgary.

> With the dessert, the family pets were brought in for our inspection consisting of 4 Airedales, a giant tufted heron & 2 lion cubs. The cubs were in a bad humour at having been disturbed at that late hour but suffered us to stroke them amongst much growling. One of them, I finally got more or less settled on my lap

where it remained while I finished my port. The giant heron created a diversion by hopping up onto the sideboard & almost demolishing the decanters.[2]

Two more days were taken with final arrangements, including buying four ponies and a mule. At O'Brien's suggestion, Gault bought a .45 Colt automatic 'for a tight place'. He spent the morning of the 21st inspecting the safari which later marched out, 124 strong, with much shouting, blowing of horns and banging of sticks on packs. The hunting party – the Gaults, Campbell and O'Brien – left an hour later on their ponies.

They reached their first camp about 5 p.m.

Never have I camped in such luxury. Our boys do everything for us & our tents are models of comfort & luxury, consisting of a bedroom, a bathroom & a sort of verandah under our fly extension, ground cloths everywhere.

We each have a tent, at least RPC and O'B have one apiece and MCG & I have a big one in which an army could be housed: 12ft x 10. We enjoyed a capital dinner of 5 courses & turned into comfortable beds about 10 pm.

The next day brought tragedy. Late in the afternoon one of their askaris, looking for hippo, fell into the river and had not come up. The waters were so muddy that it was impossible to see into their depths. Tali, Gault's boy, said that the askari came up only once and opined that a crocodile may have got him.

Until darkness fell, they dragged the river but could not find his body. There was nothing more they could do. It was a sad and gloomy party that returned to camp where each sent off a report to the Commissioner in Nairobi by runner.

On 23 December they camped near Chania and that afternoon Hammie with Campbell and O'Brien went out for kongoni. They spread out in a line and before they had gone a mile Hammie on the left spied a few hartebeeste downwind. He took a long detour to get to leeward of them and in doing so put up a waterbuck at about 100 yds range. He fired and missed. He pursued the buck and was able to get another shot, missing again. Later he came upon some kongoni but try as he would he could not get upwind of them. When he returned to camp he found that Percy Campbell had killed a reebuck and a kongoni.

They were now moving in sight of the slopes of Mount Kenya, with the Aberdare Mountains clearly in view to their left. As they came over a hill they surprised three duikers, one of which O'Brien killed at 30 yards range with his Colt automatic whilst it was in full flight – a remarkable shot.

After an excellent dinner they enjoyed a musical evening from the gramophone and set up a few rockets to celebrate Christmas Eve.

They arrived at Fort Hall [Muranga] in the middle of a steaming hot Christmas afternoon where they were asked for tea with the Governor. Hammie enjoyed himself.

> O'Brien & I went on afterwards to Stone's house where we had more whiskies & sodas and returned to camp in excellent condition for our Xmas dinner. On entering the mess tent we found that Percival had arranged a floral decoration which reminded us all of a baby's funeral. Surrounding the 'tribute' were numerous & beautiful presents & in this I was exceptionally lucky, getting a topping set of star sapphires - links buttons & studs – from MCG; a pen & book from RPC besides a number of frivolities. . . .
>
> The dinner was one suited to the occasion & worthy of the Ritz – caviar on toast, soup, fish cakes, duiker, partridge, plum pudding, a savoury, & nuts & raisins, washed down with champagne, port & brandy.
>
> I went to sleep over the port.

When they awoke next morning they discovered that fifteen of their porters had bolted during the night and their places had already been filled by women. They were now moving through foothills into a thickly populated Kikuyu district, past banana plantations and shambas, with frequent splendid views of the surrounding country. Many of the porters found their wives in the Kikuyu hills and pressed them into service. The safari now took on a new appearance with its unencumbered porters followed by their womenfolk laden with their loads.

But the porters were not satisfied. Three days after Christmas, at an afternoon halt, they lined up before their headman demanding a rupee per head and refusing to move until they got it. Gault drily commented in his log, 'O'Brien went in amongst them with his crop and soon cleaned them out'. After his experiences in the Boer War, he was genuinely sanguine about the ability of three white men to dominate 120 rebellious porters, but the tension resulting from the incident did nothing for Marguerite's peace of mind.

For Hammie there was no shortage of potential quarry but little luck. Riding toward the Rougai River, he spied a leopard in long grass and dismounted, but was too late for a shot. A few minutes later the leopard broke from thick cover within fifteen yards of him. Hammie was so startled that for a moment he forgot to shoot. He then got off two running shots, both of which missed. Later that day he failed to hit a Thompson's gazelle at 400 yards.

Next day he stalked an impala to within fifty yards and, to his disgust, missed an easy shot. He later found three more at close range and missed again. It then began to rain.

Returned to camp soaked through in very bad humour with myself at having missed 3 easy shots. Had bath & changed & a topping good lunch & 2 John Collins mixed for me specially by RPC. Feel much better.

Safari augmented today by 30 additional porters & twelve donkeys.

During the next two days his shooting did not improve, but with the new year his luck changed when he shot a hawk on the wing with his Colt automatic. Then, after a stalk up a nullah, he got within 500 yards of a herd of oryx and succeeded in dropping two. Later that day he stalked a herd of notate and bagged a 21-inch head.

They were now in thorn scrub which was very trying for the porters, few of whom had any kind of footwear. Hammie's knees were torn and cut. 'Magnificent view of Kenya above the clouds.'

After another missed shot next morning, to his chagrin he saw Campbell on a neighbouring ridge stalk and shoot two Grants' gazelle.

Returning to camp for lunch, he had a narrow escape. Beneath his decending foot he suddenly saw a huge puff adder. Instinctively he jumped back and killed it with his shotgun. Somewhat shaken, he arrived at camp where O'Brien confirmed that the snake's bite would have been fatal within 15 to 20 minutes. Hammie ordered a large whisky.

Apart from shooting two zebra, one for lion bait and another for food, Hammie had little luck in the next few days. After one frustrating morning he set out a target which he hit dead-centre with every shot but still his luck did not improve. His sense of frustration grew.

One day, as the safari neared their intended camp, they came upon a rhinoceros cow with her calf. They watched as the old cow came out from cover about twenty-five paces distant. For a moment she stood with lowered head as if ready to charge, then turned back into the scrub.

The sight of 120 porters all attempting to climb into the few thorn bushes when the rhino whisked her tail and appeared to be coming for us was too funny for words. One porter actually pulled one of his fellows from a branch to get his place. Sally, my boy, proudly told us in the evening that 'Cook & Ali & other boys were all in trees but I was near Memsahib with a big stick'(!!). Marguerite, however, had not laid eyes on him all day.

We all reached camp with terrible thirsts after our dry march, & the porters went for the river like mad. While we were waiting for lunch a mutiny broke out – the porters refusing to make camp, one fellow striking a head man. O'B quelled it, however, by giving the offender 25 with the triboco & by firing over the heads of the porters in river until they returned to put up the tents. Unfortunately I did not hear of it until it was over.

Tension in the safari was mounting with Hammie daily becoming more frustrated by his inability to shoot.

On the morning of 12 January the hunting party, Hammie, Marguerite, Campbell, O'Brien, with accompanying askaris and grooms, were riding through scrub country when Gault saw an impala and rode off to the right flank to get a shot. Having missed, he cast forward to rejoin the rest of the party but could find them nowhere.

After an hour and a half of fruitless looking for them, he came upon Marguerite who had been trying to find him. She said that O'Brien and Campbell had found rhino and were watching them for him. Again he could not find them. Later he discovered that they had come upon four rhino and had moved in to watch them at close quarters but had left no one on the track to direct him in the thick bush.

That evening Hammie good-humouredly went in to the mess tent to tell Campbell and O'Brien what he thought of their neglect of one of the basic rules of hunting. 'Went in to give them a cursing jolly,' as he put it.

Got into an argument with RPC over rhino proceedings. I mentioned that MCG had stated a certain thing whereupon RPC said 'That's a lie'. I asked him to retract. He refused, saying something about proving it in any court. I then lost my temper & threatened to thrash him if he did not take back his words, standing over him at the time. He took them back & I sat down to be abused personally by RPC for some ten minutes. Did not mind this & presently went to my tent, apologizing to O'B for the fracas on the way.

Just before dinner RPC came to our tent & attempted to make an explanation – the gist of it being that the blame for the whole thing was placed on MCG (the only one who acted with any intelligence in trying to find me). He then went on to abuse me personally for having insulted him. He . . . proposed to return to Nairobi at once & asked me to make the necessary arrangements to which I acquiesced. To his abuse I said nothing except to remark that he was taking full advantage of his position as guest & to say that I should act in exactly the same way if anyone made use of the word 'lie' with regard to anyone connected with me.

On the way back to camp from the afternoon's hunt next day, Hammie, 'found a good rhino at which I fired at 30 paces hitting him through the neck only. God knows what's wrong with me – I feel as if the whole of this trip were cursed with bad luck all round.'

The following afternoon Marguerite sighted rhino and signalled Hammie to join her. He started to stalk but rhino birds warned them and started them off at a run. He fired at the largest, missed, then stopped her with his next shot – a fine big cow with a twenty-inch horn.

His pleasure at the trophy was marred by Campbell's irritating presence.

As O'B's pony was laid up with sore back, the result of RPC insisting upon riding it without the usual numnah, I mentioned to RPC that I would have to mount him into Nairobi on the mule. As he demurred & again insulted me when I asked him if there was any misapprehension in his mind as to whose safari it was, & despite the fact that O'B will be unable to gallop lion until his pony's back is better, I made up my mind (influenced by the fact that O'B thought the mule might be useful to us) to let RPC have his pony.

Jan. 16. Newman's Camp – RPC left this a.m. about 7 o'clock. Regretted could not shake hands with him owing to his not having apologized to MCG.

For another month Hammie and Marguerite made a wide sweep through the country, looking for lion and buffalo. They sighted some but had no kills, their shooting being confined to killing zebra and antelope to feed the safari.

On 15 February they reached Fort Hall where they learnt of the disaster which had befallen Scott's expedition to the South Pole. The southern party, which Gault had been so eager to join, had been frozen to death on reaching their objective. Hammie was deeply affected by the news.

During the next three days Hammie sighted several buffalo, none of which he could hit. Then, on the evening of the third day, he caught a glimpse of a fine bull in the dense bush. He fired and saw nothing more, but Marguerite and an askari both declared that they had seen him drop. Light was failing and, with a number of buffalo still about, it was too dangerous to go into the bush after him. Next day the porters and askaris returned to the spot and found the bull dead. Hammie and Marguerite met them two miles from the camp, bringing in the head and skin.

They advanced upon us, their faces smeared in a composition of buffalo blood & mud, dancing & singing the weird chant of how the bull met his death, waving green branches in the air & shaking their sticks as spears. When they got up to us they stopped & Dama came up to me presented me with an olive branch & shook me warmly by the hand.

An hour later they came into camp dancing & singing, having apparently done so the whole way in. Amasie, my groom, the young scoundrel, was one of the two who carried in the head: he probably only seized the porter's place just outside the camp.

In the evening we broached our one remaining pint of phizz & after dinner our porters insisted upon giving us a ngoma for which they had been tuning up while we were dining. Each tribe danced together – Kikuyu, Kavirondos, Wagkambas & Merus – & spent most of their time in endeavouring to oust the other lot from the place of honour – two feet from our noses!

The ngoma was broken up in a couple of hours due I think purely to physical exhaustion.

Two days later they rode quietly into Nairobi.

After a few days in civilization the Gaults set off on an overnight train journey to Voi where they would enter the Serengeti Plain. On the first day, following their safari on mules, they were caught in a torrential downpour. It was 7:30 pm when they reached their camp to find that their tent had been pitched in a depression and was six inches deep in water. Having changed, Hammie carried Marguerite to the mess tent where, to their astonishment, they were presented with a hot dinner of four courses.

Next day, while Hammie was hunting, Marguerite was bitten by a scorpion and was in great pain. On his return, he treated the bite with a bread poultice which somewhat eased her suffering. The weather was hot and, even after the rain, the land was parched. Water became a problem. On 8 March Gault noted that they found some pools of dirty water sufficient for their use.

Hunting oryx and kudu during that week, Hammie's luck did not improve. 'How in the Lord's name I'm shooting like this, I don't know.' O'Brien loaned him one of his platinum foresights which was a bit higher than his own. Next day, while out with Marguerite, he dropped an oryx at 400 yards.

On the 14th he observed testily, 'MCG being very late, kept the safari from starting until 7:30 am.' The ticks were very bad and he picked twenty-seven off his breeches. The following morning a ten foot snake crossed his path; he disliked them. The 16th was their ninth wedding anniversary. 'MCG & I wished each other luck & M. presented me with a black silk cigar case to commemorate our anniversary – MCG drew blank.' This was not proving to be her best holiday.

On 17 March Gault shot his first lion. That afternoon the skin arrived in camp 'amidst much singing and dancing. Stretched out it measured (tip to tip) 10'8" which would be about 9'6" in the living.' Next day he followed it with a lioness.

Five days later they returned to Voi, intending to travel by rail to Athi River, near Nairobi. There was no room on the passenger train. After enduring an overnight trip on a slow freight, Marguerite announced that she had had enough; she was afraid of the ever-present ticks and was going back to Nairobi.

Having seen her depart, Gault borrowed O'Brien's 318 Westley Richards and from that moment his hunting luck changed. For two days he walked miles shooting kudu, oryx and lion, then rode into Athi River where he caught a goods train into Nairobi. The final entry in the log reads:

> After some difficulty, I got a rickshaw & arrived at the Norfolk at midnight to find the place in darkness & no one about. After an hour's search I found our rooms & wasn't long in getting to bed.
> Here ends our safari of 1913.

Hammie returned from Africa with a collection of trophies which many would have envied, including the major targets of lion, rhino and buffalo. He had seen its beauty and variety, a different wilderness rich in game, and had learned the hunting skills of its people.

Yet it had not been a success. An askari had been lost in a river, a cheerful porter had died of dysentery. Hammie the perfectionist, an undoubted marksman, had not shot well and had been outperformed by Campbell and O'Brien. His friend since boyhood had left in anger and his wife had abandoned the safari.

Perhaps Hammie felt guilty at exposing her to hardships she could not bear. Yet her excuse of a fear of ticks is suspect, as anyone who has endured the mosquitoes and black flies of the Quebec bush, as she had done, can testify. She was physically tough. But there were other strains. The African bush is not the Canadian wilderness which to Hammie and Marguerite was a friendly refuge. It harbours unknown dangers – snakes, a charging buffalo – which engender a constant sense of menace. The porters, impassive, unknowable, were unreliable – at what point would they turn on the hunters?

To attempt to join a polar expedition, to take more than five months away from his business for a safari suggests that, apart from a craving for adventure, Hammie was dissatisfied with his daily life. For days at a time he was unable to hit the easiest of targets and his log reflects his frustration over that. He cannot have been the easiest of company in the isolation of a safari camp. In that atmosphere his forgetting their ninth wedding anniversary was a major error. The tension between him and Marguerite became palpable.

And then there was Percival Campbell. His extravagant reaction to Hammie's 'cursing jolly' after the rhino incident, the self-righteousness of his attempt to blame Marguerite, the length and intensity of his verbal abuse of Hammie did not conform to the behaviour of an Edwardian gentleman. Hammie had been disgusted and very angry. Yet within a year or two they again were friends. In the light of Campbell's sexual orientation which later became apparent, it smacked of green-eyed jealousy of Marguerite.

Later still, 1913 was seen as the year when the Gaults' marriage began to deteriorate.

Did Hammie come to believe that Marguerite had lied as Campbell claimed? Was there more behind her leaving the safari in the Serengeti than is recorded in Hammie's log? Did something else happen? We do not know.

Chapter 6

THE ESTABLISHED ORDER

As Gault approached his thirtieth birthday and full control of his inheritance, one can sense an underlying discontent. Though he had risen to a succession of physical challenges, he had achieved little but victories over himself. His position in business he owed to his father and while he was gifted with undoubted administrative ability, he had not shown the entrepreneurial spirit and driving ambition for commercial success which had marked his father's career.

For him true fulfilment could probably only be found in heroic achievement – climbing an Everest, reaching a Pole, defeating the King's enemies. Coupled with this was a sense of his own destiny, the position of his family, and the duties and responsibilities which wealth and his position in society had laid upon him. He had a highly developed sense of *noblesse oblige*.

Even in the midst of such a wealthy society as Montreal's, the financial achievements of his family were unique. A current saying summed them up as, 'In Montreal there are the poor and the rich and the Gaults'. It was significant that they were known as much for their philanthropy as their wealth. They were patriotic and believed that every gentleman had a military obligation to his country. By 1911 three of them, one a lieutenant-colonel, were serving in his regiment, The Royal Highlanders of Canada (Black Watch), as the 5th Royal Scots had now become.

Hamilton Gault had a proper conceit of himself, coupled with dynastic ambitions. On returning from the Sudan in 1911 he called at the Herald's College to ascertain if he was entitled to adopt the arms and crest which were used by some of his family. The York Herald's reply was disconcerting. He had been unable to find any record of Arms for anyone named Gault. Those which Hammie had shown him closely resembled those of 'Hawker of co. Wills' and the Crest, that of 'Tounley'. He added that Gault clearly ought to have a proper Grant of Arms for himself and his family.[1]

He later wrote that, if he wished to apply for Arms, Gault should provide the Herald with the names in full of himself and his father, upon receipt of which, he would prepare a Memorial to the Earl Marshal, who in turn would issue a Warrant to the York Herald to assign Arms and Crest. When their design was settled, a Patent would be prepared. The fee would amount to £76/10/.[2]

Gault waited until he arrived in England at the end of November to forward a letter with the signed memorial and fee and to arrange for an appointment with the Herald. He must have been mystified by the reply:

> Both Arms and Crest as used by your family appear already on record here and the enclosed sketch indicates the nearest approximation to the designs which the College is able to agree to in order to avoid interference with existing rights.[3]

The Arms were duly granted and Gault's writing paper thereafter bore a crest, a hawk above a motto which acknowledged his good fortune, 'Deo Gratias'.[4]

Under the terms of his father's will, Gault would not assume control of his fortune from the trustees until 18 August, 1912, his 30th birthday and then only if they were satisfied that he was competent to exercise it. His sister Lillian's share would continue to be administered by the trustees.

Until that time the companies in which the estate held a major shareholding were controlled, not by him, but by the trustees. These were James Rodger, the chief executive of The Gault Brothers Company, and Henry Belfrage Picken and Stanley Herbert McDowell, respectively the Company's accountant and secretary. Not only were they trustees, they were Hamilton Gault's employers. They were well placed to assess both his character and his commercial and financial ability.

In the event the trustees were willing to pay over Gault's share on his thirtieth birthday and to render an account of their trusteeship, but the method of dividing the estate had not been specified in his father's will. Should it be in money terms alone or should Hamilton and Lillian receive half of every block of shares and bonds? Should all the shares, and the resulting control, for example, of Gault Realties Limited be given to Hamilton with an equivalent in another company to Lillian or should the shares be divided evenly with Lillian, resulting in problems of control.?

Not only were the trustees faced with a difficult problem; if the beneficiaries did not like their decision, it could be challenged in the courts. Eventually it was agreed that Hamilton should bring a 'friendly' action against them to obtain a judicial decision. The courts appointed valuers in October, 1912, who determined that the estate was worth $2,615,776.70. The case was heard in May,1913, but to Gault's frustration, he learned that a decision could not be expected for more than a year.[5]

With the shares which had come to him on his 21st birthday, the value of his securities would amount to some one and a half million dollars. Add to them 'Rokeby' and the estate of Mont St. Hilaire, and his total assets would amount to about $1,750,000 or ten times that in 1990's money.

Apart from that, Marguerite received $6,000 a year from her father's estate, sufficient to indulge her taste for clothes and to enable her to avoid bothering Hammie for trifles.

Apparently Rodger and his fellow trustees were satisfied with Gault's business ability: they appointed him President of Gault Brothers and to directorships in Montreal Cotton, the Van Allen Company, the Trent Valley Woollen Company, Crescent Manufacturing, Gault Brothers (Winnipeg) and Gault Brothers (Vancouver) Limited.

His clubs showed the range of some his interests. He was President of the Montreal Polo Club and a member of the Mount Royal, St. James's, Montreal Hunt, Montreal Jockey, Montreal Racquet and Royal St. Lawrence Yacht Clubs and of the Canadian Club and the York Club of Toronto.

Though Hammie was widely respected for his strength of character and generosity, and was becoming increasingly influential in Montreal's business community, some of its older members thought that his devotion to sport, his lengthy absences on 'frivolous' activities, his social life and even his engaging personality were inconsistent with the dignity and position of a man of substance. Others in Montreal were jealous of the ease with which he and and his wife moved in a Society at whose pinnacle was the Governor-General, since October, 1911, Queen Victoria's grandson and uncle to the King, the Duke of Connaught.

When the Duke and Duchess made their first vice-regal visit to Montreal in December,1911, the Gaults were among those who accompanied them to hear *La Bohème*. They were not strangers – the Connaughts had stayed with Marguerite's parents during their Canadian tour of 1890.[6] Further evidence of their easy relationship is a photograph taken at an R.S.P.C.A. gymkhana in 1912, in which Hammie took part. Marguerite, relaxed and elegant, is chatting animatedly with the Duke who enjoyed the company of attractive women.

Almost automatically, they became members of a small Government House set of friends of Princess Patricia, the Duke's younger daughter, and the members of his Household whom they often joined in private parties in Ottawa.

Being its senior field marshal, the Duke had chosen his personal staff from the most promising officers of the British Army. Since they would be living in his house, he ensured that they would be not merely competent but good company. With his beautiful daughter, they made a uniquely amusing and attractive group.

It was no secret among that circle that the Princess was deeply in love with the Duke's naval ADC, Lieutenant-Commander Alexander Ramsay, RN, and that there was little likelihood of the King agreeing to their marriage.[7] They refused to allow that prospect to depress them or their friends.

Gault found that he had much in common with Lieutenant-Colonel Francis Farquhar, the Military Secretary, a Coldstream Guardsman who had won a DSO in the Boer War. Following two years as an intelligence officer in Somaliland, he had served on the General Staff at the War Office until coming to Canada in 1913. Blessed with personal charm and a witty and attractive wife, he was very good company. Hammie and he soon discovered that they shared an interest in international and military affairs and a lively concern over the dangerous manoeuvering of the over-armed and bellicose leaders of Europe.

To the thoughtful, a confrontation with Germany seemed inevitable, though its nature was difficult to predict. The Duke of Connaught, a much more competent and influential soldier than is popularly realized, ensured that, through his Military Secretary, he was kept informed of developments in the deteriorating situation. Having come from the War Office General Staff, Farquhar was familiar with Whitehall thinking concerning the relative strengths and capabilities of the probable belligerents, British reactions to possible hostile events and the likely course of a conflict – knowledge which he perforce kept current through his duties as the Duke's staff officer. And as such, he was a link in the chain of official correspondence on military policy between the British and Canadian Governments.

Stimulated by Farquhar's wide professional knowledge and incisive mind, Gault was able to bring his own ideas about Canada's role in a European conflict into clearer focus.

Typical of the light-hearted entertainments at Rideau Hall to which Hammie and Marguerite were invited was a skating party organized by Princess Patricia in February, 1914. Her enthusiasm for winter sports was shared by her family and, perforce, by the rest of the household.

She became an expert and graceful skater, and in a time before skiing was popular, often trekked for long distances on snowshoes in the Gatineau hills.

The Gaults were house guests at Rideau Hall for the party which took place on a bitterly cold evening with the temperature at nine degrees below zero Fahrenheit. The Governor-General and the younger members of his household, in colourful costumes, opened the party by dancing a quadrille.

The men wore white sweaters with habitant sashes, polo breeches, blue puttees and red toques. The Princess and two of the ladies-in-waiting were in white-velvet dresses with swansdown tunics and caps, each with a different colour sash.

Next morning they were photographed with their guests in front of the skating hut in the grounds of Rideau Hall. Typically when being photographed at that time, no one was smiling but Marguerite and Hamilton Gault, both soberly dressed and wearing skates, appear strangely solemn beside their cheerfully dressed hosts.

They had now been married for ten years and had reached a crisis in their relationship.[8] It became manifest during their African safari but there were other possible causes. Both wanted children but none was born. Or it may have been jealousy – 'Marguerite attracted men like bees to honey'[9] and she was later to accuse Hammie of being unfaithful.

Gault remained easily distracted from business life. With the warmth of spring in 1914, he went fishing for a few days with his friend Walter Gow of Toronto, then turned once more to polo and to sailing on the St Lawrence.

In June the assassination of the Archduke Ferdinand of Austria in distant Sarajevo caused a flurry of speculation in the press which subsided with the onset of summer's heat. Then, on 23 July, an Austrian ultimatum to Serbia, followed two days later by the mobilization of her forces, warned the world that a serious crisis was developing in Europe.

Chapter 7

THE REGIMENT

In Canada the possibility of a war in Europe had long been anticipated and the prevailing sentiment was to support Britain if it should occur. In 1910 Sir Wilfrid Laurier declared, 'When Britain is at war, Canada is at war', a sentiment echoed by the Leader of the Opposition. In 1912 Sam Hughes, the Minister of Militia and Defence, was more belligerent. 'Germany needs to be taught the lesson that Canada and the other Dominions are behind the Mother Country.'

Canada's defence plans had been coordinated with those of other countries of the British Empire through the Committee of Imperial Defence in London. There were two mobilization schemes, one to fit in with the overall Empire defence plan, the second to provide an infantry division and a cavalry brigade for service in Europe if, as was widely assumed, Germany intended to attack France by way of Belgium. They had been in the hands of military districts since 1911. Defence spending in that year was seven and a half million dollars; by 1913 it had increased to eleven million. A 'War Book' was prepared for each of the major government departments which outlined the action to be taken on the outbreak of hostilities.

Groups of senior Canadian officers attended British, German, French and Swiss army manoeuvres in 1912–13. In the early summer of 1914 10,339 men and 4,553 horses of the Militia assembled at Camp Petawawa for the largest military exercises ever held in Canada. In the minds of those who attended there was little doubt as to who their likely enemy would be. Unfortunately their military ardour was not matched by their training or experience. Canada's armed forces were all known as 'Militia' but only a tiny proportion were full-time professionals.

In the week which followed Austria's mobilization peace in Europe died. Each day Canadians looked for the news from London. As it worsened, so grew the possibility that they themselves would be involved.

In Ottawa the crisis in Europe found Parliament in recess and cabinet ministers dispersed. The Governor-General, with several of his household, was in Banff, while at Rideau Hall Francis Farquhar kept open the channel of communications between the Canadian and British governments.

On 29 July the 'precautionary stage' of preparation for war was ordered in Britain, and Canada conformed. On the 30th the country was informed that, in the event of war, an expeditionary force of some 25,000 would be raised to fight in Europe. Next day the press carried reports that two Militia regiments had volunteered to a man for overseas service.[1]

As the crisis developed, Hamilton Gault considered what he should do: if war came, he was determined to take part. He was a captain in the Reserve of Officers of the Black Watch, a position which did not ensure a fighting role from the outset of hostilities. He was well aware of two widely-held military views, that a conflict in Europe would be of such violence that it could not be sustained for long, and that the Militia's lack of preparedness was such that it was unlikely that any Canadians would be ready in time to take part in the battle.

At some point in the week of 27 July he made up his mind. It seemed to him that the best prospect of getting to the war on time would be for him to raise a regiment of irregular cavalry at his own expense for service with the British Army. A precedent was to be seen in Lord Strathcona's Horse, formed in 1899. To Gault, the tactics which they used in South Africa would be particularly effective against the traditional techniques of most European cavalry.

Having decided that he could afford the cost, he discussed his ideas with several experienced officers and found them eager to join if their own units were not mobilized.

On Saturday, 1 August, he wired Sam Hughes, the Minister of Militia and Defence, for an appointment. Next day came a reply '. . . minister absent expected here tomorrow think you could see him.'[2]. Gault was on the first train on Monday morning.

During an interval in a conference on Canada's contribution to the impending war, Gault put his proposal to Hughes. The impetuous Minister welcomed the idea and assured him that the government would consider it. He thought, though, that there was a more urgent need for infantry than cavalry. Gault readily agreed to change the plan if this proved to be the case.

During the day news came that Germany had declared war on France and that Britain had mobilized. Before returning to Montreal Gault saw Francis Farquhar who had heard of his proposal from Hughes. Farquhar was enthusiastic and promised all possible support.

For all that, Gault was aware that his offer was far from being accepted officially. Any prior publicity might be interpreted as self-seeking and could well prejudice its success.

Next day, 4 August, Britain declared war on Germany. At home in Montreal Gault was horrified to learn that the Toronto *Mail & Empire* had carried a story that he was about to raise 'Gault's Light Infantry'. A telegram to the Minister brought the reply, 'Regret conversation overheard and not understood to be confidential.' It was the first indication that Gault and his regiment would do well to be wary in their dealings with Sam Hughes.

Next morning came a wire from Francis Farquhar, 'Come up at once. Stay with me if you can. Have got idea.'

By the time Gault arrived Farquhar was able to tell him that it looked very much as if his proposal would be accepted by the Canadian government. The main stumbling block was that Canada needed every trained officer and man of the Militia for the considerable force which she now proposed to send to Europe. That source would be denied to the new regiment. On the other hand there were thousands of former soldiers of the British Regular Army and veterans of the Boer War in Canada. If they were recruited, they would need only a minimum of training and could be in the field within weeks.

Gault was seeing a different Farquhar. The relaxed and urbane Military Secretary had become the decisive and enthusiastic soldier, impelled by the classic military imperative to join the battle. His was no immature wish to arrive before the chance of glory had passed: he knew how desperate was the race now starting on the Continent. While victory might go to him who concentrates his power with the greatest speed, in the case of Britain and France, failure to do so would lead to inevitable defeat.

Farquhar had outlined his ideas on paper.

THE PROJECT

1. The raising of two double companies, organized as a self-contained half battalion, strength all ranks 500 men.

2. Recruiting.
   The scheme of recruiting not in any degree to clash with the Militia, my object being to make use of the many men now in Canada who have seen service and who are not at present enlisted in any unit. These men should shake down quickly.

3. Sources of Recruiting.
   (a) Police forces such as the CPR, Toronto and Winnipeg police, etc.
   (b) Various veterans' societies or associations.
   (c) Advertisement in papers.

4. Qualifications.
   (a) Having seen active service (?)
   (b) Age 35 or less.
   (c) Physically fit.
   (d) Ex-Regular soldiers to have at least a 'fair' character certificate. Other recruits to have an analogous 'character'.
   (e) Any man drawn from the Militia to produce written permission to enlist from the O.C. his Militia Battalion.

Whatever its merits, the plan's success would depend upon the ability and drive of the officer chosen to command. When making his offer to Hughes, Gault had in mind several experienced officers of the Militia who might be prepared to join, but now it was unlikely that any of them would be available. Fortunately Farquhar himself volunteered.

Gault liked Frank Farquhar and was impressed by his intelligence and knowledge of military affairs. A mature Coldstream Guards lieutenant-colonel – an experienced campaigner decorated for bravery – would be an ideal choice to command a battalion of ex-Regulars. Gault was delighted.

The two men discussed arrangements far into the night, one subject being the regiment's name. Gault had thought of 'Light Horse' for his mounted unit and now proposed 'Light Infantry' as having 'an irregular tang to it'. Farquhar suggested they ask Princess Patricia if it might be called after her. At the foot of the notes Gault made that evening appear the words, 'Princess Patricia's Own Canadian Light Infantry'. They would have to seek the Duke of Connaught's agreement to associate his daughter with the project and to release Farquhar from his duties.

Early next morning Farquhar obtained the Duke's approval in principle. Later they were joined by Gault and Princess Patricia in a meeting which tied her name to a venture which would carry it into history.[3]

That day the Canadian Government agreed to accept Gault's offer and to cooperate with him in raising and sending to the front a full battalion of infantry for service with the British Expeditionary Force. They cabled the War Office for authority to raise it.

Nothing could be done officially until this was received, but the organizational arrangements were agreed. Farquhar would command with Gault as senior major and second-in-command. From the Duke's staff, Captain H.C. Buller of the Rifle Brigade would be adjutant. Gault got in touch with several officers who might join. Colonel Richard Turner, VC, DSO of the reserve of officers, invited to command a company, wired, 'Delighted . . .'.[4] (Two days later, he was appointed to command a brigade of the Canadian Expeditionary Force).

The press leak in the Toronto paper produced a stream of telegrams and letters at Rokeby. A telegram from Lord Grey, the former Governor-General, in London said simply, 'Well done. Bravo.' Another was from an old friend, Donald Cameron, who sympathized over the premature disclosure of Gault's offer and volunteered his services. Particularly valued were his sister Lillian's warm congratulations written from Falmouth. Percy Benson had been called out with the Territorials, a brother-in-law was commanding an infantry battalion and another with a nephew was already at sea with the Navy.

On the 7th, unaware that Gault intended to serve with the Patricias himself, Colonel John Carson of the Canadian Grenadier Guards wired him in Ottawa with the offer of a majority in the battalion which was being enrolled for overseas service.

Next day, with the arrival of the British Government's authority to raise and equip the battalion, Gault settled the financial arrangements with Colonel Fiset, the Deputy Minister of Militia and Defence.

On the 10th Sam Hughes, on behalf of the Canadian Government, and Gault signed the agreement which became the 'regimental charter'. It authorized, 'with the approval of the Imperial Government' the raising of Princess Patricia's Canadian Light Infantry to full war establishment 'with overseas base and depot in Canada'. It provided for the issue of its complete war equipment, free transportation of recruits, the establishment of a mobilization camp at Lansdowne Park in Ottawa, that all ranks would be on Canadian rates of pay and that the arrangements would continue 'until the discharge of the Officers and Men after the return of the Battalion to Canada'.

(In Britain and Canada infantrymen belong to a 'regiment' which may consist of one or more 'battalions', the basic fighting unit. Since the new regiment, Princess Patricia's Canadian Light Infantry, consisted of only one battalion, both the terms were commonly used, in a non-technical sense, to refer to it.)

One clause of the charter established Gault's financial commitment. 'As regards the expense entailed in raising, clothing, equipping, pay, transportation, feeding, maintenance and all other expenditure connected with this Battalion in and out of Canada, the sum of one hundred thousand dollars will be provided by Captain Hamilton Gault of Montreal. The remainder will be defrayed by the Department of Militia and Defence for Canada.'

The cost of equipping the Battalion was $99,043.56, in 1995 terms more than a million dollars.[5]

The agreement was unique in that it provided for a regiment that would serve with the British Army yet not belong to it. While the costs of raising and maintaining it would be met by Gault and the Canadian Government, it was not clear that the regiment was part of either the Canadian Militia or the Canadian Expeditionary Force. There was mention of a depot in Canada but no specific provision for it, nor for the supply of reinforcements to maintain the battalion at full strength.

After ten days of conception, planning and commitment came action. The day the Charter was signed Farquhar enlisted the help of local citizens in forming recruiting stations in Montreal, Toronto, Winnipeg, Calgary and Edmonton. Next day, the 11th, the first recruiting posters appeared. Their design reflected Gault's conception of his place in the project.

The first proof supplied by the printer contained the line 'Raised by Hamilton Gault, Esq.' in letters only slightly smaller than the regiment's name. The next, 'Commanded by Lt.-Col. F. Farquhar, D.S.O.,' was in smaller type. Gault amended it to give prominence to his commander and reduce the line with his own name to the smallest on the poster.

While Captain 'Teta' Buller, the adjutant, organized a headquarters at Lansdowne Park, Gault travelled to Toronto to see the Chief of Police and the Army and Navy Veterans Association. As a result of their cooperation, four days later a full company led by a stalwart guardsman, Sergeant-Major Fraser, arrived in Ottawa.

Along with a stream of congratulatory letters, Gault received many pleas from personal friends and from members of his old troop in the 2nd CMR to join the new regiment. One which gave him particular pleasure was from Joe Kurtness, his guide to Mistassini: 'Just read of your organization of regiment to go to the front. Have acted as colour sergeant at last year's camp. Would like to join you with two other Indians.'

Recruits poured into Ottawa from all over the country, though the majority were from the West where many veteran soldiers had sought a new life after leaving the army. Now they were 'prospectors, trappers, guides, cow-punchers, prize-fighters, farmers, professional and business men, above all old soldiers . . . The PPCLI recruits were responsible for many a story of these days when men drove to the nearest station, hitched their horses to a convenient post and vanished eastward.'[6]

A particularly colourful group were 'The Legion of Frontiersmen', largely from Saskatchewan. Dressed in a uniform of cowboy hats, khaki shirts and neckerchiefs, many of them were South African war veterans. A group of them in Moose Jaw, hearing that the PPCLI contingent from Calgary would be passing through Regina, wired Gault for authority to join the train, though it was obvious he could not reply in time. They persuaded an American C.P.R. employee, 'Smoke' Thompson, to place two coaches on a siding close to its junction with the main line. When the train from the West arrived, they bluffed the night operator at the Regina station that official arrangements had been made to hitch their carriages to it.

The train conductor was less willing to cooperate. A drawn Smith & Wesson persuaded him to take them to the next divisional point. There they again were obliged to convince a new conductor to allow them to proceed. At Winnipeg a telegram from Gault guaranteed their transportation to Ottawa. As a reward for his help, Smoke Thompson, who had had no military experience, was allowed to join the regiment.[7]

The Edmonton Pipe Band, in full Highland dress and wearing the Hunting Stewart tartan, announced on arrival that they had come to play the Regiment to France and back.[8]

In ten days recruiting was complete. The 1098 officers and men were chosen by Farquhar himself who interviewed each of the nearly 3,000 applicants. 1,049 of them had had previous military service. Every regiment but one of the British Regular Army (which that was is not recorded) was represented as well as the Navy and the Royal Marines. Fewer than ten per cent had been born in Canada.

Of the officers, most captains and majors were former British regulars, others had experience of active service. Unable to draw on the militia for junior officers, Farquhar was obliged to accept several who had had little or no experience. One such was Talbot Papineau, an old friend of Hammie's, a descendant of the leader of the Rebellion of 1837 and cousin of Henri Bourassa, the arch opponent of French Canadian participation in the War. (His aunt wrote, 'Imagine a descendant of Louis-Joseph Papineau at the Front. God be praised!')[9]

Gault, as second-in-command ,was responsible for the administration of the Regiment which gave full scope for his energy and undoubted talent for getting things done. As early as 11 August he was obtaining quotations from Cunard and the CPR for two ships to carry the Regiment and its horses, transport and equipment to Europe. Offers to insure the lives of the men, to sell horses, to provide boots, came to him by wire and letter from across Canada. From England arrived a more comprehensive offer, 'Shall be pleased to be of assistance in supplying general equipment for corps being raised and arrange special prices – Richard Burbridge, Harrods Ltd London.'

On 15 August, whilst recruiting in Montreal, he received a telegram from Buller with some vital information. 'Please pay men at rate of one dollar ten cents a day from day of assembly. Will settle with you later. Terms of enlistment for one year or the war.'

The ex-Regulars selected by Colonel Farquhar were surprised by his friendliness and by his knowledge of their former regiments. In their years in the army many had never exchanged more than a stilted word or two with a commanding officer. From this one they came away feeling like men, respected as individuals.

At first sight Major Hamilton Gault – six foot one, large boned, dark complexion, jet black hair, piercing grey eyes, booming voice – was an intimidating contrast to their slight, quiet-mannered commanding officer. His innate gentleness was not obvious, but it was not long before his men, with the sure instinct of the soldier, came to realize that he genuinely liked and respected them.

Gault was convinced of the direct relationship between his soldiers' morale and the way the Regiment was administered. From the outset he would tolerate none of the slackness implicit in such old quartermaster jokes as, 'How would you like your uniform, too big or too small?'.

The first evidence of this was in the way he saw to their basic interests – food and clothing. He hired a master fitter and eight tailors to ensure that, from the limited range of the army's stock sizes,they would find uniforms to fit. He hired chefs from the best hotels to organize the kitchens and took pains to ensure that competent cooks were recruited. From then until the end of the war the Regiment claimed that they could always tell when Gault was with them because the food was better.

Marguerite announced that she intended to go to England with the Regiment and to work for the Red Cross in the field. In the meantime she moved into the Chateau Laurier hotel and helped Hammie with his correspondence.

His friendship with Percival Campbell had survived their falling out during the African safari as evidenced by a message from him relayed by the Bank of Montreal in London on the 17th, 'Don't buy Brazilians over forty. Prisoner temporarily Switzerland.'

As soon as she heard that Gault was going to war, Phoebe, Percival's sister, presented him with 'Steve', a splendid hunter to carry him into battle. On the 10th she wrote to him from The Manor House, St. Hilaire, in tones unlike most of the high-minded letters he received at the time:

Dear Hamilton,

I am not going to bore you with a long-winded epistle for I am sure you must be terribly busy but I just want to tell you what a *splendid Canadian* I think you are and to wish 'Gault's Light Infantry' the best luck in the world. . . . I think Steve should feel proud of his privilege. I only hope he will acquit himself as well on the battlefield as he has done in the hunting field and, if I know anything of him, I feel sure he will. Just give a good 'view hallo' when you get near the Germans and then sail in & as Kipling would say, 'ack their bloomin' 'eads orff!' Make 'em lick the dust.

Well, dear Mr. Gault, I will say goodbye. Please give Mrs Gault my love & tell her I think she's just *splendid*.

The very best of luck possible and every good wish. Be good to Steve. Hoping to see you home *soon* with some German brushes and pates!

A few days later Guy Ogilvy, a polo-playing friend, wrote to offer his chestnut pony, Sandy, as a second charger. Ogilvy had bought him in Long Island in April, the horse having come up from Texas in the previous December. He stood at more than 15 hands and was in good hard condition. Gault had ridden the horse and was delighted to accept. Sandy carried him through the war and lived on afterwards to a good age.

As soon as the Patricias' recruits were equipped they were formed into companies and training began. For the most part it was a matter of refreshing old skills, but few of them were familiar with the Canadian Ross rifle. They were not enthusiastic. It was accurate enough, but, to someone accustomed to the robustness of a Lee Enfield, it seemed too finely made for a service weapon.

With its mobilization complete, on Sunday 23 August the Regiment held a church parade at Lansdowne Park. It was a poignant occasion, for they expected to leave for overseas before the week was out. The service was simple, the familiar sort that all had attended in the past, with traditional hymns accompanied by the band of the Governor-General's Foot Guards – 'O God Our Help in Ages Past', 'Fight the Good Fight', and 'Onward Christian Soldiers' – Psalm 121, 'I will lift up mine eyes unto the hills', the collects for the Army and Navy, and a sermon followed by 'God Save the King'.

No invitations had been issued, no announcement made but a large crowd, drawn by rumour of the Regiment's imminent departure, surrounded the parade. At the end of the service, as the skies darkened, Princess Patricia, who had been watching with her father, came forward and presented the Regiment with a colour with which to mark the headquarters of the Battalion in the field.

Designed and made by herself, it was not an official 'Regimental Colour', its design approved by the College of Heralds to be the focus of the regiment's fighting tradition. Such were no longer carried in war. She intended it simply as something of herself, to remind the Regiment that they would always be in her thoughts. Its official status would be that of a 'Camp Colour' and, as such, could be taken to the Front without infringing regulations.

Its design was simple. Centred on a crimson rectangle was a circle of blue on which were embroidered the entwined initials 'VP', for 'Victoria Patricia' in gold. Princess Patricia later told of its inception.

I was very anxious to give the Battalion some present to take overseas and I first thought of a set of Bugles, since these seemed suitable to a Light Infantry regiment; but Colonel Farquhar much wished for a Camp Colour instead, such as the Brigade of Guards have; so a Camp Colour it was.

There seemed no possibility of getting one made in the short time of two weeks which was available – so I set to work to design and work the Colour myself – I had never done any work of this kind before, and had no idea how to do it – so I just did it the best way I could! – and with the best materials I could obtain in the short time. The staff, too, was home-made being fashioned by our house carpenter from walnut wood grown in Government House grounds.[10]

It was a moving moment for men about to depart to war. The prayers, the hymns, the presentation of the Colour brought emotions close to the surface. Patriotism and a sense of dedication to a cause were deeply felt. More of the tough ex-Regulars than would care to admit accepted the Colour as a kind of knightly favour given to their charge. It was to have a remarkable history.

As the presentation ended, rain began to fall and Farquhar moved the Battalion into one of the large exhibition buildings to be inspected by the Duke of Connaught. As they marched off at the measured one hundred and ten paces to the minute of a Guards regiment, their pipe band playing 'Blue Bonnets Over The Border', more than one old soldier remarked that this was like no light infantry regiment he had ever seen. Bringing up the rear, Hamilton Gault was well satisfied.

Five days later, led by their pipes, the Regiment, in khaki and full webb-equipment but without rifles, marched through the streets of Ottawa. Waiting at the station were the Prime Minister, Sir Robert Borden, and Sam Hughes with Sir Wilfrid Laurier and Government ministers. The Duke and Princess Patricia had said farewell to them privately at Lansdowne Park.

Arriving in Montreal, they marched through streets lined with people to the docks to board the liner *Megantic*. On Beaver Hall Hill one of the men brought cheers from a solemn looking crowd when he shouted, 'Cheer up, this isn't a funeral!'.[11]

Next morning, saluted by the whistles of every ship in the harbour, they sailed for Europe, but, as they approached Quebec, a signal from Ottawa ordered them to halt. The Admiralty had ruled that ships carrying troops could only proceed in convoy. The Patricias would have to wait to sail with the first contingent of the Canadian Expeditionary Force. It spelled frustration of Gault's and Farquhar's intended speed in reaching the Front. Gault was furious, suspecting that Sam Hughes, for his own purposes, had chosen to bring the Patricias into the fold of the Canadian Expeditionary Force. Farquhar himself took the news to the men's mess room.

Regimental Sergeant Major W.H. Marsden, a Canadian regular soldier, told of the Regiment's reaction.[12]

When we were told at Quebec that we would have to disembark, it is beyond me to describe how the men took it. At one time, it looked like mutiny. The men said they would not leave the ship. . . . nearly all these men were Reservists from the Army and Navy and could have joined their units if they wished. Colonel Farquhar addressed the Battn. and told us how hard he had tried to have the order cancelled. He told us that the Governor-General had been in contact with the War Office in London but they could not interfere with the Canadian Government.

While there is no doubt that the order to halt originated with the Admiralty, it had been relayed through the Minister of Militia in Ottawa. Like Gault, Marsden believed that Sam Hughes was behind it.

He had objected to us going over before his army was raised. He was jealous of the Patricias. . . . The minister never once visited us and I am glad he did not do so, the Battn. would have booed him.

We were ordered to go to Valcartier camp and wait for his 35,000 troops to assemble there. Colonel Farquhar told us he would not take us to Valcartier, he would take the regiment to Camp Levis or take us back to Ottawa.[13]

Whatever part Hughes played in the matter, it did nothing for his reputation in the Patricias. On Gault's advice, Farquhar did indeed refuse to expose his regiment to the chaotic conditions of the improvised mobilization camp at Valcartier. Once there, they would be under Hughes' command with nothing to prevent him milking it of its veterans for NCOs for other units.

For most of September the Regiment trained at the old St. Joseph de Levis militia camp. Farquhar and Gault made the most of their time there by putting a further polish on the battalion. Training included the siting and digging of trenches, advance and rear guards, outpost duties and practice in the attack by day and night. Much time was spent on the ranges with the Ross rifle about which the Regiment was developing serious reservations.

Outwardly the Patricias, like other Canadian units, were indistinguishable from a British line regiment. It was at Levis that Gault arranged for the same order of nuns who had knitted for Wolfe's Highlanders in 1759 to produce the first of their famous scarlet shoulder badges on which the letters 'PPCLI' are embroidered in white.[14] The historical association appealed to Gault; they were unique and the men liked them.

Talbot Papineau wrote to his mother, 'I am growing a moustache – a very poor thing yet but growing rapidly. I do not consider it very becoming. However it is the Colonel's wish that we should all grow them.'[15] It was a custom borrowed from the Guards. Gault's too was developing nicely.

On 27 September the Patricias embarked in the *Royal George* which, two days later, sailed down the river to join the rest of the convoy carrying the first contingent of the Canadian Expeditionary Force and its escorting warships in the Gaspe Basin. On board were several of the officers' wives, among them Marguerite Gault who intended to work with the Red Cross. Captain Agar Adamson, an older officer, referred to her in a letter to his wife.

While there is no doubt women are a mistake on a troopship, she has been very nice generally, she has just missed being pretty, sings a bit, is very much in love with her husband, wears a new dress every night for dinner, some of them very pretty. Gault is an excellent chap, very quiet and hates to be connected financially with the Regiment. . . .

Lady Evelyn [Farquhar] is full of ability . . . have found her most interesting. She is writing a letter to each man's wife or mother and trying to make them all different which is quite a difficult job.

There was no let-up in the pace of training. The days at sea began with a half-hour run at seven a.m. followed by breakfast. Officers and men learned semaphore and map reading and bridge building with spars. Every day there were gymnastics and sports.

On putting to sea, Farquhar began the first attempt at bilingualism in the Canadian Forces when he announced that he would take no officer to France who could not read and send a simple message in French and speak and understand enough of the language for elementary military use. He claimed that the ordinary Englishman uses only some 600 words in his daily life and a man must be an ass if he couldn't learn 500 words of another language. The order presented no problem to Gault, but others had difficulty. Adamson commented, 'I am in the booby class and am getting on very badly and it is an awful grind'.

Tied to the speed of the slowest ship in the convoy, the crossing took three weeks, mostly in fine weather. For the last three days the *Royal George* ran out of tobacco or drinks of any kind – the Regiment was glad to arrive at Plymouth.[16]

Three days later, on 18 October, they moved into the sodden canvas of Bustard Camp on Salisbury Plain. If they had expected a welcome from the War Office or orders about their future, they were disappointed.

What worried Gault and Farquhar, and indeed the whole battalion, was that they were now under the command of the Canadian Contingent which would not be fit to take the field for at least three months. Until they were safely part of the British Expeditionary Force their ambition to join the fight in France could not be realized. And until that time there remained the danger that the battalion could be emasculated by calls to supply NCOs for other Canadian units.

Farquhar put the Regiment's case to General Alderson, the Canadians' commander:

The conditions of Service in the Battalion were that the men should be under forty years of age, ex-regulars or men who saw service in South Africa. 850 men fulfilled those conditions, the majority being ex-regulars.

Of the remaining 250, 219 are all picked men who have served for considerable periods in the auxiliary forces. The remainder are prize-fighters, cow-punchers, and pipers. . . . The rust is now off the old soldiers and if the Battalion is ever fit for service, it should be so in ten days.

Alderson agreed and recommended their 'early despatch to the theatre of war'.

On 4 November, at a ceremonial parade, Gault formally handed over the Patricias to the King who with Lords Roberts and Kitchener then inspected them. When the King told Farquhar, 'This is the finest battalion I have ever inspected', he probably meant it. Even the best of regular regiments has its share of young inexperienced soldiers. These were mature men. They wore 771 decorations or medals.

Kitchener exclaimed that now he saw where all his old soldiers had gone. He said that ninety per cent of the men would make non-commissioned officers and the best thing to do would be to break up the battalion and distribute them to other units as the army was so short of NCOs.[17]

However seriously he intended the remark, it came to nothing. In France and Belgium the First Battle of Ypres, which marked the destruction of the bulk of the British Regular Army, was drawing to a close. The Germans had been fought to a standstill but there remained an urgent need for trained infantry to hold the front. As soon as they could relieve them with local forces, the War Office was bringing back its far-flung battalions from the outposts of Empire. As they arrived in Britain, they were organized into divisions. One of these, the 27th, was forming at Winchester and it was in it that the Patricias found their home.

On 16 November they moved to Morn Hill on the outskirts of the city to be joined three days later by the 3rd and 4th Battalions, King's Royal Rifle Corps, the 4th Rifle Brigade and the 2nd King's Shropshire Light Infantry from India. Together they would form the 80th Infantry Brigade. The other two brigades of the division would also each consist of five battalions instead of the usual four.

While most of Farquhar's time was devoted to the training of his officers and men, Gault was concerned with ensuring that the battalion's weapons, equipment, transport and other stores were ready for war, as well as trying to ameliorate the conditions under which they lived.

Morn Hill camp was as unattractive as Bustard, cold, dismal and usually wet. Strong winds loosened tent pegs in the sodden clay and one night, despite double-staking their ropes, several tents, including the marquee sheltering the men's canteen, blew down. Three privates saw a unique opportunity and rolled out a barrel of beer during the confusion, only to see it take charge. Bouncing out of control, it crashed through the canvas wall of an open ditch latrine, followed hotly by the three men. Unfortunately for them, the sole occupant of the latrine's rail was Sergeant W.J. Beaton of the regimental police.[18]

At last, on 20 December, the Regiment marched out to war, their strength 27 officers, 956 other ranks, 25 vehicles, 82 horses, 2 motor-cycles and 10 bicycles.[19] At Southampton they boarded the S.S. *Cardiganshire* and next day were in France. After twenty-four hours on the outskirts of Le Havre, during which they were issued with additional equipment, it took them thirty hours by train and on foot to reach billets at Blaringhem.

The next few days were spent in overhauling their transport and becoming 'acclimatized', which consisted chiefly of digging trenches in the new Hazebrouck defensive line in waterlogged Flanders.

Two days after a dreary Christmas, Hamilton Gault became the first Patricia, and the first Canadian soldier, to enter the trenches facing the enemy.[20] According to the Regiment's War Diary, he and Captain C.F. Smith with two NCOs spent twenty-four hours in the line with the 3rd British Division at Kemmel, near Ypres, 'to learn the method of reliefs and gain experience. Valuable hints and information were gained'.

A veteran remembered the trenches at Kemmel. 'I was trying to get a fire going in a bucket by swinging it to and fro, to thaw us out a bit when Hamilton Gault roared, "Roffey, I know bloody well that Jerry knows we are here but you don't need to advertise the fact!"'[21]

Chapter 8

1915

The Patricias' initiation to war came in the first week of January, 1915.

The key to the northern flank of the Allied line, which now ran from Switzerland to the Belgian coast near the Dutch border, was a semi-circle of low hills which lay around the ancient town of Ypres. It was the last defensible ground before it and the Channel ports. There, in a month of unremitting violence which ended in November, 1914, the British Regular Army fought the Germans to a standstill, but at an appalling cost. On average, only one officer and thirty men who landed in France with each battalion remained. Replacements had partially restored their strength and they continued grimly to hold the 'Ypres Salient'.

If anything, the condition of their French allies was worse and it was essential that the British take over more of the line facing the Germans. So it was that, on arrival in France, the 27th Division was ordered to extend the right of the British line south of Ypres.

On the 5th the Patricias marched north into Belgium, arriving next afternoon at Dickebusch, three miles south-west of Ypres. ' Battalion much handicapped from want of boots', noted their War Diary. There they learned that they were to relieve the 53rd Regiment of the French 32nd Division in the front line at Vierstraat that night. They would be the first regiment of their Division to enter the line.

Gault had gone ahead the day before by motor with an advance party of an officer and three NCOs from each company. They had been briefed by the French general, studied the position carefully from maps then after dark, walked down to the trenches and went over them thoroughly. Gault was appalled by what he found.

The trenches had been built by the French after a successful advance and were, at best, improvised shelter of the poorest kind. Unlike the continuous lines which were developed later in the war, there were gaps between platoon positions and there were no communication trenches to provide access from the rear.

No soldier forgets the first time he comes within close range of the enemy and no battalion ever finds its first relief easy. Years later the surviving 'Originals' of the Patricias, Hammie among them, were to recall the unique horrors of that first tour in the line as one of their worst experiences of the war.

In former wars no one would have thought of campaigning in the sodden fields of Belgium in January. Armies would have snugged down in winter quarters to wait for better weather and drier ground. In 1915 soldiers were little better equipped to withstand the appalling conditions of ground and weather than Wellington's men a century before.

The Patricias who waited for dusk in a muddy field at Dickebusch were weary after two days of marching. The water absorbed by their greatcoats and kit added pounds to their weight. They were cold and their last meal, produced about 5 pm, consisted of a tin of bully beef, hard tack biscuit and tea with no milk or sugar. What was worse, the cobblestones of Belgium had so worn their boots that many men marched without soles and there was no way of replacing them.

The night was cold and black and it was raining as they moved in single file down the shell-pitted Wytschaete road to the remains of Vierstraat. Exploding shells and flares lit waterlogged fields and exposed the ruins of buildings along the road. Some 800 yards from the front French poilus joined to lead them to their positions.

With no communication trenches and few landmarks to guide them, several platoons were led astray. As Captain Stanley Jones wrote, 'it was certainly a test of discipline that our men, in some cases for over two hours, walked around in front of the German trenches without getting into a panic'.[1]

Many of the positions were reached by floundering across the Harringbeek, a narrow icy stream into whose south-east bank the French had dug some rudimentary shelters. The trenches were ditches dug across a sea of mud, too wide for protection from shellfire and too shallow to be bulletproof. At best they were knee deep in water, in many a man would be up to his waist if he stood on the bottom. They could not be drained, hence they could not be deepened. There was no overhead cover, no sandbags to raise the parapet, no revetting to keep the walls from collapsing.

French and German dead lay submerged in the knee-deep ooze of mud and water in the trenches or were half-buried in their walls.

With daylight came not only the first shots from the German positions which looked down on them from higher ground less than a hundred yards away, but the galling sight of water being pumped toward them as the enemy drained his trenches.

Because of the difficulty of controlling the battalion line from a single headquarters, Farquhar ordered Gault to command the two companies on the right of the position.

During the morning the enemy artillery opened fire with shrapnel and high explosive. For over an hour heavy shells gouged great holes in the mud and, in places, blew in the fragile walls of the Canadian trenches. Fortunately, for there was no overhead cover, most of the shrapnel exploded to their rear, the Germans evidently being afraid of hitting their own lines. Shells buried both the Patricias' machine guns in mud.

From then the position was relatively quiet and such efforts as the troops could make were devoted to surviving the elements. Most crouched in the inadequate shelter of their trenches, unable to move without exposure to the deadly fire of their watchful enemy. The only things that moved above ground were rats or bits of cloth hanging on fragments of wire before the German line.

At 10 pm on the third night their relief by the 3rd KRRC began and they moved back to spend three days in support.

> We gradually dragged ourselves out of rifle range, the men helping each other and carrying some who could not walk. About a mile away we loaded the worst cases into wagons and came on here [Dickebusch]. . . . The men had their first hot drink of tea in three days and then most of them threw themselves down and slept as they were, for the whole day. Swollen feet, dysentery and severe colds were the the chief troubles. . . . We sent 20 out of 150 in our company to hospital.[2]

The regiment had suffered only three killed and seven wounded from enemy fire but many more from exposure and from 'trench foot', an affliction almost unknown to the Army Medical Corps. The Patricias, though accustomed to the harsh Canadian winter, suffered as much as the troops from India.

With that first period in the line came the culmination of a weeding-out process which had begun the day after the battalion was formed. A small but steady stream of men were replaced because of sickness, bad conduct or for compassionate reasons. Inevitably others now found that they could not face the realities of war – the dispiriting weariness, the constant danger, the cold and misery of the trenches – and broke down. Some collapsed in tears. Some simply walked to the rear. For the most part they were viewed with some sympathy but there was one case that was different.

Major John W.H. McKinery was a large, bluff veteran of the South African War who commanded No. 2 Company. Since arriving in France, his troops had seen less of him than they should and had formed the opinion that he was more concerned for his own comfort than for theirs. They called him 'Major Machinery'.

During the first few hours in the line McKinery holed up shivering in the only dugout in his company sector. By first light he had disappeared without telling anyone in his company. He persuaded the Medical Officer that he was sick and was evacuated to England on 8 January.

Early that morning Gault visited the company and discovered that McKinery was missing. His anger and contempt were matched by Farquhar's and everyone else who knew the story. Since a charge of desertion would not stand up before a court martial – technically McKinery had 'gone sick' – Farquhar sent a report on the incident to the Chief of the General Staff in Ottawa. The Patricias viewed with disdain and incredulity his subsequent career, in which bluff and an ability to manipulate the system brought promotion.[3]

Three days' rest followed their period in support, then a return to the same trenches at Vierstraat. Gault wrote to Percival Campbell, now in London where Marguerite was helping Evelyn Farquhar collect 'comforts', woollens, cigarettes and extra food, for the Patricias. He told him first about the trenches.

> Well, to put it shortly, they couldn't be much worse – no traverses, crumbling parapets through which the bullets whistle, & almost everywhere knee deep in water & liquid mud. Our casualties so far have been small, but amongst them have been two deaths simply from exposure, so you can guess the conditions under which the war in 'these 'ere parts' is being carried on. . . .
>
> I'm glad to say that we have apparently earned a quite good reputation in the short time we've been at it, and the GOC of the Division expressed his appreciation of the work we have put in in the trenches under the enemy's fire, which the R.E.s [Royal Engineers] say is the best that any battalion of the Div. has done. . . .
>
> We've been out for the past two days having a much needed rest, but the day after tomorrow we go back for another spell of 2 days in, 2 days out, 2 days in, 2 days out, 2 days in & 6 days rest. It's a great life with a good deal of excitement & a fair share of hard work!

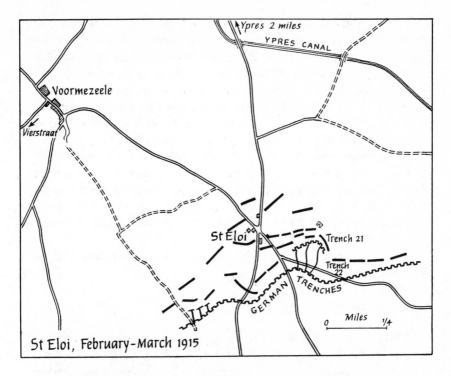

St Eloi, February-March 1915

The Patricias now moved slightly north close to the village of St. Eloi. If anything, the weather was worse, the constant rain having turned to driving sleet and snow and the trenches, still overlooked by the enemy, were no better.

During the six days' rest forecast by Gault he wrote again to Campbell:

> I shall never be able to thank you, old man, for all your kindness to Marguerite during these, for her, trying times. She tells me that you continually keep her merry & bright, but that goes without saying for your being invariably radiates sunshine. . . . Although I'm such a bad hand at expressing my feelings you need not think that I'm ever likely to forget all your kindness to the wife.
>
> . . . Appleton [Gault's butler who had joined as his batman] now carries with him everywhere he goes a heavy brass cup or bowl which he looted from a chateau & which he insists upon my using for my shaving every morning. He is more pleased with this trophy than anything else in the world & keeps it with him in his pack in addition to his sixty pounds of equipment. The d- thing weighs about 10 pounds!!!

The other night when taking up a relief, 50 to 60 yards from the German lines, a bullet came along and removed a lump of mud sticking to my sleeve as nicely as you could wish. The same day they popped a pellet through the sandbag over which I was occasionally taking a glimpse within a damn few inches from my face – a lot of them have been quite close but this one was the nearest! Don't mention the occurrence to M. & don't say anything to others as it looks silly, but to you, it may be of interest. . . .

I rather figure the war will just begin about May 1st, unless our advance is precipitated by German attacks. Every day sitting here is a day gained. What we want are men, hundreds of thousands of men, with which to press home an attack – a little brigade or divisional attack would be no use at all. When the attack is made, it must be made in depth. . . .

Must close down now for I'm due to sing at a company Gaff in a little while.[4]

Two days later, he wrote again:

The Prince of Wales looked in on us the other day (7 Feb 15) and particularly asked for our battalion, so the General sent for me and I had a few minutes with H.R.H. before he went on, driving his own Rolls Royce, a lovely car. I was most agreeably impressed with the youngster who seems to be a thoroughly nice genuine boy without any swank (naturally) and who is frightfully fed up at not being allowed to go into the trenches. They say he leads his staff a terrible life, thinks nothing of motoring to a certain town of fame there dismissing his car and walking home perhaps 15 to 18 miles to G.H.Q., dragging his wretched aides with him. . . .

Prince Arthur also looked in on us the other day, and of course discovered our room – the one in which three of us eat, sleep, work, and keep the extraordinary paraphernalia of our kits – in indescribable confusion!

However we managed to produce some potted meat sandwiches and a Buzzard cake for tea so did not do so badly. Prince A. was very cheery, and best of all – this you must keep absolutely to yourself – told me that General French was placing a good conduct mark to our credit . . . that our battalion was to be mentioned in the next despatches. Great Heavens, old boy, it's really good to be true and I'm simply all tickled to death, purring to myself like a Cheshire Cat!

Don't say anything to Marguerite about it yet, for it may not be true, and I wouldn't disappoint her in this for anything! Our fellows have worked d—d well (between ourselves, strictly) as well if not better than others – although of course comparisons are always odious – and although we may not be deserving of being mentioned still it is none the less gratifying to feel that one's efforts have been noticed and approved. Incidentally the Div. T.O. told me the other day that our Transport was miles away the best in the Division. Forgive all this 'BUCK'[5]

Two more tours in the line intervened before he wrote again:

The d—d old Huns found our H.Q. the day before yesterday – we thought it was too well hidden behind a wood for that! – and put 4 or 5 shells through. It was quite unnecessary of them to do this for the house had been barely touched before and we were extremely comfortably settled, Fannie [Farquhar], Buller and I in one room on mattresses with a table and chairs; our servants in another; the trench guides in a third; and the H.Q. men in the cellars. Buller and I were standing at the door watching the shells (15 pounders) bursting about 50 yds back, when the first shell hit the roof, then came along another taking off the end of the gable, and then crash bang came the third just in the room behind where the trench guides were, killing one man and wounding three others, and putting the 'shrap' through the shutter a few feet from our heads.

I beat it to see what had happened and to get the rest of the men in the cellars, and was just getting across the yard when along came the 4th which burst in the roof again. Although it was further from me I don't mind admitting that I did a 'duck' in short order until the tiles had reached the ground.

. . . So John French did remember us in his last.[6]

From the first day in the line the Patricias had learned to be wary of the deadly accuracy of German snipers but to allow them to dominate the Canadian line was unacceptable. A healthy respect was one thing but fear was another. The danger was that in combination with the miserable conditions of the trenches, any acknowledgement of German superiority would be demoralizing.

The first night in the line one enemy sniper was hiding in a hedge to the left of No. 2 Company and, according to Captain Stanley Jones, 'bothered us a lot'.

Sergeant Gratton of Regina marked his position the first night by the rifle flashes, then next day with his field glasses, he picked out a likely hiding spot for himself about 20 yards from the sniper's haunt. At night he crawled out, took up his position and waited. Presently, sure enough, the sniper's flash was seen, and then a man half rose to see the effect of his shot. Gratton got him.[7]

Despite such individual actions, the Germans maintained a marked superiority in sniping.

It was during this time that Gault learned some lessons in command from a remarkable commanding officer. Francis Farquhar's slight frame and gentle manner were somewhat at odds with the popular conception of a fighting soldier. It was not long before his men realized that, not only was he a strict disciplinarian, he was a front line soldier of the highest quality.

Farquhar had that divine and sympathetic spark in a command-ing officer that leads him to appear before his men at exactly the right time and circumstances, and to say exactly the right thing at a time of stress.

Message: 'German attack east of St Eloi. PPCLI relief post-poned.'. . . . That extra sentence seemed a lot to men who had not slept for five days and there was some cursing in the darkness. Colonel Farquhar, following his usual custom of considering the front line as healthy as a village lane, appeared at the back of the trench.

'And how is the merry band of sportsmen?', he remarked cheerfully. No one had heard or noticed his approach, but the replies were ready enough.

'Going strong, sir' – 'Good for another week' – 'Enjoying ourselves, sir.'

The colonel chuckled and departed while the men looked at each other and wondered why they had answered that way. But really there was no other.[8]

Farquhar refused to concede supremacy to the enemy snipers. He ordered Lieutenant Gourlay Colquhoun to form a section of marksmen to carry the war to the enemy. Their success was immediate and in two days they shot seventeen of the enemy. It was the birth of the Regiment's sniping section which was to become uniquely valuable in the future.

Another example of Farquhar's imaginative approach to command was his solution of the problem of replacing officer casualties. Promotion from the ranks was fairly common in the army, but such officers were usually commissioned into a different regiment. Farquhar began what was to be the Patricias' practice of finding most of theirs from within the ranks of the regiment. By the end of the war almost every officer on strength had risen from the ranks.

Farquhar's aggressiveness was to influence trench warfare for the rest of the war. He initiated the first of the trench raids which were to become the hallmark of the Canadians. Gault played a leading role.

The position occupied by the Patricias in February was even worse than Vierstraat. About nine hundred yards in length, facing south, it consisted of eight unconnected sections of trench extending generally eastward from St. Eloi. In the centre a German salient had forced the line to bend at a right angle southwards. After 150 yards it turned once more to the east. Opposite Trench 21 which faced west between the two bends, the Germans were sapping a fire trench, only forty yards away, from which to mount an assault.

Trench 21 was peculiarly vulnerable. One hundred yards long, it consisted of little more than a three-foot breastwork of sandbags built above a shallow ditch and could be reached only by crossing open ground at night. By day its isolated garrison of thirty men could do nothing but huddle behind their parapet. A fifty-yard gap separated its left from Trench 22 to the east.

In obtaining permission to mount a 'reconnaissance in force' against the German sap, Farquhar had three objectives in mind. The primary one was to disrupt the German work, the others, to meet aggression with aggression and to boost the morale of his men who were overlooked in their filthy ditches by an enemy who lived in greater comfort and relative safety.

The plan was simple. The assaulting party was divided into three groups of about twenty-five men each. Lieutenant C.E. Crabbe, in command of the raiders, would lead the first in rushing the German sap and clearing it. The second would protect the rear, block any communication trenches and cover the withdrawal. The third would destroy the German parapet.

On the evening of 27 February Gault and 'Shorty' Colquhoun, the Sniping Officer, crawled out between Trenches 21 and 22 to find the exact locations of the communication trenches connecting the German forward and main defensive positions. There was no cover and the bright moon made movement hazardous.

Within the German lines, they separated. Gault explored to the left for some 200 yards then returned to report that area clear of enemy posts and communication trenches and that interference with the raid from that quarter was unlikely. Colquhoun, who had turned to the right, failed to reappear.

At 5:15 am, shortly before first light, Farquhar launched the raid. Moving out between Trenches 21 and 22, Crabbe's group rushed the end of the German position and began clearing it of enemy. Above them Talbot Papineau, with three bombers, ran along the parapet, throwing bombs at any Germans they saw. Following closely behind, the other two parties mopped up the enemy and pulled down their parapet. Not to be left out of the first attack made by Canadian troops on European soil, Gault followed.

When he had thrown his last bomb, Papineau jumped into the trench:

> It was deep and narrow, beautifully built, dried by a big pump, sides supported by planks; looked like a mine shaft. A German was lying in front of me. I pushed his head down to see if he was dead. He wasn't. I told a man to watch him. Then I began to pull down the parapet sandbags. . . . Gault passed me and went along the trench.

Flares from the enemy's main position now lit the sky and a hail of machine-gun fire swept the sap and the ground between it and the Canadian line. It was beginning to grow light when the raiders began to race back to Trench 21. Climbing from the enemy trench, Papineau tumbled into the mire in which he was trapped when two wounded men fell on top of him. Gault found him, fetched stretchers for the wounded and pulled him free.

Bearer parties were bringing in casualties when suddenly one group dropped their stretcher and ran. From Trench 21 Gault, followed by a volunteer, crawled out into the withering enemy fire, dragged the stretcher into a ditch and then to a hedge where he was shot through the wrist.[9]

Agar Adamson, who was in command of the thirty men holding Trench 21, wrote to his wife.

> Though badly hit in the wrist, he still carried on for 24 hours until the CO insisted upon his going back to England for treatment. As Keenan [the Medical Officer] said, complications were sure to set in if he did not get absolute rest. It almost took force to get him to go. He has played the game magnificently, crawling from trench to trench and cheering up the men. . . . He will, I know, gladly give you a correct account of the 48 hours and how well the men

behaved, but you won't get a rap out of him about himself, so there is no use trying.[10]

Cameron and I have written a report on Gault's action . . . which I hope will get him the VC as he certainly deserves it. He thoroughly realized what certain 1000 to 1 chance he was taking of certain death and did it. I thought of doing it myself, but was not man or mad enough to attempt it. So sure did I feel that it was certain death that I almost decided to shoot Gault in the leg to prevent his attempting it.[11]

Twenty-four hours after the raid Gault finally reported to the dressing station of the 87th Field Ambulance who diagnosed his injury as a 'gunshot wound, right arm, severe'. Two days later he was evacuated to the 11th General Hospital. On 5 March he sailed on the Hospital Ship *St. Andrew* to Folkestone where he was admitted to the Queen's Canadian Military Hospital. Two weeks later he was given leave to go to London to stay for a few days with Marguerite.

By then the King had seen Sir John French's despatch which commented on the good work done by the Patricias. He was keenly interested in the details of military operations and, when he learned that Hammie would be in town, he summoned him to the Palace to ask him about the Regiment's innovative raid. On 21 March, when Gault appeared for his audience, the King found that he had a sad duty to perform.

As Colonel-in-Chief of his Foot Guards, he knew their senior officers personally and insisted on being informed immediately of casualties among their officers. That morning he learned that Francis Farquhar had been killed in action.[12]

The news came as a terrible blow to Hammie. The death of friends is one of the most difficult concomitants of war for soldiers to accept. Many succeed in erecting a barrier around their emotions to lessen the pain but they are never entirely invulnerable. Hammie's admiration for Farquhar began before the war and had developed into a warm friendship. Together they had built the Regiment and had led it in action, during which time they lived closely together.

Given the value of his experience in South Africa and his later studies, Hamilton Gault, at the outbreak of war, nonetheless had no experience of command. In this most elusive of arts, Farquhar had been his mentor and his exemplar. For the rest of his life he remained Gault's ideal of what a commander and a gentleman should be.

As his second-in-command, Gault would normally have replaced him. Despite his wound being far from healed, he immediately attempted to return to the Regiment. Predictably the medical authorities refused permission.

A few days later came news that, every major in the Regiment being a casualty, 'Teta' Buller, the Adjutant, had been promoted from captain to lieutenant-colonel and given command. In war promotion goes to the best officer immediately available.

Gault would have been less than human if he were not disappointed at missing the chance to lead the Regiment he had founded. He had come to appreciate Buller's cool competence and icy courage and they had become friends. He immediately wrote him a warm letter of congratulation.[13]

The next day Gault received a letter from Clive Wigram, the King's private secretary:

> The King was very glad to see your name in a list of officers to whom the Field Marshal Commanding-in-Chief, under His Majesty's authority, has awarded a D.S.O. for gallantry in the Field.
>
> His Majesty wishes me to find out if you are still in London, as he would like personally to invest you with this Decoration before you go out if it is possible.[14]

During April,1915, Marguerite Gault's brother, Chattan Stephens, a captain in the Canadian artillery, became seriously ill in Belgium and was moved to a hospital in Salisbury. His wife was at his side. His mother, in Montreal, decided to visit him and bring with her his two infant children and their nurse as soon as passage could be arranged.[15]

Concern for Chattan and his wife clouded the last week of Gault's convalescence and the news from the Front was bad.

On 22 April, for the first time since November, the Germans mounted a major attack to take Ypres. Clouds of choking chlorine gas had overwhelmed French Colonial troops on the north flank of the Salient and only the remarkable stand of the 1st Canadian Division at Langemarck, St Julien and Gravenstafel had prevented the enemy from reaching the town.

Press reports were grave, rumours worse, when Gault left Shorncliffe on 29 April to rejoin the Patricias. He knew from a letter from Buller that the Regiment had moved at the beginning of the month from the stinking swamp of St Eloi to the apex of the Ypres salient in Polygon Wood, four miles to the east of the town and north of the Menin Road. Their trenches were dry; they could move about by day; 'It's a paradise after St Eloi'.[16]

After two relatively quiet periods in the line, the Patricias moved into billets in the infantry barracks in Ypres. On 18 April desultory shelling of the city began. Next day it continued. On the 20th it grew to such an intensity that the barracks were no longer safe and the Regiment moved outside the city walls. From there they watched the systematic destruction of the ancient Flemish town by 2,000-pound shells fired by a German 42 cm. howitzer.

At dusk they moved forward once more to relieve the Rifle Brigade in Polygon Wood. There they remained for the next twelve days, with no relief.

They were now under frequent bombardment by heavy guns for which their trenches provided little protection. Casualties began to mount. On their second day in the line, drifts of chlorine gas reached the Patricias, but did no harm. There was no question of relief – so desperate was the battle being fought on the front of the 1st Canadian Division that every reserve battalion of every division in 5th British Corps was either used in the line or moved to cover critical points of the defence.

By 27 April the Germans accepted that their breakthrough at St Julien had failed but they had advanced so far that the British at the apex of the Salient were dangerously exposed. Sir John French, the Commander-in-Chief, ordered the three divisions of Plumer's 5th Corps – 27th, 28th and 1st Canadian – to pull back closer to Ypres during the night of 3 May. The two battalions holding the front of the 80th Brigade, the Patricias and the 4th Rifle Brigade, were to withdraw from Polygon Wood to new positions on Bellewaerde Ridge, some 3,000 yards to the rear.

Weary from twelve continuous days in the front line, PPCLI were now required to carry out one of the most difficult operations of war, withdrawal when in contact with the enemy.

The day before they moved, every man that could be spared was sent back to the new defences. Work was begun on converting the gun emplacements of an old battery position into infantry defences, while, some sixty yards to the front, a straight ditch which would become the front line was dug. The position of communication trenches was marked on the ground between them.

Late in the afternoon of 3 May Gault arrived with a small draft of reinforcements at Buller's headquarters and immediately was sent to supervise the preparation of the position on Bellewaerde Ridge.

That night, with a mixture of skill and good luck, Plumer's three divisions succeeded in withdrawing without the loss of a man. Far from interfering, the enemy continued his routine shelling of their empty

85

trenches until daybreak. By 3 a.m. on 4 May all the Patricias were hard at work, digging and wiring their new defences.

In the first light before dawn the Germans discovered that the trenches opposite had been abandoned. Their patrols soon confirmed that the British and Canadians had gone and that they had lost contact – a situation to be deplored. Their reaction was precisely in accordance with Field Service Regulations and the old Regulars defending Belle-waerde Ridge were treated to a spectacle they had not seen since their last peacetime manoeuvres.

Behind the Patricias the fresh green of the woods surrounding Bellewaerde Lake sparkled in the early morning sunshine. To the east green fields sloped away to rise again gently to the village of Westhoek standing on its low ridge. Immediately in front were the almost unmarked buildings of a farm. Apart from an occasional shout, the only sounds to be heard were the familiar ones of picks and shovels and of sledges driving wiring stakes.

Then, shortly after 6 am, shouts of, 'Here they come!' turned every head to the east. Over Westhoek Ridge, at the double, came two enemy scouts, followed by a platoon of infantry in loose formation. Behind came three more. It was an enemy vanguard.

They were met by an indifferent fire, while all the men stood up on the parapet to see the show, some of them waving their arms and cheering like mad. But the advance quickly lost interest as a spectacle, for the Germans pushed machine guns within 200 yards and bullets were soon raking the parapets.[17]

Beyond Westhoek Ridge, less than a mile distant, columns of the enemy main guard, 24 abreast, could be seen marching steadily toward them.[18] To Buller's and Gault's acute frustration, they could do nothing about this ideal artillery target – there were no batteries which could be brought to bear.

As soon as the first enemy fell to the Patricias' fire, the German vanguard extended into line and replied with their rifles. To their rear the main guard deployed in the open at the double, mounted officers directing them to the reverse slope of Westhoek Ridge where they began to dig.

This demonstration of a classical 'advance to contact' was completed in two hours during the last of which German guns began a bombard-ment of the PPCLI trenches to smother rifle and machine-gun fire while their infantry were entrenching in the open.

The enemy artillery inflicted terrible damage on the Patricias' rudi-

1. Hamilton, aged 8, with his father, Andrew Frederick Gault, his mother, Louise, and sister, Lillian. *Notman Photographic Archives, McCord Museum of Canadian History.*

2. 2nd Canadian Mounted Rifles in South Africa. *NARC PA 113028*

3. Marguerite Gault ca. 1903. *Notman Photographic Archives, McCord Museum of Canadian History.*

4. The young businessman, ca. 1905.

5. Returning from Lac Mistassini. At portages, Hammie carried loads of 150 pounds.

6. Hammie and Marguerite in the Quebec wilderness.

7. Lillian Benson, Gault's sister ca. 1912

8. Princess Patricia of Connaught,
from the painting by Sir James
Jebusa Shannon, RA.

9. Skating party at Government House, temperature 9 degrees below
zero Fahrenheit. The annotations are by Princess Patricia.
Front row, seated, L to R: — Mrs Huntly Drummond, Helen
Mathewson, Marguerite Gault.
Centre: Princess Patricia, Duchess of Connaught, Dorothy Yorke,
Daisy Combe, Duke of Connaught.
Rear: Lord Spencer Compton, Hon. George Boscawen, Katharine
Villiers, Edward Worthington, RAMC, 'Teta' Buller, Alan Graham,
Arthur Sladen, Mr. Combe, Hamilton Gault, Francis Farquhar.

mentary defences, blowing in whole sections of trench and destroying the incomplete overhead cover of the few shelters which they had begun. By nightfall, when the shelling slackened, the Patricias had lost 122 men killed or wounded.

At 10 pm they were relieved by the King's Shropshire Light Infantry.

It was a nearly exhausted battalion which, early on 5 May, moved back into brigade reserve. They had been in the line for fifteen days under constant shelling, had conducted a difficult withdrawal and had worked desperately hard to establish new defences. In doing so, they had lost one quarter of their strength. Just as there is a limit to a man's physical capacity, so is there one to his store of courage. For the Patricias, both accounts had been gravely depleted.

They were to have 36 hours of relative quiet in the reserve trenches near the junction of the Menin Road and the Roulers railway, the infamous 'Hell-Fire Corner', before moving back into the line. They had been in the reserve position for about three hours when Colonel Buller was struck in the eye by a shell splinter and Hamilton Gault took command.

His immediate concern was to prepare the battalion to return to the line the following night. Even with the draft which he had brought with him from England, their strength would be only fourteen officers[19] and fewer than 600 men.

Gault's first inspection of the line on Bellewaerde Ridge in the early morning of 7 May proved disquieting. The Shropshires had done much to improve both the front and support lines and had partially dug a communication trench to join them. But neither of the fire trenches were adequate or well placed. The more forward, consisting of two unconnected trenches lying along the ridge and its northern slope, was exposed both to the immediate front and to enemy artillery which overlooked the right flank from south of the Menin Road. They covered a front of some 600 yards.

The communication trench was crucial to the defence. Through it would move reinforcements and ammunition to the front line, casualties to the rear. Yet in no place could a man stand erect without being exposed; through most of it he would have to crawl. In a daylight action it was commanded by high ground within the enemy lines and would be of little use.

The Shropshires reported that enemy artillery fire had been heavy and so it continued. An attack might be expected at any time.

Gault, like every battalion commander who takes over another's trenches, had to accept the fact that, tactically, his hands were tied. It was as if he were garrisoning a fortress – he had no choice but to

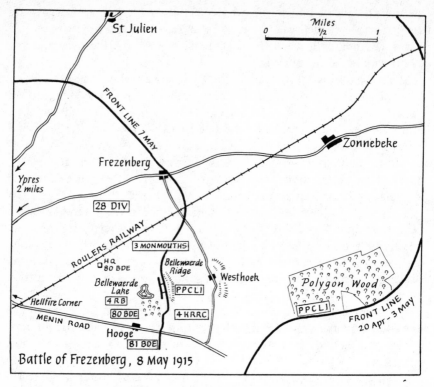

Battle of Frezenberg, 8 May 1915

conform to his predecessor's dispositions. There was nothing he could do in the short term to change the basic layout of his defences.

Two companies were needed to garrison the forward line of fire trenches with two behind in support.

The Patricias were on the extreme left flank of the 80th Brigade and of the 27th Division. On their right were the 4th King's Royal Rifle Corps manning a line which joined that of the 81st Brigade near the Menin Road. North of the Patricias were B Company of the 3rd Monmouthshire Regiment, then the 1st King's Own Yorkshire Light Infantry of the 83rd Brigade (28th Division) whose line continued across the Ypres – Roulers railway toward the village of Frezenberg.

Three hundred yards behind the Patricias and extending almost the width of their front lay Bellewaerde Lake. Access to Brigade Head-quarters and the rear was only possible around the northern end of the sprawling water. Immediately behind the lake, the 4th Rifle Brigade lay in close support to PPCLI and the 4th KRRC.

Across the Westhoek Valley, at distances varying from three to six hundred yards, Gault could see the forward positions of the the enemy opposing him and the KRRC on his right. There was nothing to indicate that they concealed the infantry of the entire German XV Corps.[20]

With the lake behind them, Gault realized that the Patricias literally had their backs to the wall. Enemy artillery could prevent any movement through the KRRC on their right. If the Germans penetrated the Monmouths and Yorkshires on their left, it would be impossible for them to retire.

During the 7th persistent enemy shelling damaged the Patricias' trenches and caused 17 casualties among the forward companies. That night Gault relieved the forward line with the two companies in support. Thus in the morning of 8 May, when the Battle of Frezenberg began, Nos. 1 and 2 Companies were forward on the right and left respectively, with Nos. 3 and 4 behind them in support.[21]

After some lively shelling in the early part of the night, the German artillery fell silent. Toward midnight Gault, with his adjutant, Hugh Niven, walked, crawled and stumbled the entire length of his two lines of defences to ensure that the company reliefs were complete and that every sentry was alert. All was quiet when, about 2 a.m., they crawled under the root of a large tree behind the support line and went to sleep.

As morning light came and grew a silence, unnatural for a battlefield, keyed the senses of the watching Patricias but no sign of movement came from the enemy.

Suddenly, about 6 a.m., a crash of shells brought Gault to his feet. He could see shrapnel bursting over the forward line, their distinctive crack identifying the exploding shells of field artillery.

As the shelling grew in intensity, Gault again went around the lines, speaking quietly to the men and ensuring that as much as could be was done to prepare for a German attack. When, about 7 am, the enemy's heavy guns opened a bombardment more violent than anything the Regiment had seen before, he knew that one was imminent. The Ridge became an inferno, and to those in the trenches the whole world seemed alive and rocking with the flash and crashing of bursting shells.[22]

At Headquarters of the 80th Brigade Gault's report of 'very very heavy shelling', and similar ones from the flanks, warned that the Germans were concentrating their fire upon the line between the Menin Road and Frezenberg.

Gault's unease about the condition and layout of his position was now brutally justified: the poor and exposed trenches were blown in; enfilading machine guns and bursting shrapnel mowed down the men. Soon the front line was virtually obliterated and the wire protecting it blown away. Two of his four machine guns were out of action and his communications with Brigade Headquarters and the 4th Rifle Brigade, who were to support him, had been cut.

With casualties mounting alarmingly, Gault ordered everyone who could fire a rifle – batmen, signallers, pioneers – into the support line. About an hour after the bombardment began, a runner reached Brigade with a message in Gault's firm handwriting:

> Have been heavily shelled since 7 a.m. Sections of front trenches made untenable by enemy's artillery, but have still about 160 rifles in front line. German infantry has not yet appeared. Should they rush our front trenches will at once counter-attack, but do not propose to risk weakening my support lines. Will advise O.C. Rifle Brigade should I require support. In lulls of gun fire there is heavy fire from rifles and machine guns. Please send me two MGs if possible. I have only two left in front line. None in support.

Gault wrote one more message. It was the last received by Brigade Headquarters that day:

> Should this continue all day, would like support this evening in case of heavy night attack. Most of my wire gone.

During one of the lulls in the bombardment, the trenches were swept by machine-gun fire while German infantry opposite No. 2 Company on the left climbed from their trenches. Apparently confident that few could have survived the fury of their artillery's bombardment, they formed for a mass attack.

Patiently schooled in 'rapid fire' – the delivery of 15 aimed shots a minute – the thinned ranks in the Patricias' front trenches opened fire. Their withering blast of rifle fire mowed into the German infantry. Not more than 80 or 100 reached cover behind hedges and in some ruined buildings a short distance in front of the Patricias' line. Most of these were soon driven out by concentrated rifle fire and were seen crawling back over the ridge into safety. But two or three German machine-gun crews established themselves in the ruined buildings.[23]

The enemy guns now resumed their bombardment, concentrating more of their fire on the support line. Gault was moving back along it from watching the action in front of No.2 Company, when he was hit by shrapnel in his left arm. He paused, tucked the wounded arm into his cross belt and hurried on to deal with the worsening situation on the right.

Small parties from No.1 Company and the right of No. 2 had fallen back to the support trench where Gault learned that most of their trenches had been completely blown in and were no longer tenable. Every machine gun was out of action.

At 9 am the next blow fell. 'There seemed,' wrote an eye-witness, 'to be an astounding silence with just an occasional rifle shot, and then we realized that the German infantry were upon us.'

On the left the remnant of No.2 Company stopped the assault with their rifle fire, causing such casualties that the enemy were driven back. On the right German infantry broke into the nearly obliterated trench, bayoneting the wounded as they came. Still parts of No.1 Company held on and succeeded in pinning the Germans to the parts of the trench which they had entered on their first rush.

As Gault attempted to see what had happened, a shell burst blew him from his feet. Hugh Niven saw that his left thigh was a mess of blood-soaked rag and torn flesh. Gault attempted to rise and, when he found that he could not, he sent an order to Agar Adamson of No. 2 Company to take command. He lay back and fainted.

Niven later wrote, 'Hammie was hit badly, his eyes were turned back in his head, only the whites showing. I did what I could and bound his thigh up tightly. I laid him flat down on his back and moistened his lips.'[24] Later he regained consciousness and Niven propped him up against the body of a dead soldier.

During the day Gault was visited by the gallant Corporal Bowler of the medical section who checked his dressings and administered morphine. One very busy soldier, Private H.G. Hetherington, remained near him.

> Soon after the bombardment started, I was the only unwounded man left in a large bay of the trench and I well remember that I fired several rifles until they were too hot to hold. There were plenty of spares lying about. Major Hamilton Gault was lying wounded in the bay for most of the day.[25]

So intense was the enemy fire that it was impossible for stretcher bearers to remove the wounded from the trenches.

The two lines of the Patricias' position had different functions which were well understood. Recognizing that if the enemy was prepared to concentrate enough power and to accept unlimited casualties, he was bound to achieve some penetration of the defences, the front line was to be held as long as possible but not 'to the last man and the last round'. The support line was vital and would be defended to the end.

The position held by the remnant of No.1 Company was now

untenable. Captain H.S. Dennison sent them back to the rear while, with another officer and a handful of men, he covered their withdrawal. Neither he nor his men were ever seen again.

No. 2 Company's situation was desperate. The Monmouths on their left had disappeared, while the Germans who had gained a foothold in No.1's position, were firing point-blank into their trench. Still their deadly rifle fire pinned down the enemy lying behind the hedge and farm buildings to their front.

But with their flanks turned and ammunition running out, they had no alternative but to fall back along the shallow communication trench. Much of this had been blown in or was choked with bodies. Many were hit as they were forced into the open. With no officers left, the withdrawal was skilfully organized and gallantly covered by NCOs and private soldiers.

While the German attack was in progress, the Patricias were astonished to see a company of the Rifle Brigade making their way through the enemy barrage toward them from the rear. Every man was laden with ammunition and with them came two sections of machine guns.

The news they brought was grave. The Germans had broken through the 28th Division and the Patricias' left flank was completely undefended. Adamson, who was already wounded, led the company of Riflemen behind the support line to the left where they counter-attacked and secured the exposed left flank.

Crisis after crisis followed. By noon ammunition was again running short and an appeal was sent to the rear for more. The Patricias lost count of the number of times the Germans tried to attack from the captured front line, each time preceded by an intense burst of gunfire and each time beaten back.

About 3 pm a platoon of the Shropshires arrived with more ammunition. Adamson scattered them along the line. Shortly afterwards the Germans made yet another assault which broke under the Patricias' fire. The enemy fell back from the captured front line leaving their dead and wounded behind. It was their final effort.

By this time the 28th Division on the left were counter-attacking in force and attracting the Germans' attention. As darkness fell stretcher bearers were able to remove the wounded and Gault was carried back to the dressing station. Learning that Adamson had again been wounded, he sent Hugh Niven, on whom command had now devolved, a note telling him how badly he felt at having to leave him to carry on. Niven commented later, 'That was the kind of soldier he was, always thinking of others . . . his spirit invaded every man's soul that day.'[26]

Lance Corporal Leonard Heddick, a medical orderly wrote to his parents about Gault's conduct:

> I never saw his equal for grit. . . . He lay all day with his body torn and bleeding, and it was only at night when the stretcher bearers could approach the trench to get out the wounded that he was carried away, and then he went last, absolutely refusing to go before the worst of the other cases had been taken. He was cheerful and grinning all over when we got him in our dressing station, and kept on grinning when we pulled the blood-soaked and ragged edge of his coat and trousers and underclothing out of his torn and lacerated flesh wounds – into which, by the way, you could stick your fist. It will be months before he will be back again.[27]

At 11.30 pm the 3rd KRRC arrived to relieve the Patricias. Together they gathered the dead who lay in the communication and support trenches; those in the front line could not be reached. They laid them in a shallow grave near Bellewaerde Lake and Lieutenant Hugh Niven, holding the Colour in his hand, said as much as he could remember of the Anglican service for the burial of the dead.

All the units of the 80th Brigade had suffered terribly in the Ypres Battles of 1915 but to the Patricias went the mournful honour of having the longest casualty list – 700 killed, wounded or missing in action.

Of all the tributes which they later received for their stand on Bellewaerde Ridge, the most moving came from their British comrades. As Hugh Niven led the remnant of the Patricias out of action, 'their comrades of the 80th Brigade turned out with one accord, lined the road, swept off their caps to the Colour and cheered and cheered again'.[28]

From the dressing station Gault was carried by four R.A.M.C. bearers through Ypres. With him were Adamson and Private Hance, 'both wounded and walking for lack of a stretcher. The town was being badly shelled and the bearers attempted to leave him and run. So forceful were Gault's remarks that they picked up the stretcher and hurried on.'[29]

By the evening of 9 May Hammie had arrived at No.7 Stationary Hospital at Boulogne. Next day he was transferred to the Hospital Ship *St. Andrew* which, on the 11th, delivered him to an ambulance train at Dover. By evening he was in the 1st London General Hospital.[30] It was there he learned that the distress caused to his family by the seriousness of his wounds was overshadowed by tragedy.

Chapter 9

PARTINGS

On the day before Gault was wounded Marguerite's mother with her brother Chattan's two children and their nurse were lost when the *Lusitania* was torpedoed by a German submarine off the coast of Ireland.[1]

They were not among the survivors listed on 8 May. Then came the news that bodies had been brought ashore and more were being washed onto the Irish coast near Kinsale. Relatives were asked to come forward to identify them.

Marguerite was not alone in facing the tragedy and in comforting Chattan and his wife, Hazel. Her sister, Mae Wedderburn-Wilson, and her husband, John, lived near Liverpool. Their daughter, Marguerite, now Lady Stirling, has told of her father's traumatic experience of looking for the bodies of Mrs Stephens, her grandchildren and their nurse. They were not in the Irish mortuary where many had been taken. Morning after morning he walked along the nearby beaches, looking at the pitiful debris which had been washed ashore during the night.[2]

Eventually Mrs Stephens body was found (those of the children and their nurse were not) and taken to Cork where Marguerite endured the grisly duty of identifying it. She and Wedderburn-Wilson removed it to Liverpool and there had it placed in a sealed coffin with the intention of returning it to Montreal for burial. In the following year it was taken aboard the S.S. *Hesperian* bound for Canada. Two days out from England *Hesperian* was torpedoed and sunk.[3]

Marguerite was not renowned for taking life seriously. Now, devastated by the loss of her mother, her nephew and baby niece, torn with sympathy for Chattan and Hazel over the loss of their children and concerned for her brother's health, she could take some comfort in the fact that, while Hammie was suffering serious wounds, his life was not in danger. She was by nature vivacious, impulsive and, according to her friends, somewhat scatterbrained.

But Hammie had been very seriously wounded – splinters in his body and his left arm and a huge gouge torn from his left thigh. He made light of his injuries and did his best to conceal the pain.

It was barely two months since, after debilitating weeks in the appalling trenches at St. Eloi he had first been wounded. He had lost many of his friends, pre-eminently Francis Farquhar. He had been through a terrible battle and endured hours of suffering propped up in a trench against a dead body. Added now was his concern for Marguerite in this horrific family tragedy in which he could do nothing to help. What emotions he concealed can only be imagined.

Marguerite outwardly accepted his attitude at face value. She had learned in the Canadian bush and on safari that Hammie would treat her physical pains with care and kindness but without an undue show of sympathy. And he wanted none for himself. They both were exponents of the stiff upper lip.

This they carried into their emotional traumas. There was nothing that Hammie could do in a material way to help Marguerite in her distress. She, in turn, wanted to be with Hammie, but she may not have realized the emotional effects of his wounds. Perhaps neither received the sympathy they needed and secretly resented it. The situation was ripe for misunderstanding.

As soon as he could move about the hospital, Hammie began to visit the Regiment's wounded. Confident of meeting any physical challenge, before he had regained his strength he went even further afield to see his men. He became exhausted and in June he suffered a relapse.[4]

The butcher's bill for Frezenberg now had to be paid. PPCLI had been reduced to less than 200 men and there were too few reinforcements available to restore them to full strength. The Canadian authorities were having enough problems rebuilding their own 1st Division without supporting a battalion of a British formation. Both Sam Hughes and the British Adjutant General were in agreement that the Patricias should be transferred to a Canadian formation where they could be more easily maintained.

A move seemed inevitable. Infantry brigades consisted of four battalions. The 80th had five of which four were British regulars. Theoretically one of these could go and military logic argued that it be the Patricias. On 9 June Lieut-Colonel R.T. Pelly, now commanding the Regiment, Hugh Niven and Talbot Papineau wrote privately to Gault recommending that the Patricias should become part of the 2nd Canadian Division.

Lieut-Colonel J.J. Carrick, Sam Hughes' liaison officer to Sir John French, the British Commander-in-Chief, saw the letter from the three officers and used it to promote the move. It was referred back officially, through channels to PPCLI, who hotly denied that they wanted to transfer from the 80th Brigade. The last thing the Patricias wished was to give the impression that they wanted to leave their British comrades whom they respected and trusted. To their embarrassment, the letter had been seen by both their brigade and divisional commanders.

The three officers each wrote to Carrick complaining of his misuse of private correspondence. Pelly's anger was obvious when he wrote, 'There is a matter I am anxious to discuss with you which I cannot express on paper owing to your dexterity in handling private correspondence'. He added that he was going to see Gault on 18 June.[5]

Gault was not enthusiastic at the prospect of joining an as yet untrained formation. In the present circumstances the danger of the Patricias being 'milked' were as great as they had been when Sam Hughes proposed moving the Regiment from Levis to Valcartier.

Fortunately, shortly before the Battle of Frezenberg, two graduates of McGill University, George McDonald and Percival Molson, obtained approval from Sam Hughes for a scheme to reinforce the Patricias. They would raise companies of university men – graduates, students, professors – specifically for the purpose. Already such a company had been trained and become part of the scheme. When Pelly saw Gault on 18 June it was already on its way overseas.

The 2nd Canadian Division had just arrived in England and was not expected in France until the end of the summer. There could be no question of the Patricias returning to Britain to join them. For the moment, with reinforcements on the way, no decision need be taken.

Two months after Gault was wounded he was given a month's leave from hospital by the medical board. With Marguerite, he went to stay with his sister, Lillian Benson, at Lydeard House in the village of Bishop's Lydeard, a few miles west of Taunton. There they were joined by Bruce Bainsmith, the machine-gun officer of the Patricias, who was recovering from wounds suffered in Polygon Wood at the beginning of May. He and Marguerite had known each other since they crossed the Atlantic in the *Royal George.*

Bainsmith had been commissioned in the British Territorial Force before the war. In August, 1914, he joined the Patricias and had been wounded three times, on the last occasion seriously. He was not an easy subordinate. As a platoon commander, he was inclined to do no more work than duty demanded, but, given an independent job, he excelled.[6] Tall, bold, handsome and amusing, he was popular among the officers and their wives.

Possibly sympathy more explicit than Hammie had expressed drew

Marguerite and Bainsmith to each other. Given the tragedies she had suffered, she was particularly vulnerable emotionally. How much time had they since spent alone together? Was their mutual attraction noticed by others? Did Gault suspect? No one today knows exactly what happened at Lydeard on 24 July, 1915. Apparently Gault discovered them in each others' arms. There was no other witness and there is no factual record. He claimed that they were in the act of adultery. Marguerite and Bainsmith denied it.

Gault was not quiet in his rage. Everyone in the house was soon on the scene, his mother, Lillian and Percy Benson, Percival Campbell and Marguerite's French maid. Bainsmith was ordered from the house. Marguerite left later. Never had Gault been wounded like this. Whether Marguerite was guilty of adultery or not, he was convinced that she had betrayed him.

For him their marriage had ended, but to obtain a divorce would be difficult. There was no question of one being granted in England. He was domiciled in the province of Quebec where divorce was only possible by act of the Federal Parliament in Ottawa and adultery the only grounds. The procedure, lengthy and costly, required an application to the divorce committee of the Senate. He was on active service and would be returning to France as soon as he was physically fit.

As far as Hammie was concerned, a solution to his personal affairs would have to wait. Marguerite, by now as angry as he, had no intention of letting matters rest. She sailed for Montreal where she consulted lawyers.

On 15 September she visited Rokeby and had Maggie Riddell, the Gaults' devoted housekeeper, pack her personal belongings and the wedding presents which had come from her family. The list ends with a note which conveys Maggie's dismay and disapproval: 'All photographs of Mrs. Gault was [sic] taken out of frames by herself and torn up.'[7]

It was only a year since an adulatory press had been full of reports of Hammie and Marguerite's going off to war together. Now with a restraint which seems inconceivable today, they recalled that romantic story and reported simply that they had each applied to Parliament for a divorce,'on the usual grounds'. It was enough. Montreal society was soon agog with a scandal about which opinion was divided. Marguerite's friends were inclined to believe that Gault had over-reacted to what was, at worst, an innocent flirtation. Most were inclined to believe the worst.

*

97

On 17 October Gault rejoined the Patricias at Morcourt on the Somme. By now most of the officers had heard of his troubles with Marguerite but none was prepared to raise the subject with him.

Talbot Papineau's mother had written from her home at Montebello in Quebec. She was horrified by Marguerite's behaviour. Papineau replied,

> You are all wrong about Marguerite Gault. I don't believe a word of the accusation against her. I know all about her innocent little flirtation. It was nothing more. I shall hope to speak to Hamilton about it some day.[8]

Papineau's comment infers that the relationship between Marguerite and Bainsmith was of longer duration and more widely discussed than the one episode at Lydeard, the details of which were known only to Gault and his family.

Agar Adamson heard from his wife of the seriousness of the affair. There was no doubt about whose side he was on.

> I am surprised that Gault's affairs had gone so far, but I always felt confident that something was up, but thought that she would cover up her tracks. She had a very bad temper. Gault is very cheery and hard working and shows no sign of secret stress, but he has always been very secretive and self-contained. The Washington Stevens [sic] were always a rotten lot.[9]

Gault brought with him several replacement officers from England, including the two organizers of the University Company scheme, George McDonald and Percival Molson, and his old fishing friend from Montreal, Philip Mackenzie. Lieut-Colonel R.T. Pelly, one of the original officers, was in command and Gault resumed his appointment of senior major. They were billeted in houses.

The Patricias had just been relieved in the line and were now engaged in training and in building roads. Before the end of the month the entire 27th Division was withdrawn into reserve. A few days later the reason became clear: it was ordered to Salonika and its brigades would be reduced to four battalions each.

With unusual consideration, General Headquarters gave the Patricias a choice as to their future: a place could be found for them in another British brigade or they could join the 3rd Canadian Division which was to be organized in the field early in the New Year.

The Patricias had changed. No longer were they a battalion of former

British Regulars. The majority were now Canadian born; Canada needed them; no one wanted a repetition of the difficulties of finding replacements for a Canadian unit in a British division. Pelly and Gault consulted Buller before coming to their decision. They chose the Canadian option.[10]

The move began on 8 November, 1915. Gault was temporarily in command while Pelly was on leave. After a farewell parade, he led them away through streets lined with the men of the 80th Brigade and the 27th Division, 'who came to salute the Princess's Colour for the last time, to shout goodbye and wish good luck'.[11]

Gault and the officers of the Patricias were not alone in viewing the parting sadly. Private Howard Ferguson, a member of the First University Company who had been with the Regiment since July, wrote of a final parade:

> Hammie Gault chose a picturesque spot on a hill overlooking an expansive valley. The trees were turning to red and gold, blending so beautifully with Hammie on his chestnut charger. There was a gentle breeze that caused a slight rustle among the leaves that autumn day, and as the sun cast its warm rays across this field of sorrow, it seemed to say, 'Cheer up, there are better days ahead.' And I doubt if there was a single man in that assembly that did not feel as I did – a parting with comrades so true and steadfast. Brigadier-General Smith bade us farewell, and the band of the 80th Brigade played us all the way to Flixecourt.'[12]

For two weeks the Regiment remained there as instructional battalion for the Third Army Officers School. Their officers' mess was in the Château de Flixecourt where one evening, its owner, M. Saint, was a guest at dinner. The Pipe-Major came in to play for the officers and did his best to coax the *Marseillaise* from his pipes. Nobody recognized it but M. Saint, who rose and stood to attention. There was an uncomfortable pause before the bewildered officers rather sheepishly got to their feet, convinced that French customs at mess dinners were even more mysterious than their own.[13]

On 25 November the battalion moved by train to Caestre, near Hazebrouck in northern France where they were welcomed to the Canadian Corps by its commander, General Alderson. They were to join the 7th Canadian Infantry Brigade which would be formed late in December. In the interim they would be billeted in nearby Flêtre.

The Patricias, both officers and men, viewed the prospect of working with new comrades and an untried brigade and divisional headquarters with some apprehension. They had been comfortable in the veteran 27th Division, knew the strengths and weaknesses of their sister battalions and had confidence in their commanders. Their feelings were much like those of the Canadian 1st Division in Italy in a later war when they were moved from a veteran British formation of the Eighth Army to the newly arrived 1st Canadian Corps.

In their new brigade they would be joined by The Royal Canadian Regiment, the country's only regular infantry unit, which had garrisoned Bermuda since September, 1914, the 42nd Battalion (Royal Highlanders of Canada) from Montreal and the 49th Battalion from Edmonton. They had arrived in France in October. At least they were not totally green and their appearance was impressive.

Their commander was to be Brigadier-General Archibald Cameron Macdonell, DSO, formerly of the North West Mounted Police and Lord Strathcona's Horse. The Patricias did not know him but they were impressed. One later described him:
'One of the most indomitable, eccentric and beloved soldiers who ever has worn the Canadian uniform. . . . He was of a breed whose passing has left this world a poorer place – colourful, fearless, flamboyant in language, canny in battle, unabashedly sentimental and emotional over his men, who in turn regarded him with joy and pride; they treasured his eccentricities, they boasted (yes, and lied) concerning his highly individual behaviour. They knew him as "Batty Mac."'[14]

Early in December Lieut – Colonel Buller, minus an eye, returned as CO of the Regiment. Pelly was given command of the 8th Royal Irish Rifles. For three weeks the Patricias remained in Flêtre, training and absorbing a draft from the 3rd University Company, then spent Christmas strengthening the defences of Mount Kemmel at the southern tip of the Ypres Salient. They were within 2,000 yards of where the Originals had first entered the line at Vierstraat a year before. In January they spent two periods in the front line, fortunately with few casualties.

There now occurred an attempt at political interference which confirmed the Patricias' worst apprehensions about coming under Canadian command. On 21 January, while Gault was on leave, General Alderson summoned Buller back from the line and told him that the Canadian Government wished to have Gault, as a Canadian, command PPCLI. They offered Buller a new battalion of Mounted Rifles. Buller replied that, if they saw fit to remove him, his place would be with his old Regiment, the Rifle Brigade. If they had no confidence in him, he would ask to be relieved of his command.

The few officers who knew of it were convinced that Sam Hughes, the Minister of Militia and Defence, resented the former independent status of the Patricias and was attempting, as a sop to his inflated ego, to impose his will upon them. Transparently, the removal of their British commanding officer was not designed to further the policy of 'Canadianization' of key appointments: Buller was being offered the command of another Canadian regiment.

They remembered Hughes' attempt to gain direct control of the Patricias by moving them from Levis to Valcartier and how, after Frezenberg, he had tried to replace their officer casualties with unqualified political friends, a move skilfully scotched by Hugh Niven. It was difficult for them, not being devious and suspicious political animals, to divine his motives, but they resented this gratuitous affront to an officer to whom they were devoted.

When Gault returned from leave and learned of Hughes' plan, he was furious. He at once saw the Corps Commander and told him that, if Buller were removed, he would refuse to take his place and would ask for a transfer to another regiment. Alderson had already suffered from Hughes' interference in the internal operations of his command. No more was heard of the matter.

Before he returned to the Regiment, Gault had consulted lawyers about the problem of his marriage. He knew that Marguerite had taken legal advice when she was in Montreal. They advised that, if he were ever to obtain a divorce, he must act quickly. If he delayed too long the Divorce Committee of the Senate would take the view that he was not seriously upset by the affair at Lydeard. What was more, delay on his part would strengthen Marguerite's hand in seeking a legal separation. He and his witnesses would have to appear in front of the Committee in person. How was he to arrange this in wartime?

Now that he was once more in the midst of the Patricias in Belgium, he was, in one sense, particularly alone. There was no one in whom he could or would confide about such a personal affair. Many of the officers knew both him and Marguerite and were keenly interested.

On 10 November Adamson wrote to his wife:

Nobody discusses the Gault affair, although all are aware of it. Martin, Cornish and I are of the opinion that someone ought to wring Bainsmith's ugly little neck. It is quite evident that Gault is undergoing a heavy strain, and that cheerfulness on his part is an effort and he rather prefers to be alone, but we keep him going and try to cheer him up.[15]

Officers returning from leave in London reported that Marguerite and Bainsmith were going out in public together, that Lady Evelyn

Farquhar was horrified and that Bainsmith had said that he hoped in a few months to marry Marguerite.[16]

Two months later, Papineau wrote to his mother:

> I am careful not to discuss the Gault affair.. When the thing first became public, I had a long letter from Marguerite Gault to which I frankly replied expressing my opinion – namely that Hamilton had exaggerated the situation but that she was principally to blame. She was evidently pleased with my view as I had another long letter in reply. Both her letters would have moved me very strongly in her favour, but I have since heard statements which make it difficult for me to retain my original opinion, so that I agree with you it is a matter upon which it is well to be without an opinion until in full possession of the facts.[17]

Early in December 1915 Gault went to England for a day to obtain permission to go to Canada for the divorce. Again in January, he went to London to make final arrangements and was assured that he would be given leave.

One virtue of his job as second-in-command was that he had little time to reflect on his personal affairs. Unlike other Canadian line regiments, PPCLI was organized as a Guards battalion. In 1916 all the Regiment's 'specialists' – scouts, machine gunners, grenadiers, signallers, pioneers, transport, cooks, paymaster, quartermaster and so on – formed a Headquarters Company commanded by the '2 i/c'. In addition he was responsible for the Regiment's funds, for the canteens and messes, for reserve ammunition and for inspecting the trenches by day and by night.

An additional task which Gault particularly enjoyed was organizing a two-day sports meet for the new 7th Brigade at Mont des Cats in early February. Apart from conventional field events, it had a distinctly military flavour. There was an 'alarm race' for the crews and teams of limbered wagons, a 'Victoria Cross' race, wrestling on horseback and grenade throwing. He was delighted when PPCLI transport won two first and three second prizes.[18]

On the 14th Gault was granted leave by the War Office. After handing over his duties to Adamson he left at two o'clock in the morning without saying why or where he was going. The one person in whom he confided was Buller.

> The CO has just told me that my surmise as to Gault's destination was correct, he is off to Canada to see his Divorce

proceedings through. Her lawyer is R.B. Bennett, MP . . . brother of our old Paymaster.[19]

The hearings before the Divorce Committee of the Senate were held in camera and began on Friday, 10 March, when Gault, Percival Benson, Percy Campbell, Marguerite and Marie Coudette, her French maid, gave evidence. Next day the Committee recalled Marguerite to the stand to clarify some points in her evidence.

On the following Wednesday the Committee gave a unanimous judgement refusing Gault's application for a divorce. On Saturday their findings were confirmed by the Senate.

Before they did so, Senator Cloran asked why the evidence in the case had not been printed to guide the Senators and was told that when the committee agreed unanimously it was not the practice to go to the expense of printing the evidence, a copy of which was laid on the table of the House. The Senator protested that eighty-six Senators could not be expected to read the one copy at once and immediately pass judgement.[20]

That copy was destroyed and today no other exists.[21] The only accounts of what transpired are in sketchy and largely speculative newspaper reports. One of the most complete was in the *Ottawa Evening Journal* of 13 March. It begins with a ploy by the defence to prove that Bainsmith was incapable of behaving as Gault alleged:

(He) . . . was severely wounded at the Flanders front. He was hit in the spine and had two of the fingers of his left hand shot off, but they were immediately afterwards sewn on, and the operation was very successful. However, the wound in his spine was more serious and it was thought that locomotor ataxia had developed. To determine this, he was examined by Dr Laidlaw, a prominent Ottawa physician and surgeon. Dr Laidlaw gave medical evidence on Saturday to the committee and it is understood that he declared against locomotor ataxia.

The suit was vigorously defended and it is stated for the defence that Captain Bainsmith at Taunton attempted to kiss Mrs Hamilton Gault, but she refused to allow this liberty. The plaintiff urges that this was by no means all that occurred. This the defence denies.

It is also alleged that the relations between husband and wife have been strained since 1913, and the defence asserts that the cause of this was not to be traced to Mrs Gault.

103

1913 was the year of the African safari which Percy Campbell left after accusing Marguerite of lying and from which she later departed when it proved to be too arduous. A reconciliation between Gault and Campbell followed. Did Gault discover that Marguerite had lied? Or was something else at the root of the alleged strain?

On the day of the divorce committee's refusal to recommend Gault's divorce he began proceedings for a legal separation before the local courts in Montreal. It would be a lengthy process. Marguerite said that she intended to apply for a divorce at the next session of parliament.[22]

Gault left Canada immediately after the Senate hearings and, by the end of the month, was on his way to Belgium.

Chapter 10

SANCTUARY WOOD

Less than three weeks after the Senate refused his divorce Gault was back with the Patricias. He found them in a hutted camp west of Ypres beside the road to Poperinghe. The weather was cold and wet and the few Originals left with the battalion reported that a tour they had just completed in Sanctuary Wood was all too reminiscent of the conditions at St Eloi. They expected to spend another week in reserve before returning to the line.

There had been few casualties in the Regiment since he left for Canada, but the influence of the University Companies upon its character and style had become more apparent. From having been a battalion of tough ex-Regulars, it was now probably the best-educated regiment on the Western Front.

The Originals and the college boys had been wary of each other at first. For the most part the men who had joined in 1914 were older and had been brought up in the rough school of the ranks of the British Regular Army. The arrival of the first university men coincided with the appearance of jam in the rations. The instinctive reaction of the 'old sweats' was to trade it for wine in local estaminets. They were appalled to see that the new boys actually ate the stuff and appeared to like it. What was worse, many of the newcomers refused their rum ration and even showed an incomprehensible preference for milk over beer.

The old Regulars soon began the education of the young by relieving them of their pay in games of skill – 'gambling' was forbidden by King's Regulations – and by object lessons in how to make up deficiencies in kit. They soon grew to respect each other. Some of the Originals were becoming too old for the rigours of war and the end of a long day's march often saw husky university men carrying two rifles.

The supply of officers was not a concern. From the autumn of 1916 until the end of the war virtually every officer of the Regiment came from within its ranks. In all 335 soldiers were commissioned from the ranks of PPCLI in the field, two-thirds of them for other Canadian and British units.[1]

The day after Gault returned there was a parade for Prince Galitzine, a Russian general, who presented him with the insignia of the Order of St Anne, 3rd Class with Swords, for his gallantry and leadership at Frezenberg. A borrowed band played *God Save the Tsar* – the Patricias' pipers could not manage it.[2]

For another week before returning to the front line the Patricias worked to improve the defences of the reserve system. On the 12th Gault gave Percival Campbell an impression of his new surroundings:

> There was the Hell of a straff on up north last evening, and since last writing there have been several shows, with the accompanying straffs on the south side. Guess we'll get in in time to get it from the centre! Have a feeling that there'll be another push against this place sometime soon!
>
> That bastard Fritz saw me riding down the Menin road the other day accompanied by the company officers and had the cheek to shell us. Two pip squeaks burst overhead about 75 yds away and the shrap scattered all round Hugh Niven and myself. First I thought Sandy was hit, then as the third burst I thought I was hit, and then all of us realizing the situation sat down in our saddles, dug our heels in and had the damndest race down the pavé you ever saw! The following day when I was walking alone over the same bit a few more shells came closer than I cared about! Healthy place this all right!!!
>
> By the way, keep my scribbles will you? I write to you whenever I can, and after the show, if I get through, they will afford me a sort of a diary of life out here, and may help to remind me of pleasant memories of the long ago.
>
> We push off tonight so don't expect to hear from me for a week or more. It's raining like the Devil, so we'll hope Fritz will want to keep in his dugout and will refrain from shelling the back roads.

That night the Patricias relieved the 49th Battalion in what was notoriously the most repulsive and hazardous position on the Western Front.

By 1916 the little hamlet of Hooge with its château and park had become the barrier which blocked the Menin Road, the German army's main avenue of advance to Ypres. Now utterly ruined, it was the focus of effort of two implacable enemies. In places their front lines were within grenade-throwing range. So deadly were the snipers who lurked in its ruins that movement by day was suicidal. To make matters worse, the trenches and posts were in terrible condition, in places full of filthy water. Whenever it rained half-buried bodies appeared above the surface of the stinking mud. Over all lay a miasma of corruption.

One company headquarters was in a culvert under the main road. At an end of the château's stables was a rifle section; at the other, the enemy. A German post was called 'the chicken coop' because of wire netting put up to catch grenades.

The Württembergers opposite were unusually enterprising and the Canadian sentries were constantly on the alert against raids after prisoners. Three such had been attempted recently on a single night, and just before the Patricias took over the line the stable post had been attacked by a bombing party thirty or forty strong.[3]

Veterans were to remember the horrors of Hooge long after time had softened their other recollections of war.

> My most uncomfortable trench trips were two forty-eight hour tours at the Culvert under the Menin road and another forty-eight hours at the Hooge stables beside that road. The water in the trenches was so deep we had to wear rubber waders such as trout fishermen use. . . . At 2 in the morning, Major Hamilton Gault came through our trench.[4]

Each night, from battalion headquarters at Halfway House, he walked, crawled and slithered to visit every post held by the battalion. 'Met Major Gault today who exchanged greetings with merry laughter and a joke!'[5] No one knew better than his men the danger to which he was exposed on these inspections. The awe which his appearance and formidable personality had inspired in Ottawa had long since given way to that companionable respect which the fighting man holds for an undoubted leader. They knew that there was little that he could do for them in the stinking swamp of Hooge but give encouragement and show that he cared. Letters and diaries spoke of 'our wonderful Major Gault', 'our friend the Major', 'one of nature's finest gentlemen'. After he had passed by, they were still cold and wet, but they felt less miserable.

Gault described his rounds to Percival Campbell:

> We usually chuck bombs at each other every other night and sniping is altogether too active. However, we hope to get things put right before long and to oust Fritz from the fire supremacy which he seems to have enjoyed for so long. Visiting rounds is not a continual picnic in this part of the world for I usually get sniped at in the brilliant moonlight nights we have recently had, and the

other evening they turned a machine gun loose when your little nephew promptly, though perhaps not elegantly or bravely, took to a 'Johnson Hole' – If you know of a better 'ole, what I says is go to it.[6]

Each day the casualty list mounted. On the 17th Lieutenant Horner and CSM Cordery were shot through the head by snipers. Next day Regimental Sergeant Major Godfrey and his batman, Private Boulter, were killed and CSM Pritchard wounded when a shell hit a dugout near one that Gault shared with Buller. In all over sixty of all ranks were killed or wounded in the week at Hooge, more than the battalion had lost in the previous six months.

Corporal Walter Draycott spoke for all when he wrote, 'A welcome relief comes at last. The 60th Battalion Canadians take over "God help them!"'[7]

The 60th were late in arriving. There was no time for the men to change boots if they were to be out of sight of the enemy before daylight. It was an exhausted battalion which covered the three miles to Ypres at a fast pace in wet and cumbersome hip-waders.[8] Some of them noticed that it was Good Friday.

Two days later, Gault wrote:

We're out in rest for a bit – just a few days – last tour was not entirely a picnic as you will see from the casualty list. One day Bosche planes were all over us flying so low that our Archies couldn't reach 'em. Following day Battn. H.Q. were shelled with 4.2's. Personally I hate being straffed with heavies, makes me pensive listening for them to come, and wondering where they are going to burst. . . .

Fritz apparently carried out an air raid the other night. We could hear his planes buzzing in the heavens and twice I caught sight of them silhouetted in the moonlight – it was rather wonderful, and as they returned over their own lines they threw out rocket signals which made the night seem like fairyland.

Several bombing shows were put on by the Bosche during our stay at Hooge. There was one Hell of a row lasting usually for about half an hour consisting of about 60 Bosche bombs bursting and about 200 of ours thrown back. I only hope ours did them more harm then theirs did to us, for we only had a very few minor casualties from this source.[9]

★

Gault received many letters from Canadians expressing admiration for the Regiment or concern for a relative in its ranks. On 24 April he answered a mother:

Dear Mrs. Robertson,

I was glad to receive your letter of March 17th & to learn that your son was serving with PPCLI. I looked him up at once & will be only too glad to do anything I can for him should the occasion arise.

As you probably know he has now got his Sergeant's stripes & is doing very well indeed in our No. 2 Coy. I have seen him several times since then, in and out of the trenches & find that his company commander thinks highly of him & speaks favourably of his work.

This life in France seems to agree very well with most of us & as a result all ranks are extremely fit and cheery.

With kind regards,

On 29 April the Patricias moved into brigade support, closer to the front, where they were heavily shelled. A week later they relieved the 49th Battalion in Sanctuary Wood, on the immediate right of their former position at Hooge.

Far to the south, in the region of the River Somme, the Germans had become aware of preparations for a massive British and French offensive. Their High Command issued orders for all their armies on the Western Front to pin down their opponents and prevent them joining the impending attack. The Fourth Army opposite Ypres reacted by raiding aggressively and attempting to disrupt the British defences by heavy shelling.

The Patricias were soon engaged in a grim duel with the German guns for their defences in the Wood. Every trench junction, every key point had been registered by the enemy who now embarked on the systematic destruction of the front line. Every night the Canadians laboured to repair the damage and to improve their communication and reserve trenches. Mercifully the defences suffered more than the men: their week in the Wood cost them three killed as opposed to eighteen at Hooge.

Yet for the Ypres Salient April and May were quiet months. In the warm May weather Sanctuary Wood, where thick foliage gave cool shade and freedom of movement, seemed infinitely preferable to the cellars and ditches of Hooge.'[10] The Patricias were relieved during the night of 15 May.

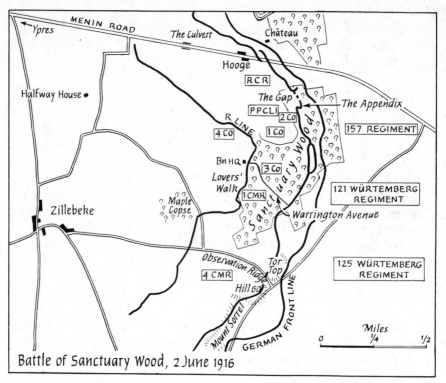

Battle of Sanctuary Wood, 2 June 1916

The 7th Brigade now moved into divisional reserve west of Ypres. The brigadier went on leave for two weeks and Buller took his place, leaving Gault to command PPCLI.[11] It was not an exacting time. The administrative machine which he had supervised so carefully worked smoothly. The men rested, ate hot meals, bathed, received clean underclothes and socks, missing kit was replaced, weapons refurbished. For the first week the battalion relaxed in the warm spring sunshine, then moved forward into brigade reserve where, each night, they provided large parties to work on the trenches.

They fully expected this interlude to end with a return to Hooge. They cheered when they learned that the programme of reliefs had been scrapped, that their Colonel had been given a choice of sectors and that he had opted for Sanctuary Wood.

The eastern tip of the Ypres Salient was held by the 3rd Canadian Division. The Germans overlooked most of their line except on the right where it rose at the southern end of Sanctuary Wood to the summit of the Ypres ridge where three small hills, Tor Top, Hill 61 and Mount Sorrel, gave the Canadians observation over the enemy. From Tor Top a prominent spur known as Observatory Ridge runs westward toward Ypres. From it and the hills held by the Canadians the low ground behind the British positions defending Ypres could be clearly seen.

General Freiherr von Watter, commanding the XIIIth Württemberg Corps, saw in the instructions to pin down the Allied troops on his front an opportunity to retrieve a failing reputation. If he were to capture Observatory Ridge the defences of Ypres would be hopelessly compromised. Not only would the British be unable to draw troops from the area, they might even be forced to delay their Somme offensive. For six weeks he made meticulous preparations to capture the Ridge.[12]

As the Patricias moved back into the line, so opposite them did the 121st Württemberg Regiment, whose rehearsals for the assault were complete.

On the Canadian side there were signs aplenty that the enemy was preparing an attack, but none to suggest that it was imminent. In particular there was no evidence of the Germans moving in reserves to exploit a success. Their only reinforcement, unknown to the Canadians, was a formidable 'travelling circus' of heavy guns and large-calibre mortars.

The first day of June brought nothing more menacing than the almost routine heavy fire of the enemy artillery.

After ensuring that the specialist platoons which came under his direct command were in position, Gault busied himself with the administrative duties which were the lot of the second-in-command. Because of the vulnerability of its rearward communications to shellfire, it would be almost impossible to re-supply the battalion during a lengthy battle. Within the position he built up stocks of ammunition and preserved rations, but containers for storing water were not supplied by the army. That problem he solved by finding a supply of gasoline tins which he had filled with water and cached in the forward area.

Always present was the possibility that he would have to take command of the battalion if Buller became a casualty; he was completely familiar with the plans for fighting the battle which one day must come.

The right of the battalion position in Sanctuary Wood sloped upward to Tor Top which was held by the 1st Battalion, Canadian Mounted Rifles. The importance of that hill and of Observatory Ridge which projects westward from it was as obvious to Gault and his CO as to von Watter. To them the two features were the most likely objectives of an enemy attack. If it succeeded, the PPCLI positions would lie open from the rear.

Nos. 1 and 2 Companies of the Patricias held the front line which lay along the eastern edge of Sanctuary Wood from the slopes of Tor Top to a four-hundred-yard gap, completely dominated by the enemy, which separated them from the Royal Canadian Regiment at Hooge. Some five hundred yards to the rear lay the 'R' Line, a well-developed fighting trench, through which the two regiments were in touch. It was held on the left by No. 4 Company

By agreement with the 8th Brigade on his right, Buller positioned No. 3 Company in its area, in 'Warrington Avenue', a communication trench which angled back from the 1st CMR's front to his reserve line. From there they would be able either to support his own front or to prevent the enemy from moving around his right flank.

By this stage of the war all except the naive recognized that, if the enemy applied a sufficient weight of shells followed closely by well-trained and determined infantry, there was virtually no trench he could not take. This had happened to the Patricias' front line at Frezenberg and it might well happen again. In discussions with his officers, Buller rehearsed the alternative actions he might take. If the enemy gained a foothold on Observatory Ridge, he said, 'There is only one thing to do – go forward and meet them.'

The morning of 2 June dawned with the enemy's familiar 'hate', bursts of artillery fire along the front. But on this day the customary half-hour of shelling did not stop. By nine o'clock it had developed into a sustained and violent bombardment which devastated the trenches of No.1 Company and the Mounted Rifles holding the hills on the right. There was nothing which could be done to counter the storm. Most of the British heavy artillery had moved south to the Somme.

A curtain of fire isolated the Patricias. Telephone lines to the rear were cut and communication trenches so accurately shelled that movement within the battalion became almost impossible. At 11 a.m. Gault estimated that No. 3 and Headquarters Company in Warrington Avenue and its adjoining trenches had lost 50 per cent of their rifle strength. The plight of No. 1 in the front line was far more serious.

For four hours the bombardment continued before lifting from the front line. As it did so, grey-clad infantry clambered from the enemy trenches and advanced at a leisurely pace towards No. 1 Company of the Patricias and the CMR on the hills to their right, some of them singing and laughing, confident that nothing could have survived the destruction wrought by their guns.

The pitifully few survivors of No.1 Company fought to the last to stem the enemy. The end came when the six unwounded survivors in the position were overwhelmed by infantry with flame-throwers who had crept around their flank. On their left, No.2 Company, though isolated by shellfire and having suffered heavily, was outside the boundary of the enemy attack. They now rose to what was left of their parapets and poured machine-gun and rifle fire into the flank of the advancing Württembergers.

Within half an hour the Germans had overrun the remnants of the Mounted Rifles on Tor Top, were advancing along Observatory Ridge and had begun to bomb their way down the vital Warrington Avenue and its neighbouring trenches. No. 3 Company fought for every inch of the ground. For an hour and a half their epic defence went on; at its end scarcely a man survived to tell the story. After the battle little heaps of the Regiment's dead were found, back to back in the trenches, every few yards where they had built block after block until weight of numbers forced them to give way.

Soon after the German attack down the Avenue began, while Gault was working desperately to prepare a blocking position farther back, a bursting shell blew him from his feet, shattering his left leg and lacerating the other. He was carried unconscious back to 'Lover's Walk', a fire trench in the R Line. There, with other wounded, he was attended by Captain J.B. McGregor, the Patricias' medical officer who earlier had been blown out of his Regimental Aid Post. It was impossible to move stretcher cases to the rear.

During most of the long hours of that afternoon and evening Gault was conscious, his mind clear, and he continued to play what part he could in the battle. Sometime after three o'clock he was told that Colonel Buller, carrying a rifle, had been killed while leading a counter-attack up Warrington Avenue. While he had stopped the Germans in their tracks, the situation of the Patricias was desperate. Casualties had been enormous. Two companies were without officers and command had devolved upon Captain Martin, the adjutant, who was now organizing the defence. While the line was holding in front, the Germans had taken Observatory Ridge and were threatening to envelop the Regiment's rear.

Gault realized that a gap lay open to the enemy on the right of Warrington Avenue. He summoned his old friend Philip Mackenzie and ordered him to take two platoons of No. 4 Company to cover it[13]. At one point, when an enemy breakthrough seemed imminent, Gault had himself propped up on his stretcher and waited for them with two loaded revolvers in his lap. Later in the day a runner from The Royal Canadian Regiment, Private R.J. Blatchford, brought a message along the R Line to the PPCLI.

I was amazed to find ... Hamilton Gault lying there on a stretcher, fully conscious, directing his men, and absolutely refusing to leave. Finally the Medical Officer had to administer injections and it was then that I myself directed them overland to the Medical Station. . . . There is one man I know should have received the Victoria Cross for bravery and devotion to duty . . . Andrew Hamilton Gault. . . . I was the only person outside of his regiment present. What a thousand pities I had not reported his gallantry to my own Commanding Officer.[14]

By mid-afternoon the main German thrust had halted and everywhere along the front they began digging in to consolidate their gains. The Canadians watched them in disbelief, incredulous that they should fail to administer the coup de grace by driving north from Observatory Ridge behind PPCLI and the RCR to the Menin Road. By six o'clock it was too late. Canadian reserves sealed off the Ridge and prepared to counter-attack.

For the Patricias, the battle went on. Major Donald Gray of No. 4 Company had taken command and sent Lieutenant Louis Scott to report the battalion's situation to Brigadier-General Macdonell. On his way he came upon a wounded soldier, Private Brazell, clutching Princess Patricia's Colour to his chest. He had rescued it from a smashed dugout where it lay with its dead escort. Scott removed it from its staff, wrapped it around his waist and helped the soldier to an aid post before setting out through the continuous barrage of shellfire which lay between him and Ypres. (It was returned to the battalion as its remnants marched out of the line.)

The enemy now attempted to break through 'The Appendix', the fire trench on the left of the Patricias' line. Three times the much depleted No.2 Company beat them off, then at night, when in imminent danger of being surrounded, they withdrew across country with all their weapons, their wounded and their equipment to the R Line in the rear.

Counter-attacks by reserve units made little progress against the enemy's superior artillery and the Patricias continued to hold their positions until, on 4 June, they at last were relieved. The cost in casualties had been almost the same as at Frezenberg but, as there, they had prevented a military disaster.

The German infantry had taken Observatory Ridge as their commander had ordered. Below them lay open the flat ground before Ypres, the unattained objective of so many attacks since October, 1914. It was well within the capacity of the well-disciplined Württembergers, supported by their excellent artillery, to advance into the flats and totally disrupt the Ypres defences on which the left of the BEF was anchored.

Yet, with such a stunning success almost within their grasp, the Germans hesitated.

Their probes downward from the Ridge behind the Patricias and further west to Maple Copse were met by the fire of Mackenzie's two platoons, sent earlier by Gault to cover the opening. And to their right there was no sign that the Patricias' resistance was weakening.

The officer commanding the Germans on Observatory Ridge decided not to risk advancing beyond his objective without the approval of higher authority. Had PPCLI pulled back, or failed to guard their rear, it might well have been another story.

Ten days after the Patricias were relieved, the Canadian Corps attacked and drove the Württembergers from the lost positions. German prisoners later said that General von Watter was congratulated on 3 June for his success, but within two weeks was relieved of his command.[15]

When, in the late afternoon of the battle, it first became possible to move stretcher cases to the rear, Gault refused to be evacuated before his wounded men. When he later lost consciousness, Ray Appleton, his devoted butler, batman and friend, as at Frezenberg, found two stretcher bearers and began the long carry toward the dressing station three miles to the rear. Private George Milne recalled seeing, 'the ashen-grey face of Hammie Gault as they carried him out past us on a stretcher during the late afternoon of the 2nd. I never thought he would live.'[16]

On the way to the rear one of the stretcher bearers was killed by a shell splinter. Eventually Appleton and the second man with their heavy burden came to a light railway which traversed the swampy ground and loaded Gault on to a handcart. Barely had they begun to move when a shell burst in front and cratered the line. They carried Gault the rest of the way on a stretcher.[17]

As the Patricias moved out of the line on 4 June it was rumoured that Gault had died and, next day, newspapers carried a report of his death.

In Bishop's Lydeard his mother and his sister Lillian were frantic for news. They knew that he had been dangerously wounded, had seen the press reports, then heard nothing more. Eventually, on 9 June, his mother received a telegram from the War Office. They regretted to inform her that her son who had been wounded, was listed as 'seriously ill'.

By 1916 women knew the implications of that expression. Lillian set off for France to find him.

Chapter 11

OUT OF ACTION

At least twelve hours had elapsed after Gault was wounded before he received even the emergency surgery necessary to stabilize his condition. By that time shock and loss of blood from the wounds in his legs, buttocks and back had almost fatally undermined his strength. He was unconscious when, on 4 June, he arrived at No 7 Stationary Hospital in Boulogne.

For four days surgeons attempted to save his shattered left leg but on the 9th were forced to amputate it above the knee. His condition had deteriorated further by the time Lillian found him on the 10th. He was allowed no visitors and was far too ill to be moved to England.[1] Another operation followed on the 13th and for some days he was given hour-long antiseptic baths in an attempt 'to kill the poison in his system'. Several shell splinters still remained in his body.[2] A worrying week went by before he was allowed visitors.

A message to him spoke of the Regiment's concern:

> Keep us posted in your address and we will send you all particulars of the regiment. All ranks send you greetings and regret your serious wound and look forward to the day when you are able to return and command your old regt now one thousand and thirty strong. Major Adamson[3]

Gault now held a unique unofficial position in the army. As the founder of PPCLI and because of his seniority in the Regiment, he was, as a matter of course, consulted on a variety of matters which affected it. As his suggestions had been sought on the Regiment's reinforcements and on its future after leaving the 80th Brigade, so was he asked for his views on who should succeed Colonel Buller and on the employment of other officers. Those in authority valued his opinions as much because of his qualities and experience as a soldier as any proprietorial rights which he was seen to have over his Regiment.

An example of his easy relationship with senior officers can be inferred from a four-page, hand-written letter from 'Batty Mac',

Brigadier-General A.C. Macdonell, Commander of the 7th Canadian Infantry Brigade.

Forgive my not writing sooner but I have simply been kept on the go refitting etc & now we are going back into the line again, I feel I must have a chat with you before leaving.

I do hope & trust all is going well with you & was comforted to know you were in the dear old No. 7 Stationary Boulogne. . . . I also heard your sister was with you & of course that will cheer you tremendously. . . .

The PPCLI will always be able to look back on the last fight proudly. No Regt could have done better & few as well.

After Col Buller's glorious death & your wounding, Donald Gray took hold well & carried on. All the officers with Hugh Niven in the Appendix having been killed or wounded (he himself wounded) Donald sent up Glassco. Hugh came out & got his wound dressed & started back & was wounded again, got dressed again & again was wounded, this time they evacuated him by main force. The standard was brought back by Scott, about 6pm 2nd inst., who after he had something to eat & drink went back & was eventually a casualty (wounded). I wrote to poor Lady Buller & gave her particulars & to the Duke as I knew his regard for Buller & keen interest in your Regt. . . .

On the 7th when the Pats marched out of Camp 'A', we tried to cheer them out but most of us like myself got too choked when we saw their numbers. They themselves marched proudly with their standard at their head & led by their pipe band.

Sir Malcolm Murray came at the Duke's request & visited the Regt yesterday. We had a parade of the men who had been thru the fight & he made them a short but very good speech. I think that all the men were pleased.

Col Elmslie is now B.G. Commanding the 8th & we hear Loomis has 2nd Bde, Lipsett has the Divn, a splendid choice. . . . Please let me know at once if there is anything we can do for you.[4]

Gault spent a full month in Boulogne before he was strong enough to be moved by the Hospital Ship *St Denis* to England and by train to the I.O.D.E.[5] hospital at No. 1 Hyde Park Place in London. His life was in no immediate danger but months of further surgery and recuperation were to follow before he was discharged at the end of November to a long convalescence.

Among the patients in the hospital was his cousin, Gordon Blackader, an officer of the Canadian Black Watch who had also been wounded at Sanctuary Wood. As the weeks went by, Blackader's condition weakened and he realized that he would probably not recover. His concern for the future welfare of his wife, Kathleen, was heightened by the possibility that she might be denied an inheritance due to her from her mother's estate. Before he died on 10 August[6], he obtained Gault's promise to pursue Kathleen's interests and an assurance that she and her infant daughter Patricia would not lack financial security.

Kathleen had been a daily visitor to the hospital, small, bright, bravely vivacious and sympathetic. Now, like other young widows, she was a tragic figure in black, her large eyes shadowed by exhaustion and grief. Gault's sympathy and sense of family obligation were aroused. Knowing what she had lost in what he saw as the cause of her country, he willingly assumed the responsibility which he had promised to his cousin.

For a time Marguerite too almost gave way to her sympathies. On 14 August Agar Adamson wrote to his wife from France, 'Miriam Scott tells me that Mrs Gault is all for returning to the fold and her rooms are covered in photographs of Gault.' Be that as it may, the *Canada Gazette* of 23 September gave notice that Marguerite intended to apply at the next session of Parliament for a divorce on the grounds of her husband's adultery. This was an echo of the petition of a year ago, which was withdrawn in March. As then, no hint exists as to whom the other woman might be, if there was one. In November the *Gazette* gave notice that Gault too intended to seek a divorce.

But while the War went on, so the Regiment continued to be the centre of Hammie's life. Soon after he arrived in London, wounded Patricias, officers and men, called to see him and, despite his condition, were seldom turned away. Adamson, still temporarily in command of the Battalion, was concerned. 'Hope Gault isn't overdoing the seeing everybody bit as he did the last time and then broke down. He is an obstinate dear good chap.'[7]

Gault had confidence in Adamson's ability to command, a feeling which the latter did not share. On 24 July he wrote to bolster his morale:

> You are far too modest in yourself old boy. Please remember that there is none better suited to command the Battalion than yourself and, besides this, there is now no one else to handle the job.

Again, four days later:

10. Officers of PPCLI, Lansdowne Park, Ottawa, August, 1914.
Standing, L to R: Capt A.S.A.M. Adamson, Lieut L.T. Bennett, Major J.W.H. McKinery, Major C.B. Keenan (MO), Lieut
C.E. Crabbe, Major R.T. Pelly, Capt D.F.B. Gray, Lieut H.W. Niven, Major A.H. Gault, Lt-Col F.D. Farquhar, Capt H.C.
Buller, Lieut E. Christie, Lieut C.A. Wake, Major J.D. Hay Shaw, Capt C.F. Smith, Major C.Q. Court, Lieut D.E. Cameron,
Major J.S. Ward, Lieut F.F. Minchin.
Seated: Capt McDougal, Lieut H.E. Sulivan, Lieut B.F. Bainsmith, Lieut J.L. Carr, Lieut F. Fitzgerald, Lieut T.M. Papineau,
Lieut P.V. Cornish, Lieut M.S. DeBay, Lieut C.H. Price, Lieut F.L. Eardley-Wilmot.
Not in Picture: Lieut C.J.T. Stewart, Capt D.O.C. Newton, Lieut W.G. Colquhoun, Lieut S.L. Jones.

11. Lieutenant-Colonel Francis Farquhar, first commanding officer of PPCLI, killed at St Eloi, 20 March, 1915.

12. Lieutenant-Colonel H.C. 'Teta' Buller, second commanding officer of PPCLI, killed at Sanctuary Wood, 2 June, 1916.

13. Princess Patricia's Canadian Light Infantry, Lansdowne Park, Ottawa, August, 1914.

14. The Camp Colour embroidered by Princess Patricia in 1914 and carried by the Regiment in all their actions in the First World War. Known affectionately as the Ric-A-Dam-Doo, it was consecrated as the Regimental Colour in 1919 and decorated by the Princess, with a wreath of honour.

15. Hamilton Gault, from the portrait by Glyn Philpott, 1919.

16. The Originals at Frezenberg, from the painting by W.B. Wollen.

17. Kathleen Blackader.

18. Patricia Blackader who became Hammie's ward.

19. Hammie and Kathleen, with Clive Benson, in the car in which she was killed.

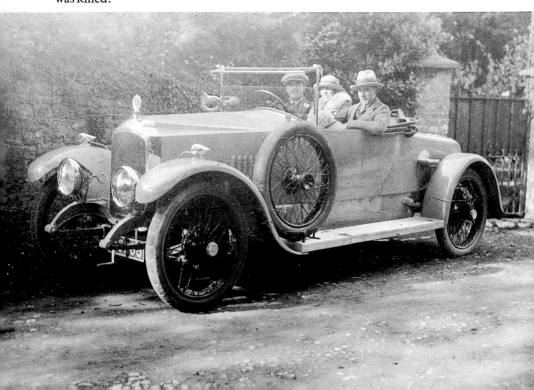

... as far as I am concerned I want you most emphatically to carry on; on no account do I want to see an outsider commanding the regiment as long as we have qualified officers to do so and although I know it is a rotten job at times and a bit disheartening when you get all kinds of conflicting orders from higher authority, I feel that you are the one man for the job. So that's that.

... from what I hear, I conclude there is no chance of Pelly coming back to the Regt. so this absolutely clinches matters.

Gault was wrong about Colonel Pelly. On 3 August he left the Royal Irish and resumed command of PPCLI.

At that time Gault's doctors had become concerned that the stump of his left leg was not healing satisfactorily and decided that a further amputation was necessary. The operation was successful but it was a setback to his recovery and to his mobility. He had been getting about the hospital on crutches and had been able to go for a drive in Hyde Park with his mother. But two weeks after the operation he wrote wryly to Mrs Adamson who had earlier called to see him, 'Please forgive this pencilled scrawl: I am still taking, or rather again taking, the rest cure on my back.'[8]

At last, on 7 September, he was able to leave the hospital and travel to Taunton to stay with his mother, but his medical problems were not over. A month later he spent five days in the Granville Hospital at Ramsgate, having six more pieces of shell removed. In mid-November he returned to the IODE Hospital for a further week's treatment and was then fitted with an artificial leg.

Impatient to return to the war, Gault grudgingly endured the months of convalescence and adjustment to his disability. The earliest he could hope to return to the front would be in the following May. In the meantime there was little he could do in England and much to be attended to in Canada – including Kathleen Blackader's inheritance and his divorce from Marguerite.

The effect of the latter on the attitude of friends in Montreal was of particular concern. Many, he knew, sided with Marguerite and would not forgive him for his accusations against her. As is usual in public scandals, disapproval was heard more clearly than silent agreement. Being anxious to avoid a rebuff, he sounded out men of substance as to the welcome he might expect in Montreal. A prominent Canadian banker and leader of society, Sir Frederick Williams-Taylor, replied:

... You may be sure you are not forgotten in Montreal and that you are highly regarded in many more quarters than perhaps you suspect. I can say quite frankly that I take off my hat in profound respect, not unmixed with envy, to a man who has played the leading part you have in defence of the greatest traditions of the British race and the British Empire.

Such reassurances helped him decide on a visit to Montreal early in the New Year.

In September and early October the Patricias took part in the battles of the Somme, then marched north to occupy a position on the slopes of Vimy Ridge. A week later they provided a guard of honour for the Duke of Connaught who had just retired as Governor-General of Canada. One of his last acts had been to write a personal letter to the Prime Minister, Sir Robert Borden, confirming an earlier discussion. In it he appealed to the Canadian Government not to disband Princess Patricia's Canadian Light Infantry at the end of the war.

After outlining its history, he continued,

They have fought in many an engagement and have on every occasion brought honour to the Canadian name. On many occasions their losses have been very severe and two successive Commanding Officers, Lt.-Colonel Farquhar and Lt.-Colonel Buller have been killed at the head of the Regt and many other officers have also fallen. Major Hamilton Gault, the Founder of the Regt. and the second in command has been four times wounded. There is no Regt. in this war that has made a greater name for itself. The Regt. bears the name of my daughter, a member of the Royal family and daughter of Canada's Governor-General. May I hope that special consideration may be given to the services of so distinguished a Canadian Regt. and that you will not forget the appeal of, Yours very sincerely, Arthur[9]

On 31 October, the day after the Duke's visit, Colonel Pelly left the Regiment to instruct at the Senior Officers School in Aldershot and Agar Adamson was promoted to command.

In a letter to his wife the new Colonel revealed a poignant gesture which reflected Marguerite's affection for the Patricias.

Lady Evelyn [Farquhar] has sent 20,000 cigarettes to the men for Xmas, and if you can keep a secret which only I am supposed to know, Mrs. Gault (junior) has sent 135 wrist watches, one for each of the original men left in the Regiment to be given 'from a woman who loved the old Regiment' but whose name must not be mentioned.[10]

Gault spent Christmas, 1916, at Bagshot with the Connaughts and Princess Patricia.

For two months Adamson had been commanding the Regiment as a major. He wrote frequently to tell Gault of the Regiment's exploits and of the problems of command. About one subject he was quite clear: should Gault return to France, fit for duty in the line, he would be delighted and would happily turn over the command of the Regiment to him.

In return, Gault told Adamson of his thoughts on the subject:

> . . . there is of course nothing that I would sooner do than get back to the Battalion At the same time I know that I shall never be able to get about nearly as freely as I used to with this damnable swinger which I now have, and the question arises in my mind whether it would be in the best interests of the Regiment for me to do so.
>
> There is another thing too that bothers me and that is the thought of you who have been carrying on for so long and doing so damned well; my return to the Battalion would also stop or put a block in the promotion of so many officers who so greatly deserve it. I want you to talk the matter over freely with the General and you may rest assured that I shall be quite content with any decision that is come to . . . in the interests of the only thing that counts, namely the Regiment. I told the General when here, exactly what I felt about it and also told him that I don't want a position anywhere unless I can properly do my job and carry my own weight. Nothing would worry me more than that of being tolerated or of being given a position simply on account of past associations. . . .
>
> I go really pretty well on the level and each day go for a two or three mile walk to get myself fit. But I'm done on the rough going and the other day while pottering with a gun around the hillside coverts could not have managed to get on without assistance. I think I've told you the worst; the best is that I can get on in the saddle; but if I can't get back to a fighting job in France or to a temporary job with the idea of finally getting back to the line, I shall have a shot at the flying game.[11]

The question of who should be named to command PPCLI was settled as far as the Army was concerned, when shortly afterwards,

Adamson's promotion to lieutenant-colonel was confirmed. He immediately wrote to say that he still hoped that Gault would return to France and take command of the Regiment.[12]

On 2 February Gault sailed for Canada in the SS *Missanabie*. His arrival in Montreal coincided with a week's campaign to raise money for the Red Cross and the 'Patriotic Fund' which helped needy families of soldiers overseas. A crowded luncheon in the vast dining room of the Windsor Hotel, attended by most of the prominent businessmen of Montreal, had assembled to receive donations when General Wilson, commanding the Montreal District, entered, followed by Gault and a group of wounded officers from overseas.

When the distinguished father of the Princess Patricia's Canadian Light Infantry was recognized, the whole room rose to their feet as one man, waving napkins, cheering and calling out his name. When all were seated again the General rose to deliver his short address of welcome home to the wounded officers, but he was not permitted to finish before cries of 'Gault!', 'Gault!' rang out from all over the room until the Major rose to his feet. This was but the signal for all present to let their enthusiasm for a very gallant officer and his heroic regiment break loose once more and for fully five minutes Major Gault was unable, because of the cheering, to begin his few words of thanks, words in which he cautioned those present not to forget the returned soldier in after years when the glamour and romance of war would have died down and the citizen would be inclined to be less enthusiastic than he was at the moment.[13]

Gault's words reflected his concern for the soldiers he had come to love and respect. He reminded people of their obligation to them:

Many of them come back dismembered and maimed for life. I only hope that in the enthusiasm of their return your generosity will not be forgotten in the years to come. It is so easy to do things for a man upon his return to his country. It is also easy to forget in the fifteen or twenty years, or the next generation what that man's services have been. I hope that in the great generosity of this hour, you will not pauperize the home-coming soldier by your unlimited charity.

[The disabled soldier] should return to a country where he should find his people ready to find employment for him, and in saying that, I realize that employers of labour would have to do a great deal more than is expected of them in an ordinary commercial way. They will have to make places for them. They will have to find employment for the soldier that the soldier can do. The men who have given of their best should be made to feel that their services have not in any way been forgotten.[14]

His words were widely reported and brought a request from the Canadian Association of Returned Soldiers to take an interest in the organization. At that time it counted some 2000 members in most of the principal centres of the country and was about to form a national organization with a Federal Charter. Gault had no difficulty in supporting the aims of the Association: of perpetuating the comradeship of service in the War, of remembrance and of loyalty to Canada and the Empire. Of particular appeal was the clause which read 'to ensure that provision is made for due care of the sick, wounded and needy among those who have served, including reasonable pensions, medical care and proper provision for dependant families of enlisted men.'

His intention of returning to active service prevented him from becoming an active member of the Association, although he advised its Montreal District on the drafting of its constitution. After the War he took an active part in the affairs of the Royal Canadian Legion whose efforts over the years have resulted in Canada having the most enlightened system of veterans' care of any country in the world.[15]

Like other soldiers who had fought the enemy in the field, Gault had little sympathy with the way civilians at home treated former friends of German extraction. A popular member of Montreal society before the war, and a friend of Gault, was an immigrant named Baumgarten. He had made a fortune in sugar, built a splendid house and entertained lavishly. Like Hammie, he was a member of the Montreal Hunt Club. Open-handed and gregarious, Baumgarten's main interest was his position in Montreal society. But he remained a loyal son of the Fatherland and in July, 1914, at a dinner party in his house, he proposed a toast to the Kaiser. When war was declared a few days later his former friends cut him dead.

Things remained in this sad state for more than two years. When Gault learned of the way this decent and generous man had been treated, it offended his sense of chivalry. With another wounded and decorated Montrealer, he arrived at Baumgarten's house in an open carriage to pay him a formal call. Within days others followed and Baumgarten's isolation ended.

On 1 March the hearings began before the Superior Court in Montreal of both Gault's and Marguerite's petitions for legal separations. When they ended on the 17th, Mr Justice Weir reserved final judgement but on the basis of their marriage contract which provided that Gault was obliged to 'provide for (her) necessities and support and to pay all expenses connected therewith without (her) or her revenues being answerable for the same or any part thereof', he ordered Gault to pay Marguerite $5,000 towards her costs and an interim 'alimentary allowance' of $1,400 per month.

In his judgement two weeks later, Weir ruled that Gault had failed to prove the allegations against his wife and granted her a separation on grounds of 'ill-usage and grievous insults offered to her by her husband.' He confirmed the alimentary allowance which, added to her personal income, would give her $24,000 per year. After paying it, Gault's annual income would be reduced to $43,000. With the costs of the separation and of the past and impending applications for divorce added to the judgement, freeing himself from Marguerite had become an expensive operation.

The next chapter in the dissolution of their marriage was scheduled for the third week of April when hearings before the Senate of Marguerite's petition for divorce and Gault's counter-suit were to open. She alleged that he had committed adultery but no details of her complaint have survived.

With his charm, his wealth, his matinee-idol looks and reputation for gallantry, Gault was undoubtedly attractive to women and he enjoyed their company. There had been endless opportunities for extra-marital dalliance had he chosen to take them.

Among his wartime letters, those from women reveal nothing of a romantic nature except one. Of it, Gault preserved only a few lines with a fragment of a four-leafed clover and a verse.

> I went out to pick daisies the other afternoon and enclose the four-leaf clover that I found. May it bring you good luck.
> One leaf is for hope, and one is for faith,
> And one is for love, you know,
> And then there's another one, just for luck,
> If you search you will find where they grow –
> Molly Make Believe

There are two possibilities. Though he was an honourable man with uncompromising standards of behaviour, he may have lapsed. On the other hand, Marguerite's initial accusation in 1915 could have been a tactical legal move taken in the hope that Gault would withdraw his petition in order to protect the name of the co-respondent. After his application for divorce was dismissed by the Senate she may have decided to enter a new petition to strengthen her application for a separation.

Whatever lay behind it, it seems that she was not confident of proving her case because on 25 April the Senate Divorce Committee reported that both she and Gault had withdrawn their petitions.[16]

An earlier comment of Agar Adamson, might have been echoed by many of his friends:

> Poor old bird, he certainly has not started well in his legal ventures – he had better stick to soldiering. I hope she does divorce him and he gets a thoroughly nice woman to marry him. I feel so beastly old, when I think he is seventeen years younger than I am, full of money and much fuller of sense, except in his choice of THE WOMAN.[17]

Gault's sick leave in Canada had been extended until the end of April. On Sunday the 15th he attended a reception given by the village of St Hilaire which had erected a fountain in his honour. When presented with an illuminated address by Mayor Oscar Dessautells, he replied in French. After thanking, 'you, my friends, amongst whom I hope to make my home in years to come', he added an eloquent plea that the names of all men of the Parish who had gone to the war should also be inscribed on the fountain.

Next day he wrote to Adamson, anxious about the casualties which the Patricias had suffered a week earlier in the attack on Vimy Ridge. 'Expect to sail for England the 29th April or 3rd May, and, please God, will be back with you all by the third or fourth week in May.'

When he arrived in England, he found that, because of his disability, no one was prepared to send him to France. By a stroke of luck he learned that Major-General Louis Lipsett, the GOC of the 3rd Canadian Division, was on leave in London. He wrote to him asking that he give him a letter to the effect that employment would be found for him in France. Lipsett replied that he could not do this, that all appointments were made by Corps Headquarters from lists which they kept. He would ask them to include Gault but,

> . . . this may cause a delay in getting you out.'
> The only appointments I can directly nominate anyone for are my own A.D.C.s. I have three on my staff at present and I see I am allowed 4. I am enclosing a letter definitely asking you to come out

as A.D.C. Shew that to the [Medical] Board & ask them to pass you fit for it. That ought to get you out almost at once & then you will be well placed to move into anything else. You will be in just as good a position to get another appointment as if you waited here to be sent for.[18]

That this was a wangle must have been obvious to anyone in authority who became aware of it. Majors as senior as Gault simply did not become aides de camp to divisional commanders. But the Army tends to be tolerant of a contrivance which enables a man to get closer to the enemy. Nonetheless, the wheels of administration ground slow and, despite Gault's impatience to be back in the field, it was not until 20 June that he sailed for France.

Chapter 12

BACK TO THE FRONT

On the evening of 20 June 1917, Private Armishaw, one of the 'Originals' of the Patricia's transport, was plucked by his sergeant from an estaminet behind Vimy Ridge, ordered to get himself properly dressed and report to the orderly officer for special duty. As luck would have it, the latter was the glacial Slim Allan, the former Regimental Sergeant Major who had been commissioned after the Battles of the Somme.

> After he had found fault with everything about me, he assured me that for once I was to look like a soldier even though I would never be one.
>
> However, he calmed down and told me that I had been picked to go to the railhead and bring home to the Regiment none other than Major Hamilton Gault. I proceeded to tell him that Major Gault was not able to come since he was without one of his legs. At that moment along comes Slim Rippin driving the notorious Bushytail hooked up to a dog cart and I was ordered on my way. This convinced me it was no horseplay as was usual in such turn outs . . .
>
> I finally arrived at the railhead and found that the train would not arrive for a couple of hours, so I gave Bushytail a haynet and headed for the nearest estaminet for a further vin blanc . . .

There followed a contretemps with the military police who doubted his story and threatened to confiscate Bushytail and the dogcart and incarcerate Armishaw in the local 'slammer' if the Major failed to arrive on the train which was just pulling in.

> Moments later I located Hammy and after my best salute, I told him that I was here with a conveyance to take him to the regiment.
>
> He was, to my surprise, very active and looked every bit the

gallant soldier he was, and believe me I was thrilled at being chosen to get him safely back to the Regiment.[1]

Gault found the Patricias in Toronto Camp on Vimy Ridge in readiness to support the 3rd Division's advance around Lens. Agar Adamson was in command. 'Batty Mac' had just left the 7th Brigade to become GOC of the 1st Division in place of Sir Arthur Currie who had been promoted to command the Canadian Corps. Talbot Papineau had returned to the Regiment from the staff a few days earlier and, with Percy Molson and Charlie Stewart, was there to welcome him.

General Lipsett told Gault that he could spend as much time with the Regiment as necessary to discover if he was fit for service in the line. After a few days, according to Adamson, the prospects for this seemed bleak.

> Gault has turned up and bunks with me, plus one leg on and a second in a box looking like a coffin. I am parading the Regiment for him today to make a speech. He rides in a special saddle quite well, but poor old thing, he cannot carry on on rough ground and is constantly falling down and won't be helped.[2]

If Gault was depressed by his disability, he gave no sign of it to the Regiment.

> He was soon back with two wooden legs, Hubert and Herbert, and he would have us believe that they were an improvement on the one that had been taken from him.[3]

The day after his arrival he and Adamson attended the First Army Horse Show where the Patricias' transport won second prize. Prince Arthur of Connaught told them that he had found a new pipe major for the Regiment to replace Colville who led the original band from Edmonton to Ottawa and now was ill. His man had been piper to Queen Victoria. He said it would be nice to keep him in the family.

They returned to be met by heavy shelling and ordered the men into the Vimy tunnels.

> Gault and I remained in the open [ie in a tent] as he was in bed and it takes hours to get him dressed. Poor old fellow, he feels the loss of his leg very much and is most depressed and to me, depressing. He tries so hard and won't be helped, as

obstinate as ever. I feel it is quite out of the question his taking the Regiment.[4]

The effect of another wound, that caused by Marguerite, was causing difficulties. Gault now wanted to excise any reminder of her from his life. At his request, when the Regiment was formed, Princess Patricia had personally designed its cap badge with its centre a stylized 'Marguerite'.

> He wants for 'private reasons' to change our badge. The Princess refused and he wants me to write asking her to change her mind. Is this not a difficult job to tackle? Nobody would ever understand the reason. The men love the badge and I don't think after so many good fellows have died with it, if not for it, it should be changed because one lady has lost her bed and board. So far, I have refused.[5]

Gault later unburdened himself to Adamson who found it 'very painful', but made it clear that he could not agree to changing the badge. He told him that at the beginning they were all very fond of Marguerite and so, of course, was Gault, that she, as they knew her then, was a part of the institution and the emblem chosen at that time should remain.

What he did not say was that, if the badge were changed, the resentment felt by the Regiment would inevitably be directed at Gault. Fortunately Adamson's opinion prevailed. The Regiment, including its founder, continued to wear the 'Marguerite' until after the war.[6]

Gault now divided his time between the Regiment and divisional headquarters where there was work aplenty for an experienced senior major. General Lipsett did not employ him as an ADC but used him to organize the Dominion Day Sports, the unveiling of a memorial to the men killed in the Battle of Vimy Ridge, as president of the canteen Boards and as inspector of the divisional schools of instruction. Every job he was given he did well, but his heart was not in them. He longed to be with the Regiment, but, if that proved to be impossible, he would apply to become a pilot in the Royal Flying Corps.

An unexpected opportunity to test his physical fitness for command came on 4 July. Adamson was taken ill. The Regiment was in the line in front of Avion. Gault persuaded General Lipsett that, as he was as fit as he would ever be, he should take command until Adamson returned.[7]

Talbot Papineau was with his company in the front line:

Hamilton Gault actually walked up yesterday and came in to see me last night. It is extraordinary how he can get about, and his enthusiasm![8]

Lipsett gave him his head for three days, then, on the night of the 7th, ordered him out. It had been long enough for Gault to realize that his disability seriously limited his usefulness in the line. In low trenches he could not stoop or crawl.[9]

He returned to divisional headquarters, saddened by the experience and by the loss of Percy Molson who had been killed by a shell. But he remained determined to find a fighting role. He told Percival Campbell,

This last week has been full of incident! On Monday a fellow came up to see me with a message from your friend Branker to the effect that they'd take me in the R.A.F. if I wanted to go.

I still feel like nothing on earth and sometimes think I've made a mistake in coming out to this blasted country again. If it weren't for the Battalion, I'd switch for I'm handicapped with this swinger more than I would admit to anyone but you. The Flying stunt is attractive if only I could compete on anything like even terms & I can only find that out by trying.[10]

He failed to say that he had broken his artificial leg in a fall playing polo the day after he came out of the line and was now wearing his spare.[11] A press report a few weeks later spoke of other mounted sports:

The most striking figure at the recent horse-race on the Western Front was Major Hamilton Gault, a gallant Canadian. . . . He rode his horse with great éclat, and, what is more, notwithstanding his terrible wounds, has been actively engaged in fighting the Germans.

More than once he had been in the line since his three days in command:

On a few occasions, I had the honour to accompany Colonel Gault on brief tours of our front. . . . He had permission from Divisional H.Q. to go as far as our reserve line but on at least two occasions he couldn't resist the temptation of having a look at our front line. Once while going forward we met Maj Papineau. Col Gault stopped for a chat with him and the enemy chose that moment to drop a big black shell just outside the trench. I hit the duckboards and even Major Papineau flinched a little but Col.

Gault stood erect as if on parade and calmly said, 'That one was close, wasn't it?'[12]

By September Agar Adamson, at 52 one of the oldest battalion commanders in France, was feeling the strain of months of action and was sent on extended leave to England. He arranged for Gault to command the Patricias whilst he was away. On the 9th, the day Gault arrived at Bois des Alleux where the Battalion was resting, Charlie Stewart, the second-in-command was taken ill and Hugh Niven took his place. For ten days they remained there, training under the hot September sun, then relieved the 43rd Battalion in brigade support near Neuville St Vaast.[13]

> Hamilton Gault walked to the front line today but the conditions were perfect and he could not do so under other circumstances. He is just trying himself out but I think, with regret, that it would be a mistake for him to attempt to command the Battalion permanently, and even his temporary command is a mistake as it is upsetting & nobody knows just where they stand. Also those likely to succeed to command should be given practice when an occasion such as this one presents itself.[14]

If Gault was indeed physically unfit to command, Talbot Papineau's comments to his mother had some validity and foretold trouble to come.

After a week in support, the Patricias relieved the RCR in the front line. Papineau observed:

> Hamilton Gault stumps about the trenches once every day. His devotion to the Regiment is very real and he works hard.[15]

It was a quiet tour in the line – rest by day, patrols and working parties to improve the defences by night. The weather was fine. Unusually the Regiment had only four casualties. On 30 September they again exchanged places with the RCR by moving back to the support line.[16]

During the last ten days of Gault's command the Battalion was withdrawn from the line for a week's intensive training in the techniques of the attack. It ended with orders to move north to join Plumer's Second Army, but Gault was not to go with them. He was to take command of the 3rd Divisional Wing of the Canadian Corps Reinforcement Camp, which trained and held a pool of men to replace casualties.

Adamson returned within a week, to lead the Patricias in the Battle of Passchendaele. On 30 October, in capturing the Meetcheele Ridge, the Regiment won two Victoria Crosses. Among their 363 casualties was Talbot Papineau, killed while leading his company in the assault.

Gault had shown once more that he was a capable battalion commander, in the line, in reserve and in training. His physical disability had not been a significant handicap in the conditions of ground and weather of the early autumn of 1917. Perhaps he carried away from the experience a false confidence in his ability to command under all conditions, but, among some of the officers of the Regiment, there remained serious doubts.

For the moment he had a new and challenging task. In an endeavour to improve the availability, training and morale of the reinforcements held in the rear to replace casualties, General Currie brought forward most of the men from the notorious base depots at Etaples. Gault was in command of the 3rd Division's share, a unit of some 1,800 men of all arms, with the task of improving their training to a standard acceptable to the fighting units. He threw himself into it with enthusiasm and energy.

To the front line soldier, few things were less inspiring than the sight of the average draft of 'reinforcements', tired, bewildered, untidy, noticeably lacking in martial spirit, their military skills forgotten. In transit camps and depots, too often they were treated as a lumpish mass, a necessary inconvenience, with indifference or varying degrees of harshness. Gault never saw soldiers in that light. To him they were individuals, deserving of respect, and he treated them with consideration.

> Many of us have vivid memories of passing through that camp – his gallant figure riding out to meet a new draft (Gault was a beautiful horseman . . .); his gaiety and kindliness with all ranks stationed there for a day or a week or longer; his continuing to play outdoor-indoor baseball in spite of his physical disability; his generosity to the French peasants near his camp; his 'Hamilton Gault Theatre' in an old barn which he personally purchased and had converted to a theatre for concert parties from Britain and cinema, to keep the troops under his command and the nearby French population entertained.[17]

There were relatively few battle casualties in the Canadian Corps during the winter of 1917–18 and, in consequence, many of their intended replacements spent several weeks in the Wing. Gault organized the unit, which held some 100 reinforcements for each of the Division's twelve infantry battalions and the equivalent of ten percent of the strength of the artillery, engineers and other arms, into ad hoc battalions and gave them basic tactical training. Besides improving his men's chances of survival in the line, it gave them a sense of purpose and was to prove valuable during the great German offensive of March, 1918.

The Division was conducting a continuing series of courses to meet its need for NCOs and specialists, such as bombers and machine gunners, and to improve the tactical training of its officers. These now came under Gault's command and, with the Reinforcement Wing, were referred to as 'The Divisional Schools'. In November, 1917, Gault was promoted to the local rank of lieutenant-colonel.

On 22 February, 1918, the King appointed Princess Patricia to be Colonel-in-Chief of PPCLI. It was an honorary position which she was to hold for the rest of her long life. Gault, like the rest of the Regiment, was delighted. What they did not know was that the King had given his approval only after being assured that the Regiment would become part of Canada's permanent forces after the war.

A month later Agar Adamson, found by a medical board to be physically unfit for service in the front line, left the Battalion. Later he revealed to his wife some of the financial responsibilities which his position had involved. He and Gault had arranged to share certain expenses to which the other officers could not be asked to subscribe. Adamson told her that it was difficult to get Gault to agree a settlement because he always wanted to pay for everything himself. Finally he had succeeded and now owed Gault £120 which he was sure was entirely in his favour.[18] Nowhere were the expenses covered by army regulations.

> While I was getting Colonel's pay, allowances and Command pay I could generally put in 25 pounds a month for things generally expected of a CO in a well-run Regiment. And for things it was not possible to ask the junior officers to chip in for, as most of them had no money and their pay was small and I insisted on their being well dressed. . . . The actual extra expenses have been for extra rations, Tommy cookers in the winter when the men were having a bad time in the trenches. . . Warrant Officer's uniform for Regimental and Company Sergeant Majors, the upkeep of the pipe band. (Gault has paid 90 percent of this.) Officers' cheques and a few unfortunate circumstances arising over deceased officers' private affairs which we wished to keep from their people, extra vegetables, men going on leave who had not the money to do it

with. . . . How do other Regiments get on? There always seems to be someone who does it and in many cases much more so than the PPCLI.[19]

On 27 March, Major Charles Stewart, who had returned to the Regiment after Passchendaele, took command until a new CO was appointed. But the generals needed to deal with the matter had other things on their minds. Less than a week before, the Germans had launched a massive offensive against the Allied armies. They struck a succession of blows over the next four months but none fell directly on the Canadian Corps whose frontage was perilously extended to free other troops to reinforce the sagging Allied line.

At the end of March, when the Corps was holding a front of ten miles with two divisions, General Currie formed two additional infantry brigades from the Corps Reinforcement Camps and various engineer units. Gault was immediately involved in forming a third line to either reinforce or make a final stand in the event of the enemy breaking through the forward defences.[20]

During the months of the German offensive Gault commanded a fighting unit, which he organized, trained and deployed. It did not meet the enemy, but then, for most of the time, neither did the 3rd Division which was held in reserve. The experience was little different from commanding an infantry battalion.

The question of Adamson's successor had received little attention in the midst of the German offensives. Brigadier-General Hugh Dyer of the 7th Brigade, believing Gault to be unfit, recommended Stewart. General Lipsett of the 3rd Division agreed, but Currie, the Corps Commander, thought Stewart lacked the necessary balance of character and told Lipsett to consult Gault.

There was no doubt in Gault's mind that Stewart would fight the battalion boldly and well in any kind of action. But out of the line, when the flow of adrenalin eased he had shown little interest in its day-to-day management. He was a soldier of Falstaffian tastes who too frequently shed mundane administration for a roaring party in the Mess. More than once the Regiment had had to extract him from trouble when he was on leave in London. More than once, after drinking too much, he had been hidden from a visiting general. He was impulsive and prone to speak on serious subjects without much thought. He was unlikely to represent the Regiment well within the Corps and would probably be regarded as a lightweight, if not a buffoon. He seemed incapable of maintaining a judicious distance from his subordinates – to draw the line between friendliness and familiarity, between authority and indiscipline – an essential quality of a commander. But in Gault's view, one of the worst results of his careless running of the Regiment would be that the men would suffer.

After much heart-searching and consultations with Adamson, Gault could offer no other solution than that he himself, as the senior major in the Regiment, should take command.

General Currie agreed and on 18 June Canadian Corps Orders announced: 'Major (Acting Lieut-Col) A.H. Gault to be temporary lieut-col and to command PPCLI with effect from 28 March, 1918.'[21] He was to be replaced at the Reinforcement Wing by George McDonald of the Patricias who would be made an acting lieutenant-colonel. Three days later Gault reported to the Regiment at Cotte where, since 7 May, they had been in reserve, training intensively for open warfare.

Stewart being on leave, he was met by McDonald, the acting second-in-command who asked to speak to him privately. When they were alone, he delivered a shattering blow. Brutally he told Gault that the Regiment as a whole no longer knew him and the officers thought him physically unfit to command. They wanted Stewart, a first rate fighting soldier, who had commanded them for the past three months, was known to them and enjoyed their confidence. Furthermore Dyer, the brigade commander, thought that, with one leg, he was unfit to command and had asked for Stewart.

Gault was stunned. He looked on the Regiment as a band of brothers who would welcome him with open arms – now this rebuff. Did McDonald speak the truth? He was certainly not going to ask subordinate officers in the Regiment to confirm it. If they had been gossiping about his fitness to command, it was a serious breach of discipline. That he could deal with, but there was something more serious. How had McDonald learned the details of something as confidential as the brigade commander's opinion of him and his recommendation of Stewart to command the Regiment? Were they correct? He must first call on General Dyer.

Much as 'Daddy' Dyer admired Gault and regarded him as a friend, he was indeed of the opinion that, with only one leg, he was unfit to command. As gently as he could, he told him so and confirmed that he had asked for Stewart whom he had so informed at the time. As to how McDonald knew of his views, he could only suggest that it had been through Stewart.

Their conversation ended with Gault telling the brigadier that he intended to go at once to divisional headquarters to see General Lipsett.

When he left brigade headquarters, he was near to despair. Since his marriage had been destroyed, he had focused all his love and aspirations on the Regiment which now had rejected him.

To take command was his undoubted right – many would say his duty. He had the strength of character to impose his will on the Regiment and to deal with breaches of discipline. Never in his life had he turned his back on a fight. There was no question but that higher authority would support him.

But there would be no breach of discipline – the Regiment would obey his orders. What was at stake, was its spirit – the selflessness, the mutual respect, the willing obedience which had been its strength. If his officers and his brigadier regarded him as being unfit to lead, to him there was no alternative but to refuse the command which had become his life's ambition.

Lipsett accepted his decision. He returned to the Battalion for the night, then, next day, went to see Agar Adamson whom he trusted as a friend and whose advice he valued.

On the day before Gault had arrived to take command Adamson had been shocked to hear from McDonald and other officers what was in store. He sensed at once that the matter would have to be resolved by higher authority who no doubt would ask for his views. He decided that until then he would listen and express no opinion, difficult though it was to conceal his anger at this first sign of discord within the Regiment since its foundation.

His first reaction was a feeling of sadness that Gault, 'the most unselfish of us all', should be the cause of it and that others were 'thinking of themselves rather than finishing the war and licking the Germans'. It was evident that too many officers were becoming greedy for promotion and 'that the best of them is inclined to forget what he came out here for.'

The only view he expressed at the Regiment was that, if they did a little more fighting and less training, they might realize that, as life meant little, they should not clutter their minds with thoughts of what was due to them for their services.

I consider that Charlie Stewart is selfish in the matter and ought to be ashamed of himself for having discussed it with anybody. Most of the Regiment are saying how badly he has been treated and openly sympathize with him. The discipline of the Regiment seems to me to be good but the morale, as this incident shows, must be very bad indeed.

. . . I am ashamed of C.S. and the other officers whom he should never have allowed to be on equal terms with him in matters of policy. He will never be anything but an irresponsible boy without any of the reserve and dignity that should go with the Command of a Regiment and will never be able to do more than command a fighting company , and that he would always do well and gallantly.[22]

Adamson, as selfless in his devotion to the Regiment as Gault, could not understand why Stewart would not stand aside as he himself had done for Pelly and was prepared to do for Gault.

After Hammie had left him on the 22nd he wrote:

> He is in a desperate state, always feeling that he was part of it and always wanted by it. Stewart has never consulted him on any matters and just gone ahead on his own sweet way. He has often referred to me on matters of policy. But, in important cases I have always suggested getting Gault's views. This he has never done. I am most annoyed and disgusted and fear that G. will do something that most of us would do but should not do. He ended by promising to be at a certain spot in 48 hours time to again listen to my point of view. The poor old fellow is broken-hearted and desperate. The one and only thing he had to live for since the war is gone, and also the one thing he banked on as his friend and understanding him, has also gone. I am writing to the General to give him special leave at once which may help him to get down to normal conditions.[23]
>
> . . . the only consolation I can find is that it may mean the life of Gault which I do not think he values very much. But such a magnificent fellow is worth saving although he will be very unhappy as his whole soul was wrapped up in the Regiment.

Gault was not given leave, but two weeks later, with the other reinforcement wing commanders, was sent to England for ten days. There they were to inspect the training of recruits and coordinate their work in France with that of the reserves in the United Kingdom. By the time he returned, Gault had accepted that he could never again fight as an infantryman. He applied to command a battalion of the Tank Corps.

For weeks, during which he immersed himself in work, there was no reply; everyone concerned was involved in preparations for the great offensive to be launched at Amiens.

On 8 August the Canadian and Australian Corps, with almost every tank the British possessed, delivered the deadly blow which marked the end of hope for the German Army. That evening, as the Patricias waited in a wood to resume their advance, Gault arrived on a motor cycle 'beaming with excitement', to cheer them on, then sadly returned to his schools at Forfay.[24]

His mood was not improved by a letter he received two days later from Lieutenant-General Sir Tom Bridges at the War Office offering him the job of British Provost Marshal in New York.

The Patricias had a relatively easy time in the first few days of the Amiens offensive, then, at Parvillers, No.3 Company, having captured their objective, were counter-attacked in overwhelming force on both flanks. They fought their way back to the Canadian lines, causing heavy casualties to the enemy. Initially Sergeant Bob Spall's platoon was isolated and, in covering its withdrawal, he gave his life and won the Regiment's third Victoria Cross.

Two weeks later the Patricias attacked south of the River Scarpe; their objective, deep in the German defences, was Jigsaw Wood.

On the first day they came under the direct fire of German artillery which was plainly in view on their right. Eric Knight, later to become the well-known American author of the 'Lassie' stories, wrote to Gault in 1939 to tell him of his experiences that day, as a signaller in the Patricias. Gault had been told that he must not go near the front line but he had interpreted 'near' to mean 'in'.

> At Jigsaw Wood, we were held up in a bit of a trench all morning, and we watched Jerry pull down some new batteries up the hill right in daylight the beggar did it; and then watched the reserve Jerries come down for counter-attack, and the telephone line blew out, and every time we mended it, it was out somewhere else. We were just at the 'what-the-hell's-coming-off' stage and you came down the communication trench, with no gas mask, no tin hat. It was a nice sunny day, and you were saying: 'Oh, we've lots of men here. We ought to jump over and put a bombing raid on him.' You were so damned cheerful about it – that by God we just went over and did bomb them out.[25]

The Regiment was exhausted by the three-day battle and it was to be nearly four weeks before they attacked again.

The Canadian infantry had suffered heavy casualties and Gault was fully occupied with replacing them and with his courses for new officers and NCOs. Early in September he received a copy of a letter from General Hugh Elles, commander of the Tank Corps:

> I have had Gault's case before me already and I have had very reluctantly to turn him down. The fact is that although a Tank

Battalion Commander for 7 or 8 months in the year has a pretty easy time compared with the normal Infantry Battalion Commander, he has a very long and continuous physical strain when once his people go into battle. I have tried an Adjutant with a wooden leg, a boy of tremendous spirit who can do 5 or 6 miles on his feet, but the strain of the last operation has broken him down altogether. All our movements are in the dark and I have had my battalions over the top as many as 7 times since August 8th.

I know about Gault's record and would very willingly take him for a sit down job but I take it that is exactly what he does not want and as he has a sit down job already he would prefer to do it with his own people.

I am more than sorry to have to turn away such a good man.[26]

It may have been some solace to Gault that the work he was doing at the reinforcement wing was appreciated. When Hugh Dyer was replaced as commander of the 7th Brigade he wrote to him from England:

I was very grieved to leave France without once more gripping you by the hand & thanking you once more for all you have done for me & all you have been to me in my work, the men you trained, the influence you had on all the Officers who passed through your hands had more to do with the efficiency of the dear old Brigade than anything else I know of. Again from the bottom of my heart, I thank you.[27]

Later an officer of the 49th Battalion (Edmonton Regiment) spoke of his time at the Divisional School:

Colonel Gault certainly gave us the Devil when we needed it but he was the best C.O. I knew in France.[28]

In September Gault went to England for two weeks' leave. When he returned he learned that Stewart had been killed by a shell during the Battle of the Canal du Nord and that, later, the Regiment had suffered 359 casualties, virtually as many as at Sanctuary Wood or Passchendaele, in capturing the village of Tilloy on the outskirts of Cambrai.

Once more, through death, the problem had arisen of who was to command the Patricias. Not one major was left in the Battalion and, of those not with it, none was fit or immediately available. Sir Arthur Currie decided that Major George McDonald, who had been wounded, would be promoted to command upon his return from Canada in about six weeks time. Until then he accepted Gault's recommendation that Captain A.G. Pearson should command in an acting capacity.

Pearson, who had joined as a private in 1914, had won a Distinguished Conduct Medal and a Military Cross and had been wounded at Frezenberg, at Sanctuary Wood and in the attack on Vimy Ridge. On the last occasion his injuries were so severe that he was nearly discharged from the Army. He appealed to Hammie who made him his adjutant at the Reinforcement Wing. With persuasion, a Medical Board agreed that he was fit enough to command for a limited period.[29]

For Hammie a change was in the offing. Major-General Louis Lipsett, the GOC of the 3rd Canadian Division, was an officer of the British Regular Army which now asked for him to return to lead their 4th Division before being promoted to the command of a corps. Believing that Gault would benefit from a change, he invited him to join his new headquarters. By 10 October arrangements were complete and he wrote to Hammie to welcome him. Three days later he was killed.[30]

Gault wrote to Adamson:

> I wish you had been able to get to Lippy's funeral; I half expected to see you there – As you know , I had formed a great admiration and regard for the little man and almost feel I have lost a brother. Damn it! This show seems to kill off the best and leave those that can or could be best spared![31]

While on leave in England Hammie had lunched amicably with Marguerite. She had been seeing much of an Italian air force colonel, Count Luigino Falchi, and was now as keen as her husband to end their marriage. Both had learned that it was possible to divorce in France and they decided to act at once.[32]

Marguerite moved to Paris where her brother, George Washington Stephens, had a house, thus, under the law of the time, establishing her domicile there.

On 25 October Gault was granted a week's leave in Paris. By the time he returned he had retained a French lawyer and arrangements were in hand. All that was necessary was for him to return in two weeks' time for a hearing in a local court.

Two days after the Armistice the Civil Tribunal of the First Instance of the Department of the Seine in Paris heard the case and on 20 December, 1918, pronounced a judgement of divorce.

Chapter 13

COMMAND

During the night of 10 November, 1918, the 42nd Battalion (Canadian Black Watch) with a company each of PPCLI and the Royal Canadian Regiment fought their way into Mons, where British troops first met the Germans in 1914. Next day, as the guns fell silent along the Western Front, the 7th Brigade paraded before Sir Arthur Currie to mark the end of the war. With them was a detachment of the 9th Lancers who had been there in 1914.

Some felt it a pity that none of the infantry of the original BEF was present. The end of the fighting had come too quickly for such a gesture to history. But in a sense they were represented. As the Patricias' regimental history put it, 'Is it an immodest pretension that one battalion parading that day in the City Square was linked through its "Originals" with almost every unit of the old British Regular Army?'[1]

Gault returned from Paris on 16 November to find that once more the question of who should command the Regiment had arisen. With the end of hostilities, the authorities in Canada refused to allow George McDonald to return overseas. Pearson was not well and did not wish to continue in office indefinitely. Both he and Clark, his brigadier, wrote to invite Gault to return. They found him less than willing.

He answered that if he was not fit to command the Regiment when it was fighting, he was not fit to command now. Pearson enlisted Adamson's support in arguing that in this he was wrong and that he was both wanted and needed. Finally they persuaded him that it was important to the Regiment that its final days should be as devotedly and carefully managed as its formation.

All was not well. Since the disaster at Tilloy the Battalion had not regained its full strength. New officers with no previous association with the Patricias had been drafted in from a pool of reinforcements and there had not yet been time to mould its new men into the ways of the Regiment. With the Armistice of 11 November, the fundamental incentive essential to discipline in a citizen army was removed. Men accepted that they must soldier on, but began to wonder 'for how long?' Increasingly they found military routines and duties irksome. The key to morale, as ever, was leadership.

Gault was aware that some of the officers, particularly those who had joined from other units, did not want him back. For the most part these were subalterns. It was understandable that they would have preferred someone who had been with them through the past months of hard fighting; since before Passchendaele, Gault had been but a visitor to the Battalion. They had seen enough of him to realize that he was a stickler for maintaining the highest standards of dress, behaviour and performance in the officers. They appreciated that these affected the honour and good name of the Regiment, but thought that Gault's demands were excessive. They chose to believe that he regarded the Regiment as his property and that the polish he wanted on its image was a reflection of his vanity. They had been much more comfortable under Charlie Stewart's relaxed regime.

On 22 November, 1918, at a parade in Mons, Pearson relinquished command to Gault. There is no record of the measures he subsequently took to tighten the discipline of the officers but one effect was immediately visible to their men. Following a popular style of the day, some officers had clipped square the ends of their moustaches. To Gault they looked ridiculous and he ordered them to get rid of their Charlie Chaplins and either grow proper ones or nothing.[2]

If some of the officers were less than pleased by Gault's arrival, the men were delighted. One veteran recalled, 'He joined us at Mons and, good gracious, the first thing he did was look into the messes and, even before seeing him – you knew Gault was back because the food was better.'[3] Significantly, too, they had grown disenchanted with some of the new officers and NCOs whom Stewart had accepted during the past few months. To them Gault epitomized all that was admirable in the old Regiment and they liked his style.

> As was to be expected, officers and NCOs without experience were not the most popular soldiers. Sometimes their actions were comical, if not tragic. I was leading a working party one night when a German flare went up. The next second I spotted my officer tearing away across the common in the path of the flare. He eventually returned but made no mention of his behaviour; nor did I refer to it.[4]

Private Eric Knight, who had come to the Patricias from the mounted section of the Signals, remembered one of them:

He had the most terrible seat on a horse God ever gave to a man, and if there was anything worse than his seat it was his hands. I hated him for being on a horse and flubbing it when I would have given a month's pay for ten minutes on it. I wonder if officers ever understand the minute regard, the complete understanding of their character and lives that some of the enlisted men get from this long daily contact. . . .

One of our greatest kicks on regimental parades was to watch [Gault] come on at a lope and draw a horse up with just the precise amount of gentle flamboyance that befits a damned good regiment drawn up for its commander.[5]

The 3rd Division had not been chosen for the Occupation Force in Germany and the Battalion was to remain in Mons for several weeks until plans for demobilization were complete. Gault organized sports, games and educational classes for the men, along with enough drill and military training to keep them fit and occupied. During this time, one incident demonstrated Gault's flair as a leader and his ability to rise to an occasion.

On 27 November he was in command of an impeccable Guard of Honour of four hundred men drawn from each battalion of the 7th Brigade. In the Grande Place of Mons they were to greet the heroic King Albert of the Belgians who was returning to the newly liberated city after four years of war. The square and the surrounding streets were jammed with ecstatic crowds, cheering through their tears of joy.

After his formal reception by the Guard, the King entered the Hotel de Ville. When he emerged, instead of ordering a Royal Salute, Gault had his men doff their helmets, place them on their bayonets and raise their rifles high as he led them in cheers for the King – a flamboyant gesture which exactly caught the mood of the moment.

The original demobilization plan called for Canadian troops on the Continent to sail directly home from French ports.[6] If Princess Patricia was to see her Regiment before they sailed for home, she would need to come to Belgium. Already she had consulted her father as to how she might express her admiration for their gallantry and had a proposal which she wished to discuss with Hamilton Gault. Through official channels, he was ordered to England on 'two weeks' special leave' with a view to arranging a visit by the Princess in the New Year. On 2 December he left Mons expecting to find the Regiment there when he returned.

While he was away the Patricias were allotted vacancies for leave in

London and Paris. Major Pearson decided that those for officers and NCOs should go to men of long service, with the result that each of the rifle companies was left with only one or two officers, most being woefully inexperienced. The men were enduring a boring time in indifferent billets. The reason for their existence as soldiers had been removed and, having shared so much danger and hardship with their officers, many felt deserted by those they most respected.

For the moment the chain of comradeship was broken. The new officers, insensitive to that mutual respect between all ranks which was the key to the Patricias' unfailing discipline, fell back on rank as their source of authority and their soldiers resented it.

Orders then came for the 3rd Division to move north-east to billets east of Brussels. On 11 December the Patricias marched from Mons to Genappes, then, next day, continued to Nivelles where the entire 7th Brigade was billeted, a total distance of 34 kilometres. In accordance with divisional orders, the men were in full marching order, armed and wearing steel helmets. When they arrived at Nivelles on 13 December the Patricias found that the resentment which had begun to simmer within the Battalion had reached boiling point in other regiments. The following is a summary of the official version of the part played by the Patricias in what ensued.

Late in the afternoon some hundred men of different units gathered in the town square and were harangued by two or three speakers who complained that, with the end of hostilities, there was no need for them to wear helmets and that they should not have to carry their heavy packs on the march. During the evening the crowd increased and about two hundred gathered at Brigade Headquarters. A small group, including one Patricia private, were allowed in and spoke with the Brigadier, after which the crowd dispersed quietly.

Early next morning a crowd from other units visited the Patricias' billets inciting the men to attend a mass meeting at 8:30 am in the town square. When the Battalion paraded at nine o'clock an entire company was missing and was presumed to be at the meeting. With a few exceptions, the men of the other three companies remained in their billets, ready to turn out on parade.

After being addressed by five or six agitators, the crowd in the square made a second round of the brigade's billets, trying to enlist support, during which they broke into guardrooms and released prisoners. The guards did not resist and later all the prisoners reported back to their units.

Later that afternoon, the brigade commander ordered PPCLI to march from Nivelles to Genval, near the battlefield of Waterloo. One company and part of another, with the battalion transport, moved without difficulty, but when the other two reached the town square a mob surrounded them, broke into their ranks, tore packs and equipment from their backs and unhitched the horses from the company cookers – the most violent incident of the 'mutiny'.

The two Patricia companies were ordered back to their billets where they remained until 11:00 pm when, with the exception of about fifteen men, they again paraded and marched to Genval. The missing men later reported to an NCO and rejoined the Battalion.

During the night calm was restored and next day the other units of the brigade left Nivelles without trouble.

So went the official reports of the brigade and the battalions concerned. In each one can detect a cover-up – commanding officers defending both their men and their own actions in the sorry affair. But General Loomis, the divisional commander, storming back from leave late at night on the 16th, was under no illusions. His mood was not improved by the knowledge that he would have to report the details of this discreditable business to the commander of the 4th British Corps under whom his division was now serving.

He first vented his displeasure on the assembled COs of the 7th Brigade (Major Pearson for PPCLI), then visited every unit and spoke to the men. His formal report to the commander of 4th Corps on 26 December was terse.

The alleged complaints which were voiced by the men were trivial. There were no real grounds for complaint. The whole matter was one of discipline, training and efficient Officers and Non-Commissioned Officers. It was not a condition of recent growth.

The measures which I am taking are not exactly those which I would recommend if the Division were not preparing to move back home and if the fighting was not finished. The benefit of the doubt is now, in a large measure, being given to certain officers who, if the Division was not shortly to be demobilized, I would strongly recommend that they be removed from their commands for inefficiency.

I am able to report that all who are guilty of crime or misdemeanour are being brought to judgement, and the spirit of the units has been improved and is now good. Agitators are being dealt with.

That the affair at Nivelles was much more serious than officially reported can be inferred from the disciplinary action taken. Ninety-four men were dealt with by their commanding officers for absence without leave or under the Army's catch-all charge of 'conduct to the prejudice of good order and military discipline'. One NCO and seven men, including two PPCLI privates, Butler and Nicholas, were found guilty by a court-martial of mutiny without violence and were sentenced to five years' penal servitude.

Neither the Patricias' war diary nor their history make any reference to the troubles at Nivelles nor to Gault's actions when he returned to them on the 16th. They say little more than that they undertook a programme of 'training, sports and educational classes' and that they remained at Genval until after Christmas. In reality, Gault shook the battalion by the scruff of its neck.

He began by speaking to the officers, then to the sergeants and finally to the men. Then he paraded them in full marching order with every bit of operational kit they could carry and led them on a totally pointless twenty-mile route march. They returned to Genval singing.

If any of the officers knew how serious the affair had been, they never told Gault. The number of absentees from the rifle companies when they left Nivelles was far larger than reported. A former private recalled, 'A bunch of us were spectators when battalion headquarters moved out leaving us stranded.'[7] The officers had temporarily abandoned control of their men.

After the war the 'Mutiny' became a folk tale spoken in whispers between veterans, growing more lurid with time. In 1939 the author heard two former sergeants tell of the Pipe Band arming themselves and taking charge of the Colour to prevent it falling into the hands of the mutineers.

In July, 1939, Hamilton Gault for the first time received a reliable account of what had happened from the point of view of the private soldier. Eric Knight, the American author, was the PPCLI private who spoke to Brigadier-General Clark on the night of 13 December, 1918.

In a letter written from his home on the banks of the Hudson, he recalled the young idealists who then made up the ranks of the Patricias. When Gault and the other veteran officers left to go to England they were left in the charge of 'other men with badges that came and gave orders. We felt as if we had all stuck together in the war – officers and other ranks -and the minute the armistice was signed, you left us.

'The minute you went away, it wasn't a regiment with another set in command – it was an integrated whole, put together in a white-hot blast furnace during five years, that had had the most important mechanisms removed. And, as we used to say, *'cà ne marche pas'*. It suddenly didn't work – and we didn't march.

The comradeship and cheerful discipline which marked the Patricias had been replaced 'by a variation of the Prussianism that we had, we supposed, come to defeat'. Discontent spread through the ranks of the battalion and, as always in such situations, there were those who called for dramatic action.

We talked it over among ourselves, and worked for many days to keep the hotheads down. And then the hotheads got loose – and like all hotheads, after they had spilled the beans, they ran to us and asked us how you could pick them up.

At Nivelles most of the private soldiers joined in refusing to march; those companies which were reported to have fallen in in good order were sadly under strength. Then rumours of retribution began to spread.

They said artillery was round the town ready to fire on us. I told them it was nonsense, civilians were in the town and British artillery hadn't begun tricks like that yet. They said they had no food and wanted to loot the shops. Some of us said we'd shoot any man looting. It was our doing, and it would have to be our hunger. . . . I was afraid that they would do something that surpassed the schoolboy prank that it was, and become ugly. Somebody had to do something. . . .
I went and talked to the Brigadier. He seemed heart-broken, and I was tremendously sorry for him. A half dozen of us began to scheme how to push the others the way we wanted without their knowing it. We discussed the food situation with them incessantly. After talking food supply for about half an hour with several hundred hungry men, their mouths were beginning to drool. After talking food for a whole day, they began to feel as if they were dying of hunger. And they were ready to promise anything if we could get it all straightened up. We said we would.

Knight took a bicycle, found where battalion headquarters was at Genval and rode back to the men. There was little argument. They formed up in column of route and marched off in good order to rejoin the battalion.
At that point many of the men had serious doubts about the wisdom of giving themselves up.

I was tired of men . . . who said we should have stayed where we were (when any fool could see that we had achieved all we could hope to achieve by merely indicating in a concrete way to authority that there was something wrong with the regiment) . . . I was tired of hunger and not sleeping, and I was tired of authority thrust on me who had no real desire for it. . . .

And then, as I had expected, the voice of Olympus had sounded, and you were back, coming down the street of Genval with your eyebrows in a straight line, and I knew someone was in for hell, and I didn't want it to be me.

And when you lined us up in the hotel and started talking to us, and told us what fools we had been – it was all over and some of the men actually began crying.

There were still a few thick-skulls who wanted to know if we should obey – we were sentenced to a full-pack march. That was funny. . . . I told them they should say their prayers every night for a long time that that was all we had to do, and the best thing they could do was to like it.

I don't know whether or not you remember that route-march. The moment march-at-ease came, and you were up there on the horse at the front, the regiment was a regiment again just like it used to be, and the column started singing 'Ricky-Dam-Do'(sic) and there wasn't a single word of disobedience from any man I ever knew in the ranks from that day to the day you told us the regiment was dismissed from service. . . .

After twenty years, it doesn't matter much perhaps – only I don't want you to feel bad about anything the regiment did, even when you weren't there.

And anyhow, what did you say to the commissioned personnel the day you got back to Genval?

Well, that's all. You won't remember me – the only time I think you looked directly at me was when we were playing football at some godforsaken place after the war and you came out and played goal, and a little Belgian chap asked you why you didn't play forward. You said:

'*Par-ce-que j'ai per-due mon jambe, et c'est impossible pour moi a courrir en-core.*'

I remember the words exactly, and then you turned to me, playing full back, and laughed. I laughed, too, because you spoke such a meticulously military French, with all the words in a neat row, standing on parade.[8]

Knight's account is a remarkable tribute to the Regiment, and to Gault. The fact is that, badly commanded, within a few days it ceased to function. And then, most remarkable of all, the moment the men were left on their own without a single commissioned or warrant officer in charge, the spirit woke in the Regiment again. It pulled itself together, route-marched fifteen miles in good order without the loss of a man, and presented itself for duty.

Gault could hardly be blamed for the temporary break in the discipline of the Regiment. He had been in command for less than ten days when he was sent to England and had had no part in sending such a high proportion of its experienced officers and NCOs on leave at the same time. But in a remarkable display of unflinching leadership he, overnight, restored the Patricias' pride in their Regiment and in themselves as soldiers.

The day after a white Christmas Gault led the Regiment on a five day march westwards toward the sea. Early in January they arrived at St Leger on the Belgian border where they remained until the end of the month. It was not until the 23rd that they knew that the Canadians would be repatriated through Britain and that they would be among the first to leave.

The Patricias had always treated the Princess's camp colour, which they carried into every battle they fought, with the respect due to an official 'Regimental Colour' and that is what they wanted it to become. Gault obtained official approval and on 28 January, 1919, 'the Ric-a-Dam-Doo', as they affectionately called it, was consecrated on a snow covered Belgian parade ground.

On 7 February PPCLI sailed in the S.S. *Dieppe* from Le Havre where they had landed four years and two months before. Their term of service in the field had exceeded that of any fighting unit from overseas on the Western Front and of most battalions raised in the British Isles after the outbreak of war.[9] After landing at Weymouth, they entrained for Bramshott Camp south of Guildford to wait for a ship to Canada. All were granted eight days' leave which Gault spent with his family in Taunton.

On 21 February Princess Patricia came to see her Regiment. There had been no occasion like it in Britain for years. A luncheon guest list of politicians and generals was drawn up but the Colonel-in-Chief insisted that it should be a family occasion. Only members of the Regiment might attend.

Accompanied by Agar Adamson, she was greeted by Gault and the Battalion on parade. Apart from those two officers, only 42 men were present of the 1100 who had received her Colour in Lansdowne Park. On its shell-scarred pike she hung a wreath of laurel in silver gilt inscribed:

> To the P.P.C.L.I. from the Colonel-in-Chief,
> PATRICIA, in recognition of their heroic
> service in the Great War, 1914–1918.

The honour remains unique and replicas of it are borne to this day on the Colours of each battalion of the Regiment.

After Gault, on behalf of his men, had thanked the Princess every steel helmet went skywards on a bayonet point as the Regiment cheered.

A week later Princess Patricia was married at Westminster Abbey to Commander Alexander Ramsay with whom she had fallen in love in Ottawa before the war – the first 'Royal Occasion' since before the War. An immaculate Guard from the Regiment with its Colour greeted her and the King and Queen as they arrived. The Abbey's aisles were lined by Patricia NCOs and every officer of the Regiment was a guest.[10] That day Gault gave his NCOs lunch at the Trocadero and the men at another hotel, followed in the evening by a farewell regimental dinner for PPCLI's military friends at the Carleton.

Before the Regiment left to embark at Liverpool, Gault and Hugh Niven, who had re-joined from the staff, went to London to tidy up some regimental business. Several officers, since killed, had had accounts with Fortnum and Mason through whom they received regular parcels of food and cigarettes. Gault was concerned that these might have been left unpaid and determined to settle them. When the Managing Director heard what he wanted, he said that there were no unpaid accounts of deceased Patricia officers – they had died to keep Fortnums open on Piccadilly.[11]

When Hammie arrived with the Regiment at Halifax in the *Carmania* he was handed a telegram inviting the Patricias to parade down Fifth Avenue in New York. A similar one came from Montreal but he refused both in the interests of uniting his men with their families without delay. On 19 March they were welcomed in Ottawa by the Governor-General, the Government and most of the population. After an inspection in Confederation Square, Gault led the Patricias on foot the three miles to Lansdowne Park. There the local military staff told him that there was no question of his being able to give his men a dinner at which he could thank them for their service – when he dismissed them from parade, they would immediately be swept up by the demobilization machine and most would have left Ottawa by train before nightfall.

Gault began to say farewell to his men:

> I believe we have all returned to Canada better fitted to take up
> the duties and responsibilities of citizenship in the country we love

20. The candidate for the Conservative and Unionist Party addressing Devon farmers at Dulverton.

21. Percival Campbell, with Miles Wood on his right, on the *Promenade des Anglais*, Nice.

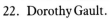

22. Dorothy Gault.

23. Dorothy checking the engine of the Gaults' Gipsy Moth, G-AAGA.

24. Discovering the *Luftwaffe* being formed despite the Treaty of Versailles. Gault took this photograph of Dorothy with Nazi airmen in 1933.

25. Flying Members of Parliament meet Hitler. Dorothy Gault is on the German Chancellor's right. Gault, in the back row, is obscured.

26. Hammie with his Leopard Moth, G-ACSI, in Egypt, 1934.

27. Lillian and Percival Benson, Freiburg, Germany, March, 1933.

28. Hatch Court.

so well. Difficult days may lie before us in the re-establishment of life, but if they are faced with the same steadfastness of purpose which has characterized the years which we have passed through, I feel confident that you will succeed in whatever you may undertake to do.[12]

As he spoke simply and movingly of his regret at the prospect of being separated from the comrades he had known for so long, the Battalion broke into a roar of spontaneous cheering which continued for several minutes. Gault was so overcome that when it subsided he could not speak. Taking a firm grip on himself, he called his Patricias to attention and dismissed them to civilian life.

Hammie's next few days were occupied with planning for the Regiment to become part of Canada's Permanent Force which was being increased from one to three regular infantry battalions. He was to remain in command temporarily until a new CO could be appointed. Eventually they were to have their headquarters in Winnipeg with companies in Vancouver, London and Toronto but, until recruiting began, he would have an office in Ottawa.

The selection of the Patricias had been decided before the end of the war but the second regiment had not been named. Gault strongly recommended that it be the 22nd (French-Canadian) Battalion, a view which found support at Militia Headquarters.[13] No one was more pleased than he, when on 1 April, 1920, the new '22nd Regiment' (now Le Royal 22e Régiment) joined the Patricias and the Royal Canadian Regiment in the 'PF'.

With initial arrangements made, he went home to Rokeby in Montreal. Any doubts about his reception were dispelled by a flood of invitations from his friends. The Hunt and Mount Royal Clubs gave dinners in his honour. His friends dined him and he dined them. Adamson who stayed with him for several days commented,

> The wealth of Montreal is very great, society quite small (all English speaking) and some of it very charming. Gault comes home every night enraged with the extravagance and want of national responsibility of the leading people. Sir Herbert Holt, Sir Mortimer Davis etc., all old men, will dance till 4 o'clock in the morning, damn labour and labour unions and refuse to discuss the problems of the moment. Gault has called a meeting of the Board of Trade to give them his views of the situation and try to get the responsible people to take some responsibility and stop playing with the labour fire until it is too late.

He has been offered a seat in the British House of Commons. I advised him to take it but he feels he owes something to Canada from whence his fortune came. He is a very high minded fellow with the greatest sense of duty. I wish there were more of them in Canada. . . .

His wife is in town but I have not seen her. . . . Gault is going to England at the end of June.[14]

When he accepted the temporary peacetime command of the Regiment, Gault had imagined it would be for two or three months at most. By May headquarters had been established in Stanley Barracks in Toronto where a small number of soldiers were over-officered by men of experience. The Militia Department had approved the appointment of Colonel Pelly, one of the 'Originals', an officer of the British Army, to command, subject to his reverting to the rank of major and acting as second-in-command for a probationary period of six months during which Gault would be granted leave. This it seems was a Machiavellian device of the Militia Department to slot Pelly into an acceptable position in the seniority list.

Hammie duly went on leave and finally gave up his command on 20 January, 1920. The deal with Pelly had fallen through and he was succeeded, not by another Patricia, but by Lieutenant-Colonel C.R.E. Willets, DSO, a highly competent officer of the Royal Canadian Regiment.

In the King's Birthday Honours List of 3 June, 1919, Gault was appointed an Officer of the Order of the British Empire. No citation exists today, nor any record of who recommended him for the decoration. But he must have been angry or hurt by it because he took the unusual step of resigning the appointment.[15]

Like most front line soldiers, he regarded the decoration as one for 'base wallahs'. Among that unique fraternity who performed their duties within close range of the enemy, the OBE was said to be awarded for 'Other Buggers' Efforts'. His DSO, his four mentions in despatches and his two foreign decorations were awarded for gallantry in the face of the enemy. He received no recognition from his country for raising the Patricias, nor did he expect any. But if the Canadian Government did award him an OBE for that, he would have been right to regard it as an insult.

Chapter 14

MARRIAGE

In June, 1919, when Gault went to England on six months' leave, he hoped to find a new course to follow in his life. His interest in business had been waning fast when war broke out and now was virtually extinct. The family interests were well-managed and needed little supervision by him. Some form of public service, possibly a parliamentary career, seemed attractive. He was confident that a candidature in either Canada or England would be his for the asking. But where did he want to live?

Today, with Canada's independent identity so firmly established, Gault's position may seem strange. Many Canadians, not exclusively those of British stock, enjoyed a dual patriotism. To them to be loyal to Canada was not inconsistent with loyalty to Britain, the Empire and to the Crown which bound them together. Passports proclaimed that Canadians were British. Many Canadians represented British constituencies at Westminster, just as many born in Britain were members in Ottawa.

Gault saw the Empire as a force for peace and stability in the world and felt strongly that it should be nurtured by its parts. In the war just finished, it had demonstrated its strength and its power for good. Whether he served his country in Ottawa or in London, he would work to strengthen the Empire and its member countries through trade and mutual support.

Like most veterans, Gault found Canada as much changed by the war as he was himself. Much of the savour had gone from life in Montreal as he remembered it. So many faces of those who had laughed and argued with him, of his polo, sailing and fishing friends were no longer there. Wherever he went, the shadow of Marguerite fell across relations with mutual friends. He was distressed by the rising unemployment which was making a mockery of the promise of jobs for Canada's returning soldiers, and by the venality of the wealthy and influential who would do nothing to avert it.

But before he could decide on a career, he needed to come to terms with himself. As far as he might, he refused to concede that the loss of a leg limited him physically, but it did. At an extreme, it was obvious that never again could he contemplate going to the South Pole or climbing a sheer rock face. Probably he would never again play top flight polo. The day of that sort of physical challenge was over. But what were his physical limits?

And there had been other injuries. Marguerite's betrayal was the worst and the rebuff by the Regiment in 1918 still stung. Both had injured his pride, but that was easier to heal than the rejection of his love and affection.

While he was at Lydeard in October a line was drawn under his relationship with Marguerite with the news that she had married her Italian airman, Luigino Falchi, and had gone to live in Italy.

Since the summer of 1916, when his dying cousin had asked him to ensure his wife's and daughter's financial security, Hammie had been conscientious in seeing to Kathleen Blackader's interests. And he saw much of her. She and his sister Lillian were close friends and she was often a guest at Lydeard when he was there, convalescing or on leave. She was particularly fond of his mother whom she called 'Granny Gault' and whenever she came to Taunton would buy her a posy from an old gipsy flower-seller at Paddington Station.

For their part, the Gaults were full of sympathy for their cousin, widowed at twenty-one, and her small daughter, Patricia.

As the months following Gordon Blackader's death went by, Kathleen's vivacity and sense of fun gradually returned and when Hammie came to Lydeard on leave in September, 1918, his interest in her changed.

She was undoubtedly very pretty. Slight, small-boned, five feet four and a half inches tall, with a good figure, she dressed well. Short-cropped light brown hair framed an oval face. Her complexion was clear but for a mole on her left cheek. Above her full mouth and straight nose, large hazel eyes, rather vulnerable, looked directly at him.

Unlike Marguerite and Lillian who were superb horsewomen, she had never ridden. Neither did she have their air of sophisticated assurance. But her appearance, gentle and very feminine, was deceptive.

In 1912, when she and her parents were staying in the Black Forest, she was invited by a German officer for a flight in a military aeroplane. To even think of flying in an aircraft of that day, all wings and wire and popping engine, was challenge enough for most people but she accepted. Dressed like a Gibson Girl in a white blouse and a long black skirt with a straw boater tied by a veil beneath her chin, she was strapped to a seat resembling a kitchen chair while the rudimentary flying machine bumped into the air and circled before returning to the landing ground.

In a day when few women skied, she learned in Switzerland and when Gault offered to teach her to ride she was delighted.

In 1919 Kathleen took Pat to Montreal to spend Christmas with her Blackader in-laws, and as Gault's leave was drawing to an end at the time, he escorted them across the Atlantic. He re-opened Rokeby and from there, almost daily, sent his coachman with an open sleigh to take them up onto Mount Royal, Kathleen to ski, Pat to play in the snow. Often he joined them.

He had not lost his love of the wilderness. While expeditions like those to Mistassini, which involved packing heavy loads over difficult portages, were beyond his capacity, he was still drawn by its wild beauty and its offer of solitude.

One day he took Kathleen and Pat for a winter picnic on Mont St Hilaire and there, standing on a promontory overlooking Bruneau and Montreal, asked if this was where he should build a house. The question was more than half-serious. If his future was to be in Canada, though he might not be able to live on the Mountain, it would always be his refuge. Before the war, Gordon Blackader had designed a chateau with towers surmounted by coppered coned roofs to stand beside the lake. Gault now commissioned Ernest Barrot to plan another. There would be several designs before he was satisfied.

By this time the day-to-day affairs of the Patricias were out of his hands, although before he finally retired he did what he could to ensure that its new life as a regular Regiment was established on a sound footing. He remained deeply concerned for the welfare of its old soldiers and took the first steps toward forming them into a mutual help association. As an extension of this, he took up once more his association with the Montreal branch of the embryonic Canadian Legion.

Aside from the Regiment and the welfare of ex-servicemen, as the decade ended he focused his attention on Canada's public affairs, a process of re-education to prepare for the future. He read widely on its trade and international relations and deliberately set about obtaining the views and opinions of business and political leaders.

During the months they were in Montreal, Hammie and Kathleen were often together in the friendly atmosphere of his Blackader cousins' home. In the spring she and Pat would be returning to England; the future without them seemed bleak and Hammie's thoughts turned to marriage.

Early in the year he obtained an assurance from Senator W.B. Ross, Canada's leading expert on the subject, that his Paris divorce was valid.[1]

In the spring he accompanied Kathleen and Pat once more to England where she shared a house in London with General Garnet Hughes (the son of the Patricias' bête noire) and his wife, Irene. Hammie repaired at first to Lydeard but soon took a flat in London and brought his two wartime chargers, Sandy and ZiZi PomPom, to town so that he and Kathleen could ride together in Hyde Park. A few weeks later, after receiving assurances from his lawyers in England that there was no impediment to his remarriage, they announced their engagement.

On the day of the first post-war Royal Tournament, Hammie collected Kathleen and Pat in a carriage. On the way, the child succeeded in marking his immaculate dark blue trousers with her white buckskin shoes. Her mother was upset, but not Hammie: already he had become the indulgent father.

In early autumn, when Kathleen was leaving Paddington for one of her frequent visits to Taunton, she stopped as usual to buy a bunch of violets for 'Grannie Gault' from the gipsy flower seller. The old woman took her hand, looked at it and said, 'Oh, you poor child – you haven't got much longer'.

That evening Kathleen laughed as she told Lillian Benson about it, but was serious when she asked her if she would take care of Pat if anything happened to her. Lillian willingly agreed.

A few weeks later, on a bright November morning, Kathleen and Pat squeezed into the front seat beside Gault in his large open Vauxhall to follow the West Somerset Foxhounds who were meeting in the Quantock hills north of Bishop's Lydeard.

The lane outside the village was narrow and covered with wet leaves. Hammie drove slowly as he edged past hunt followers on horse and foot. He had driven about a mile when, rounding a curve where the road dropped down a gentle slope, the heavy car suddenly skidded out of control on the slippery surface. It partly mounted a bank, then veered across the road to the other side and overturned. Gault was trapped by the steering wheel, Kathleen, pinned by the back of the seat, was face down on the road. Pat began cry.

Kathleen asked Hammie if he could get out and he said no, that he was caught. He asked if she was alright. She answered, 'Pat is being crushed. Can you get her out?' After struggling for what seemed an age, Gault managed to work free. Desperately he tried to lift the car but failed.

Hammie was not immediately worried about Kathleen – she showed no sign of being seriously hurt and her own anxiety, and Hammie's, was for Pat who was further underneath the car and screaming. With all the speed he could muster, he ran up the road, calling for help. He met the keeper of Cothelstone Lodge who returned with him to the car. A boy working in a field was sent running to the nearest farm.

In the meantime Kathleen managed to quieten the child and asked, 'Patsy, can you squidge out?' Seeing light by the driver's side, she said she could. She asked, 'Are you coming?' Her mother said, 'Yes' and the little girl crawled out into the sunshine. Moments later Gault returned.

He could see that Kathleen was unconscious, her face faintly blue. Frantically he tried to raise the car with the jack. Two men appeared. Together they lifted it and rolled it onto its side. Kathleen had stopped breathing; her heart was still.

When Doctor Frossard from Bishop's Lydeard arrived, he found Hammie seated by the roadside in tears, with Kathleen lying in his arms.

Someone fetched a hurdle. With the help of police, they carried her body back to Lydeard House. An inquest next day found that she had died from suffocation as a result of pressure on her rib-cage and that her death was accidental. She was buried on 11 November in the local churchyard.[2]

Kathleen's death was a double blow, for added to Hammie's sense of loss was an inevitable feeling of guilt. Much as others might accept that it was accidental, much as his mind agreed, there remained the knowledge that it was he who had lost control of the car, that it was he who had failed to rescue her from beneath it. Could he have done more?

'If only. . . .' No one who has been involved as he had been in an accidental death can ever rid themselves completely of the feeling of responsibility, no matter how irrational.

The accident had shattered his hopes for a settled personal life, with Kathleen and Patricia at its centre. Not only had he lost a wife but a daughter as well. He was determined to take full responsibility for Pat, but given the state of his life, he could not himself make a home for her. Lillian, his sister, was equally determined to keep her light-hearted promise to Kathleen. Pat remained at Lydeard to be brought up as a sister to Doris and Clive Benson. Gault became her guardian and assumed responsibility for her financial security. Pat came to call Lillian, 'Mum', Hammie was her devoted, 'Bing' or 'Bingo.'

For a time, he seems to have withdrawn into himself. In December Princess Patricia, now Lady Patricia Ramsay, wrote him a letter of condolence. In February she wrote to Lillian, 'as I don't know where he is' with a message for him about a new colour for the Regiment. In May she wrote, 'I assure you, you are often in my thoughts in your sorrow & loneliness'.

The loneliness was not to last much longer.

Three years earlier, whilst on leave at Lydeard, Gault had spent a few days hunting with the Taunton Vale. One day they met at Hatch Court, a handsome Palladian house belonging to W.H. Lloyd, a member of the banking family. Staying with the Lloyds was their nineteen year old niece, Dorothy Shuckburgh. With her fair hair and fine features, slim, elegant and vivacious, she was undoubtedly attractive and she rode beautifully. Hammie appreciated attractive women and was intrigued. His interest grew when he learned that she was no social butterfly but was employed by the British army to break and train cavalry horses at their remount depot in Warwickshire.

He saw her a few times in the company of other people, found her interesting but, as he was still married and considerably older, there was no question of a closer relationship. Attractive as she was, she would probably soon be swept up by some discerning young man.

What he did not realize was that Dorothy had been completely bowled over by him. On one of the last days of her leave, she packed herself a lunch and rode from Hatch to Lydeard House, some twenty miles there and back, in the hope of catching a glimpse of him. She later admitted that, if they had met, she would have been completely tongue-tied.

Two years later Gault met Dorothy by chance when he was riding near Hatch. They had a long conversation, mostly about hunting and horses which Gault found strangely disturbing. Already he felt committed to Kathleen but Dorothy was unaware of that relationship.

In December, unaware that he was in Canada, she wrote him a note from Lancashire (which does not survive) but for three months received no reply. In March, 1920, Gault answered 'Dear Miss Shuckburgh', apologized for the delay which he attributed to the winter mails and his 'erratic wanderings' and hoped that she had enjoyed her 'sojourn in the north without becoming entirely estranged from the banks and bull-finches of the west country where perchance we may meet in the dim and distant future.

'With kindest regards and many renewed thanks for your letter, Very sincerely yours, A. Hamilton Gault'.

It offered sparse encouragement but what little there was may have tipped the scale that summer when Dorothy was hotly pursued by the handsome and eligible Hugh Cole-Hamilton. She was tempted to marry him but could not rid herself of the fascination of Hammie Gault.

Early in August, 1921, Gault met Dorothy again at an evening party at Lydeard.³ She told him that she would be staying at Hatch that winter to hunt. As he would be in Canada, he offered her 'Sandy', his charger throughout the war, to ride, saying that she would be doing him a favour by giving the horse regular exercise, but they made no firm arrangements.

On 8 August Dorothy wrote to Hammie from her home at Halton Hall near Lancaster,

> I have been thinking a lot about Sandy . . . I have bought a big bay mare which I think when she has been ridden a bit will probably sell pretty easily so in that case I should of course *love* to have Sandy for December & January . . . but what is worrying me is that I am – as usual – so horribly vague – cos you see if the big mare doesn't sell, I suppose I oughtn't to have him, so if you hear of a more dependable person than myself, oughtn't you to let them have him?
>
> I think I may have to run up to London for three days towards the end of the month in which case, if you are anywhere near, p'raps we could meet & talk it over more definitely as I suppose you will want to know before you go away that he is going to get some sort of regular work this season . . .

Hammie promptly wrote to ask her to dine with him in London and to help him buy a birthday present for his niece, Doris Benson. Dorothy asked him to call her at her club, The New Century, in the evening of Wednesday, the 17th. During Friday, with Percival Campbell hovering in the background as a discreet chaperone, Gault asked her to marry him and she accepted. They agreed that, since it was only seven months since Kathleen's death, their engagement would be kept secret from all but their mothers.

Hammie had fallen romantically in love, a condition which continued for the rest of his life.

In less than a week, without seeing her again, Gault sailed from Liverpool for a ten-week stay in Canada. Every day they wrote, making up the gaps in their courtship by correspondence. So little did Dorothy know him that she was uncertain how to begin her letters. In the ones arranging their meeting in London she had quite properly addressed him as 'Dear Colonel Gault'. Perhaps she found 'Dear Hamilton' too formal and intimidating and may not have known that old friends called him 'Hammie'. So there was no salutation. The first began abruptly,

'Here are two photos to choose from . . .' It closed shyly with, 'There is no way of ending that appeals to me so I write, Your Dorothy.'

Hammie spent his first two weeks in Canada fishing with friends at Pointe au Pic on the St Lawrence, then moved to Montreal to attend to business and other interests there. He played tennis frequently and took up golf.

In her letters Dorothy told him of her progress in training her new bay mare, 'Maple Sugar', and in another, mentioned that she intended to sell her in order to be able to afford her trousseau. Hammie at once offered to buy the mare, drawing the response, 'You don't seem to have quite grasped the difficulty about my selling a horse to my fiancé in order to buy my trousseau! Men (even the very nicest in the world) are very dense!'

In Canada the Conservative Government was facing a general election in December and their leader, Arthur Meighen, asked Gault to stand as their candidate in Montreal West. He assured him that a man of his stature could look forward to an early ministerial post. Hammie was not enthusiastic, but, faced with appeals to his sense of duty to Canada and his obligations to family tradition (his uncle Matthew had held the seat in Sir John A. Macdonald's government), he demurred. His cousin, Charles Ernest Gault, a Conservative Member of the Quebec Legislative Assembly, weighed in with others to persuade him to accept.

Still he hesitated. If he agreed to run, he would be setting the pattern of his future for, win or lose, it was not in his nature to take up a challenge only to drop it at the first disappointment. He would be committing himself to a career in Canadian Federal politics.

His sense of duty told him that, potentially, there was much that he could do for Canada. Yet while he might win Montreal West in December, nationally he foresaw a resounding defeat for the Conservatives. The prospect of some five years as an opposition MP with no outlet for his executive ability and energy, no prospect of furthering the policies which he supported, had little appeal. His month in Canada had not improved his opinion of many of the Conservative party's prominent supporters which had so marred his return to Montreal from the War in 1919. In truth, he did not much want to be associated with them.

But now he had another to consider. On 9 October he cabled Dorothy:

Without my seeking Government have asked me to stand for my uncle's old electoral division in coming general elections early

December. If returned would mean our residing largely here and would entail great sacrifice for both of us in every way. Personally inclined refuse nomination on account our scheme of things but would willingly take on duty of public life if you wanted me to do so. Only consideration is your happiness. Must give immediate answer. Please consult your mother fully and cable me your views . . . My love to you. Hamilton

She replied:

Am willing but if you really feel inclined refuse I really much prefer original plan also. Love. Dorothy.

Gault's business kept him in Montreal until the beginning of November but he remained there for another two weeks so that he and Pat Blackader could attend a memorial service for Kathleen on the 15th. Arriving in London on the 30th he met Dorothy accompanied by her mother and her aunt, on the platform at Paddington.

Before he told the rest of the family of their plans, he took Pat for a walk in the garden at Lydeard and asked her if she would mind if he married again. She said of course she wouldn't.[4] His engagement to Dorothy was announced in *The Times* on 20 December.

It was over thirteen months since Kathleen's death but some who were close to Gault were unhappy. His brother-in-law, Percy Benson wrote:

I have been feeling very uneasy lest you might think me wanting in sympathy or lacking in wishing you well in your engagement to Dorothy though I feel certain that you have proved me sufficiently not to misunderstand my feelings.

I am *very* fond of Dorothy & I most earnestly wish you & her many many happy years together but my heart was very much little Kathie's & I miss her all the time. The day you arrived, Bristowe & the other gardeners spent the afternoon in levelling the turf & decorating her grave with chrysanthemums under my direction. One's deepest & most abiding feelings are generally those least capable of discussion or of reason & even at the risk of your misunderstanding me I know you prefer that I should not make a pretence to you – we have been far too intimately connected for that. Percival [Campbell] in a letter which came today put my feelings in a nutshell when he said, 'My heart & mind are still so full of last year that I cannot yet see things properly in this new direction but if it is all for dear old Hamilton's happiness, it is alright.'

Those are entirely my feelings & as I have always prayed for your happiness & welfare so I shall always continue to do.[5]

Hammie replied:

> I was glad to hear from you and understand full well how you feel over my engagement to Dorothy. I can hardly expect you to appreciate that which I can only understand but dimly. I loved little Kath, loved her truly and tenderly as a big brother loves his little sister – there was nothing I would not have done for her – but even from her I did not disguise the fact that there was a vision of one whom I had met but a few times in my life and by whom I was strangely attracted, one who at that time had seemed unobtainable, one whom I should in all probability never meet again – that one was Dorothy Shuckburgh.
>
> When we met again by chance last summer I was impelled by an impulse stronger than myself not to go away from her again without first knowing if this strange attraction did not dwell within her as it had done within me against my will for just on two years. You know the rest. To Kath I was never disloyal even in thought – I would willingly have given my life for her, would do so now could I but bring her back – and though we shall never understand in this life, the whys and wherefores of things, I believe that in some future incarnation all will be made clear & that at this moment Kath understands the motives which actuate our beings. This is no apology, but tonight I feel that I must speak to you of matters too intimate and sacred to be mentioned openly between us.[6]

Dorothy's parson uncle, Harry Shuckburgh, made it plain to Gault that it would not be tactful to invite him to officiate at their wedding:

> You and Dorothy have my very best wishes, but of course, the fact that you have had to divorce your wife worries me, as I dare say Dorothy has told you, and holding the views I do, the question of re-marriage is a difficult one.
>
> As I say, you both have my best wishes and may God's blessing rest on you both.[7]

Hammie's unease about his unconventional divorce in Paris continued. At the time of his engagement to Kathleen his lawyers had assured him that his Paris divorce was indeed valid. In what might be seen as a belt and braces move, he had since asked them if his remarriage would be recognized as legal in England and elsewhere. On 28 February, 1922, Sir John Simon, the former Attorney General and Home Secretary, gave his opinion that it would.

Most Church of England clergymen would have found it 'difficult' to marry them but fortunately Gault had a friend in the Reverend Hugh Chapman at the Savoy Chantry who had written:

> . . . we will arrange all the details which shall be as perfect as possible for her dear sake, Always your affectionate, "Padre".

The wedding took place quietly in the Chapel Royal on 7 March,1922, and immediately afterward, Hammie and Dorothy left for Sicily. In Taormina they were met by Percival Campbell who by now was living permanently in the beautiful Casa Montebello, but, not unnaturally for a honeymooning couple, they preferred to stay in a hotel.

It was a practice which they were to follow in future visits to Taormina. The reason may have been the presence of Campbell's close companion, Miles Wood, at the Casa, although, curiously, both were frequent guests of the Gaults in England. It became a source of some wonder and amusement to other members of the family that Dorothy apparently never realized the nature of the relationship between Percy and Miles. Hammie was far from liberal in his views of homosexuality but in this case his affection for his old friend outweighed his disapproval.

Gault's chauffeur, Jasper Durman, joined them in Sicily with their touring Rolls. A few idyllic weeks of lazing on the beach and exploring the island were followed by the further enchantments of Venice.

On their return to England they moved into Hatch Court which they had leased from Dorothy's aunt. For the first time since 1916 Gault began to feel that there was an element of permanence in his life.

But the honeymoon was not over. In the early autumn Hammie took his new wife to Canada. Outside Montreal they stayed with the Campbells at their Manoir from which, across a sweep of fields edged by trees, they could see Mont St Hilaire rising green against the sky. They spent hours exploring their mountain, its lake and woods and the sites where, eventually, they might build a house.

From Somerset they had brought two couples of hounds for Campbell's pack and Dorothy was fascinated to see the hunt, well-mounted, some in pink, older women elegant on side-saddle – a picture of England – assembling in a typical Quebec village beside the general store and the verandahs of its white painted clapboard hotel.

For a few days 'Bau' Peck lent them his gem of a Quebec stone cottage which they used as a base to explore the area further but Hammie was keen to get away into the bush.

Down the St Lawrence from Pointe-au-Pic below Quebec they canoed with four friends and some guides into the woods to fish. Summer was ended, the leaves on birch and maple were turning and even in the bright sunshine it was heavy-sweater weather. At night they camped in lean-to tents.

It was not the arduous trip which Gault had enjoyed before the war but it was a good beginning to Dorothy's indoctrination into the wilds. When it ended, they said goodbye to their friends and, with two guides, set off by canoe to find deer. That night they camped by the river. When they awoke their tent and the woods were inches deep in snow. Paddling on, about midday they reached the log cabins which were to be their base.

Hammie was in his element and was delighted to find Dorothy as enthusiastic as he. No account of their hunting trip survives except a few photographs – Dorothy on snowshoes – on a horse with a holstered pistol at her waist – with a Mannlicher, their three guides and a skinned carcase in front of the kitchen hut, the snow having disappeared. That Dorothy loved Canada there was now no doubt and they resolved to return next year.

The Gault's visit to Canada in 1923 coincided with one by the Prince of Wales. Hammie, who had known him during the war, gave a party for him at Cartierville. As on other such occasions, the Prince was less than discreet in his behaviour. Colonel Paul Hutchinson who was there recalled that Hammie 'should have been annoyed that evening with Edward of Windsor but could not have been a more charming host to the Prince.'[8]

Later the Gaults returning to England in the *Empress of France*, saw a good deal of the Prince during the voyage. Dorothy danced with him more than once and though, like so many others, she found him amusing and attractive, she kept her guard well up.

In Somerset Hammie put aside thoughts of his future career in favour of enjoying married life and a winter of sport in the hunting field.

Chapter 15

A NEW LIFE

In May of 1923 Bonar Law, the British Prime Minister, retired because of ill health. Stanley Baldwin, who succeeded him in that office and as leader of the Unionist and Conservative Party, was immediately faced with a worrying economic recession. Industry was in decline and unemployment had risen to nearly one and a quarter million. Exports were diminishing in the face of tariff barriers erected by Britain's competitors who further exacerbated the situation by selling their products at uneconomically low prices in the UK. The solution, as Baldwin saw it, was to impose selective tariffs on imports. Behind their protection, Britain's beleaguered industries could regain their markets and solve the distressing problem of unemployment.

But Bonar Law had promised the electorate that he would not change the existing tariff structure without reference to the people. In October, 1923, Baldwin called a general election to obtain their mandate.

In Taunton there was dismay among the local Conservative Party officials. The seat was held by a Liberal who had won the last election with a substantial majority and their prospective candidate had just announced that he was going to try elsewhere. No other party was competing. Desperately casting about for a replacement, they approached the new squire of Hatch Court.

Having turned against a political career in Canada, Gault was not enthusiastic about undertaking one in England. It was not that it would be un-Canadian to do so; Bonar Law was a Canadian and so were several other members of Parliament. But to do so involved a commitment to live in England, as opposed to Canada, which, so far, he had not made.

He knew that Dorothy would cheerfully move to Canada if that was what he wished, but, without knowing the country well, she preferred Somerset. Life there was congenial and all his closest relatives, to whom he was devoted, now lived nearby. In Montreal, with its memories of Marguerite, he had not been universally welcomed. His instinct was to hold on to what he had.

But there was more to be considered. What did he want to do with his life? Where could he be most useful? In Canada he had found no fulfilling outlet for his energies, no role which satisfied the calling of public service. There was little which attracted him in political life on either side of the Atlantic. Paradoxically it was his disenchantment with the myopic attitude of British governments toward the Empire which tipped the scale.

Like so many of his generation in the Dominions, Hammie was an unashamed Imperialist. The British had built a great empire and in the Dominions had founded a family of self-governing countries which turned naturally for their trade and hopes of prosperity to Britain. They had been educated to buy British goods, yet to them it appeared that the 'Mother Country' gave them no preference but 'bought cheap' without regard to the resultant damage wrought to their economies.

The War had revealed the Empire's latent strength. In Gault's view the economic recession which followed it could be defeated if its Dominions and colonies joined together with Britain in, if not a free trade bloc, then a system of mutual preferential tariffs.

Time was short in which to make a decision. Gault spent three days in London consulting Canadians prominent in business and politics, and leaders of the Conservative party. Their advice was that he could do much for Canada and the Empire by changing the attitude of the government in Westminster and there was an urgent need to do so.

In a later letter to Lord Beaverbrook he recalled, 'As one of my advisors . . . you may recollect that my chief reason for entering the political arena in England . . . was in the hope of helping towards a closer rapprochement of Imperial relations.'[1] While that proposition was of little interest to the Labour or Liberal parties, at least the Conservatives under Stanley Baldwin were lukewarm and might be persuaded.

On his return to Taunton he accepted the Tory nomination. Privately he did not give much for his chances. His opponent had won a substantial majority at the preceding election, had proved to be a good constituency M.P. and only three weeks remained in which to change the voters' minds.

Gault immediately embarked on a speaking tour of his largely rural constituency. At village meetings in Hatch Beauchamp, Churchingford, Corfe, Pitminster, Creech St Michael, West Monkton, Kingston St Mary and dozens more, he was introduced as, 'a man who represents not only our little island of England but the British Empire whose aim is to protect British industry and reduce unemployment by protective tariffs against foreign but not Empire goods'.

Gault proved to be a fluent and convincing speaker on the issue of tariffs and unfair foreign competition. He was applauded when he acknowledged that Hope Simpson, his opponent, was universally and deservedly popular, and cheered when he added, 'When speaking at Bath, he said the first duty of England was to reconstruct Germany. I say our first duty is to reconstruct our own country and find employment for our own people.'

If the Conservatives lost the election, the Labour party under Ramsay MacDonald – the official Opposition in the last Parliament – would be likely to form the next government. Gault vigorously attacked their policies of nationalization and a levy on capital and it was evident that Somerset audiences wanted no truck with their 'revolutionary ideas'.

At Milverton, Hope Simpson's home, Gault faced an audience which contained many Liberal supporters. They greeted him with a mixture of mild applause and good-natured booing. He was laughing as he said, 'I am much gratified at this hearty reception in what I am told is a veritable stronghold of Liberalism. I suppose that this is because I come here as a missionary with the intention of converting the "reddest" of Liberals to the sounder doctrines of Conservatism and bring you into an economic Garden of Eden.' He failed to win them over but it was obvious that they liked him.

Not all his audiences were so civilized. At Rockwell Green, near Wellington, the experience of Conservative candidates in the past led him to expect an unsympathetic reception but not the jeering at his disability in the chant of, 'Half a man and half a tree, he's no good for our M.P.'[2]

No well-known English names could be brought in to support him, but in one of the most unconventional of campaigning ploys, Major-General J.H. MacBrien, Chief of the Canadian General Staff who was in England for an Imperial Conference, spoke for him, 'not politically but as a life-long friend'.

Before a large audience MacBrien extolled Hammie's virtues as a citizen and soldier, warmly supported his ideas on Empire cooperation and trade and said it would do the Taunton voters credit to have him as their representative in Parliament.

Jimmy MacBrien had certainly overstepped the line between friendship and political support but nobody seemed to mind.

Unlike Hammie, Dorothy had had no experience of public life. She was young, shy and self-effacing but highly intelligent, attractive and perceptive. She was a brilliant rider and had shown that she could certainly keep up with Gault both in the hunting field and in the Canadian bush. Soon after her marriage she came to realize that she must also develop a role of her own in life as well as playing a full part in his political and other ventures if she were not to be overwhelmed by his forceful and magnetic personality. The press were willing to help. A full page photograph of her in a glossy women's magazine noted that, 'she has just returned from Canada where she has entertained the Prince of Wales'.[3]

Dorothy was on the platform at most of Gault's political meetings and occasionally spoke on his behalf. On election day they visited every polling district in the Taunton division.

The result of the poll was no surprise. Simpson won with a total of 13,053 votes but Hammie had reduced his majority from 2,913 to 1,255. At Westminster the Tories had lost their majority and Ramsay MacDonald, with the support of the Liberals, formed Britain's first Labour government.

The Times commented, 'Colonel Hamilton Gault made a plucky attempt to win Taunton and succeeded in considerably reducing the Liberal majority. But he only had three weeks in which to make himself and his policy known to a scattered country constituency.'[4]

In the new year Gault began a local campaign of meetings and lectures to improve the party's organization and to win more supporters. To broaden his knowledge of issues of the day and make plans for the next election, in August he attended a two-week course run by the Conservatives at the Philip Stott College in Northampton. While there, he obtained a promise from Stanley Baldwin to come to Taunton to support his campaign.[5]

In 1924 Russian Communism was seen in the West as an immediate and serious menace to world peace and stability. The Third International, the organization through which the Communists extended their doctrines abroad, had proclaimed its aim of defeating capitalism by world revolution.

At one extreme, the London *Morning Post* of 26 August printed a report from Dublin that Jim Larkin, the Irish Labour leader, returning from two months in the USSR, had told an enraptured crowd of supporters that the International had appointed twenty-five men, of whom he was one, to govern the world. The Red Army was ready to march to support Irish workers and Russian ships would shortly arrive in Dublin harbour.

There was no shortage of such nonsense being preached to the gullible. On the other hand, reminders of the excesses of the Bolshevik revolution and the brutal murder of the Russian imperial family could still send shivers of apprehension through Britain's voters. When MacDonald agreed to a treaty with the Soviet Union under which

Britain would guarantee a loan of several million pounds, the Opposition became apoplectic.

On 8 October the Labour government fell when the Attorney General, allegedly influenced by the extreme left of the party, refused to prosecute a notorious Communist agitator who had been charged with inciting troops to mutiny. MacDonald called a snap election for 29 October.

This time Gault's campaign was better organized and supported. As promised, Baldwin came to speak in his support to a large audience in Taunton and spent the night at Hatch Court. When Gault spoke at meetings in the villages of west Somerset, he had three issues to hammer – support of agriculture, Empire preference and the threat of Bolshevism.

Many voters saw Labour as sympathetic to the Communists and would never forgive the Liberals for enabling them to take power at the last election.

When the result of the poll in Taunton was announced, Gault had won with a vote which exceeded the total cast for his two opponents.

The *Sunday Express*, admittedly partisan, wrote:

> Colonel Gault won the hearts of the Somerset farmers, and is also popular with the industrial section of his constituency. His amazingly vigorous personality penetrates the remotest corner of it, and his imperialistic programme was taken up with enthusiasm.
>
> 'My first thought,' said Colonel Gault, 'is the strengthening of the Empire by bands of Imperial Preference, and by bringing the scattered units into a composite whole.
>
> 'I can also see a self-contained Empire, almost independent of the troubles of the Continent of Europe. I also see in this the solution to unemployment. We must strengthen our colonial trade. We must find overseas an outlet for our ever-growing population. . . .
>
> 'I place side by side with my Imperial ideas,' he said, 'the determination to champion the farmer. I realize the need of a restored rural life and the building up of the agricultural industry. I am looking forward to standing up for the farmer in the House of Commons.'[6]

In the Commons Gault found himself in the company of sixteen other Canadians or Anglo-Canadians. Six more had been defeated in the election.[7]

On 25 May, in his maiden speech, Gault spoke in defence of the Budget. His military reputation was well-known and it may be that Members were curious to see how this paladin would perform in their arena. That they stayed to listen says something for his personal magnetism as well as for the content of his speech which was an exposition of his belief in the benefits of Empire cooperation.

He began by advocating that tariffs should be used as an instrument for the direction of trade and the stimulation of commerce which should tend to increase production and so bring the cost of living down.

A partial solution to the problem of the million unemployed in Britain would be to support emigration to those parts of the Empire which were crying out for development.

He said that Imperial Preference and Imperial Development went hand in hand, claiming that the greatest consumers of British manufactures were the overseas British, and that the more that is produced in the Dominions, the more they are able to export to Britain and take from Britain in return.

> The New Zealander buys upwards of £16 of English goods per head per year, the Australian over £10, and the Canadian just over £3. (I have a word to say upon this matter later on.) In South Africa nearly £4 worth of English goods per head of population are bought; while Germany buys only fourteen shillings per head and America only ten. . . .
>
> For years past the Overseas Dominions have been giving to England substantial preferences, which amounted to some £12,000,000 in the last year, and in exchange England has had nothing of this character to offer. . . . If the Dominions are not able to look for an expanding market for their products in the United Kingdom, they may be forced into other economic channels and orbits to the detriment of England's exports, and the consequential detriment of England's purchasing power.
>
> Co-operation is the key word of to-day. Can we not introduce it into our business dealing with our kith and kin across the seas to our mutual advantage? . . . Whatever policy is necessary to secure this end must emanate from the centre, from the heart of the Empire, and that is here in England. . . .
>
> Let us not forget that the beginnings of our maritime supremacy were created within the protective scaffolding of our navigation laws. Is it not possible that by a scaffolding of Imperial Preference the compound parts of the Empire may be brought closer together,

and that we may evolve into a great civilisation wherein not only the greatest individual freedom will be found, but where complete freedom of trade may exist? . . .

New Zealand, Australia, and South Africa have all expressed their desire for closer economic union through the medium of Imperial Preference. Only Canada has refrained from pressing this point . . . explained I think, by the fact that since the late Sir Wilfrid Laurier . . . made advances for a closer economic union 15 years ago – advances which were rejected by the then British Government – the Canadian Government has refrained from re-opening the question. I am, however, satisfied that the preference included in this Bill will be taken by the great body of Canadian people as a gesture from the Motherland towards the closer economic union of the Empire. It is for these reasons that I whole-heartedly support the principles embodied in . . . the Bill, believing, as I do, that they will help to bring back this country and the Empire as a whole to the high road of peace and prosperity again.

In Britain, Canada and the rest of the Commonwealth, many today regret that the policies advocated by Gault were not pursued with more enthusiasm.

But junior back bench Members have few opportunities to intervene in debates in the early stages of a new Parliament and it is by their work in the direct interests of their constituency that voters tend to judge them. At the time of his maiden speech, Gault was working behind the scenes to correct an injustice.

A few months earlier several Taunton men were sent by the local Labour Exchange to the Derby Forest Timber Company where they were employed after depositing money as a 'guarantee'. After they had worked there for some time, the manager decamped without paying their wages. On the grounds that they had been 'employed', the local Labour Exchange refused to pay them unemployment benefit for the time they had worked for the defunct company – the men lost not only their guarantee money and wages but also the dole they would have received if they had remained out of work.

When Gault learned of the case, he questioned the men himself, then wrote to the Minister of Labour. After several interviews and frustrating correspondence with the Minister and the civil servants of his department, Gault persuaded them to submit the men's appeal against the disallowance of their claims, to the Court of Referees. It ruled against the men.

Fortunately, there was an authority, the Umpire, to whom an appeal could be made in cases where strict adherence to rules resulted in injustice. Gault persuaded him to review the case: the Umpire decreed that the men had been the victim of a fraud, hence had never been employed. They received their unemployment pay and Gault a boost to his rising reputation in Taunton.[8]

Though he had seen nothing of his regiment since he left Canada, Hammie kept in close touch with it by correspondence. His position of honorary lieutenant-colonel of Princess Patricia's Canadian Light Infantry carried with it none of the rights or duties of command – those were defined by statute and remained solely with the commanding officer of the day. Possibly unique among the holders of such honorary ranks, Gault was recognized both by the Patricias and by the military establishment as the guardian of their traditions and was invariably consulted about matters which related to them. An early example occurred in 1924 when the War Office invited units of the British army to seek alliances with regiments in the Dominions.

Lieutenant-General Sir Henry Fuller Maitland Wilson, K.C.B., K.C.M.G., Colonel Commandant of the Rifle Brigade, otherwise known as 'Fatty', lost no time in seeking to form one with the Patricias. In a letter to Hammie he said how proud they would be 'to have an alliance with your Regiment which so distinguished itself in the Great War. . . .' Remembering how, at Frezenberg, the 4th Rifle Brigade had saved the Patricias from extinction, Gault's response was never in doubt. After quickly consulting the Regiment and their Colonel-in-Chief, he replied that nothing would give them more pleasure. The King approved the alliance on 3 December, 1924.

Three years later Gault took Dorothy to hunt in the Rocky Mountains and to see the Patricias about whom she had heard so much.

At Winnipeg, the headquarters of the Regiment, where they stopped on the way to the Rockies, and at the detached company stationed in the old garrison town of Esquimalt, near Victoria, British Columbia, they were warmly welcomed. Hammie came away happy that the Regiment's morale and standards were being maintained, though their strength and training were severely limited by the Government's savage economies.

It was between these two brief but happy visits to the Patricias that Hammie and Dorothy spent three weeks hunting in the Smokey River country, one of the best districts in the Rockies for bear, sheep and goat.

At Devona, west of Jasper, they met their guides in a picturesque western scene. An Indian teepee was pitched beside a roped corral in which the three men, wearing chaps and stetsons, were attempting to load and saddle an assortment of horses.

They watched intrigued by the rough and ready methods used for making a horse stand still with his pack on his back. There was one who bucked if let loose and broke his rope if tethered. Dorrell, the head guide, tied him to a strong but whippy young pine tree so that each time he plunged, the top of the tree whacked him on the head. Dorrell quietly commented, 'That'll teach you old boy.'

Mounted on typical cayuses, they rode westwards for six hours to a salt lick where for two days they camped, surrounded by poplars leafed in autumn gold. Riding into the hills, they watched and photographed mountain sheep and goats high above them in the mountains. It was their last camp among deciduous trees for, as they moved higher into the mountains, only pine and spruce clothed the lower levels.

In a diary of the trip Dorothy wrote that they rode for three miles through an astounding wilderness, a network of windfalls which no English horse could have stood up in for ten yards, much less have crossed at a good speed as their cayuses did.

At Hay River they camped among pines high above the water – 'an evening of purple and primrose fading into the dark blue of night, lighted by the most brilliant and numerous stars.' The only sounds were the wind in the trees and distant mournful howling of coyotes.

On the eighth day, above their camp at Rock Creek, Hammie spotted some mountain sheep sitting on a crag, miles away. He and Dorothy, with Dorrell, rode as close as they dared, tied their horses to some stunted spruce, then stalked the sheep across a tumble of rocks and ravines. Hammie was unable to crawl with his artificial leg, so he scrambled forward as best he could, sometimes with Dorrell and Dorothy pushing and pulling him, at times rolling forward in his eagerness to get on.

From about noon until after three o'clock he kept moving in this fashion until they got as close to the sheep as it was possible to do without being spotted. Hammie took careful aim. His shot hit the ground below a ram which departed at high speed around a shoulder of the mountain. It was a repetition of his shooting experience on his first African safari.

Hammie's determination sometimes verged on the foolhardy. Seeing some inaccessible goat, high on a mountain, he insisted, against Dorothy's protests, on trying to climb a steep slope covered with loose flint rock and stones. Dorothy later said,

We got into the middle of this stuff – I fighting every inch of the way and wanting to cry like a baby with anxiety – before he admitted that there wasn't much point in going any further. So then back we climbed, trying not to look at the stones which went crashing into the ravine below. We were both very cross when we reached safety, and I couldn't eat my lunch.

The next day was eventful as we decided to try for a goat we could see straight up the very steep grassy slope of the mountain opposite camp. Dorrell and Harry (our excellent cook) took a rope and Hamilton scrambled to an unbelievable height with the aid of these two and their rope, I doing odd jobs behind, such as stopping Horace slipping. At last Harry went on, skirting round the peak the goat had been on, only to find he'd gone. . . . It took ages to get down again, but we all enjoyed it and were glad to get out of the snow and biting wind which came on after we got high up.

The next morning they faced a strenuous ride across 'Hard Scrabble', a pass so named for the tumbles of rock and boulders and great smooth slopes of rock which make it difficult for pack horses to keep their feet. As they climbed towards it they found another world of ice and snow and great rock walls. Near the summit they scrambled forward, hand in hand over the rocks, to photograph the train of horses. Fortunately none of them fell.

Hammie's bad luck at shooting continued. After a long, hard stalk after caribou, he picked out a good bull and, to his surprise and fury, missed it. While Dorrell went after the horses, Dorothy was left, 'to enjoy Hamilton's sorrow which was not mild . . . a bad day!'

On 2 October it began to snow and was bitterly cold.

We went goat hunting and after a frightful rocky scramble to get within shot of a small herd, we found that by the time we had reached the top, the goats had gone down to where we started from and were watching us. Once they see you it is hopeless, so Hamilton took a wild, long shot at a billy which went very near him indeed, but only speeded his departure. The snow was coming down really hard by then so we started for camp and Hamilton shot a deer for meat en route.

In the morning, the snow was deep and, though it was an impossible day for hunting, they rode out to look for a moose. They found nothing and rode back to camp through a soft white world, very beautiful but dangerous for riding and cold.

Next day Gault, Dorothy, Dorrell and Felix, an Indian guide, spotted a fine bull caribou with some cows. It was a difficult shot – three hundred yards range with underbrush partly obscuring the target.

The suspense was awful while we waited for the psychological moment to fire. At last Felix said 'now', and Hamilton shot hitting the bull, who just stood and looked toward us. He fired again and hit again, we couldn't see where, feeling pretty sure it was all over. Hamilton and Felix went on scrambling over the rock slide to finish him off. On getting within about fifty yards, Hamilton fired, too high. He had forgotten to alter his three hundred yard sight. Then he discovered, much to his horror, that he had left the rest of his cartridges in his saddle pocket.

While Dorrell rushed back to the horses, the supposedly dead caribou walked slowly but firmly away into the thick bush. Hammie was less annoyed at losing him than horrified that he would creep away and die slowly. Casting about, Dorothy and Felix picked up the caribou's trail.

Hamilton shouted to me to go on and finish him, so rather against my will I started off on the most awful hunt, running and jumping after the Indian who was just like a goat. . . . After keeping up this pace for nearly a mile, Felix suddenly put the rifle into my hand and said, 'There he is, shoot!' Not realizing the three hundred yard sight was still up, I shot where I could see the huge beast disappearing among the dark trees. I missed and rushed on to within a few yards, Felix following and beseeching me not to go too near as he might charge, a possibility which I had completely forgotten. I finished him then, poor chap and felt rather small about it, but he was so badly hit already that he couldn't have gone much further. . . . I was so awfully glad Hamilton had got what he wanted. . . . we rode back to camp feeling we had all had a good day – except the caribou- whose head was riding on Dorrell's horse.

By now the weather was bad – cold, grey with snow falling in little flurries and they were faced with again crossing Hard Scrabble to reach their next hunting ground.

We had not got very far on the climb to the summit, when a real blizzard began. The wind and snow on my cheek bones, which were the only uncovered part of me, felt as if the skin was being flayed off. The pack horses kept trying to turn round and make for the old camp and we could hardly make them face the driving snow. Our own horses kept floundering shoulder deep into drifts which varied the monotony of the ride. As we neared the pass, the storm cleared away and we were able to get over comparatively easy, though the deep snow provided one or two thrills – such as a pack horse losing his footing and rolling down a thirty foot slide of snow covered rock, pursued by me with the cine-camera in hopes of getting a picture. As I was slithering and falling myself, he was up again before I could get him.

On the far side they trotted and cantered down the snow-covered and rock-strewn slopes to make camp at Sulphur River, where they were snowbound for two more days. When the weather eased, they hunted for goat and sheep through the snow, cold and soaking wet. Hammie's luck changed. He killed a moose near Monaghan Creek at 150 yards with his first shot.

By that time they were three days behind schedule and decided to return by the shortest route to Jasper. There was no more shooting. When Gault spotted a fine bull moose, Dorothy stalked him with her camera. Closing in on him she walked in plain view toward him until Hammie warned her not to go too near.

I think I got a good one of him as he looked right at me and stamped his foot and then turned round and flew. He looked lovely and very imposing standing out in the open swamp with the woods behind him. I love photographing animals and the stalk is just as exciting as if you were going to shoot and you don't get a flat feeling afterwards.

On the last day, it began to pour with rain as they were making camp and their teepee was very nearly blown into the river.

We had had such peace in it and had been so gorgeously tired and slept so soundly on our air beds which Hamilton has a perfect genius for blowing up. We had also read to each other nearly every other night, nice things like the Jungle Books and the Three Musketeers and the Light that Failed. . . . I think Kipling ought to keep off love stories . . .

I felt positively alarmed when I looked across the Athabaska [River] and saw the Brewsters and a lot of civilized women in fur coats and things. It was only then I remembered I had on a hat of

Hamilton's with a woolly scarf inside it to keep it from coming over my ears. They all regarded me with interest and I didn't wonder at it after I had seen myself in a glass. Apparently very few women go on long hunting trips. Hamilton looked far more respectable than I did. He had shaved off his beard the night before.

Chapter 16

THE CONTESSA FALCHI

Ten months after her divorce from Hammie in Paris Marguerite married her airman, Count Luigino Falchi, and moved with him to Italy. In the early 1920s she gave birth to a daughter.

A few years later, with her sister, Mae Wedderburn-Wilson and her family, they were staying at their villa on the Via Bolognese outside Florence when the children came down with typhoid fever. Both Marguerite's child and Mae's daughter Barbara succumbed.

Falchi had already proved unreliable and now he failed to provide the moral support which Marguerite desperately needed following this tragedy. In the words of her niece, 'the marriage was a disaster.'

Marguerite soon came to realize that it had no future, that there was only one solution – she and her husband should part. That proved difficult. She was now an Italian citizen. Since Falchi was a Catholic, there was no possibility of divorce within that country. Even to obtain a legal separation was difficult, though, in return for a payment of $5,000, Falchi did sign a letter agreeing to an informal separation and not to press for his entitlement to a share of Marguerite's property. But Marguerite found that she could not leave Italy without a passport and could only obtain one with her husband's consent, which he refused.

In Rome Mae Wedderburn-Wilson was seriously ill. Much against her conscience and her natural sense of caution, she allowed Marguerite to borrow her British passport on the promise that it would be returned to her from Paris. (The matter so preyed on her mind that her family later claimed that it contributed to her early death.)

In appearance the two sisters resembled each other closely enough for the photograph and the physical description which a passport then contained to deceive casual inspection.

Whilst Falchi was away, Marguerite, tall, elegant – a figure no Italian could fail to appreciate – swept through the railway station in Rome followed by a train of baggage porters to board the Paris express. She charmed the conductor with an outrageous tip, explained that she was tired and asked not to be disturbed. At the border an official, with the conductor at his elbow, opened the door of her compartment, examined the passport and handed it back with barely a glance toward her.

From Paris she returned to Canada where, unknown to Gault, she obtained a British passport in the name of 'Marguerite Claire Gault, wife separate as to property of Andrew Hamilton Gault.'

In the years after their divorce Marguerite had written to Gault occasionally , usually about relatives and mutual friends, so he was not surprised in August, 1927, to receive a letter from her postmarked Montreal, just as he and Dorothy were about to board the *Empress of France* to sail to Canada. Its contents were shattering.

Falchi had refused to give her a divorce and threatened to sue for restoration of conjugal and property rights. Her lawyers in Montreal had informed her that the Privy Council had recently ruled that a wife's domicile was always that of her husband and that, consequently, she could not have established a separate domicile of her own in Paris while Gault's had remained in Montreal. Since that ruling, none of her friends believed that she and Gault were legally divorced or that she was married to Falchi. She asked him to cooperate with her in asking Parliament to rule that their divorce in Paris was invalid, that her marriage to Falchi was void, and then to grant them a divorce.

She added that, if he refused to cooperate, she would take action in the Courts.

The implication was obvious: to agree would be to admit that his second marriage was bigamous. Gault was secure in the knowledge that, before their wedding, he had a written opinion from Sir John Simon that his marriage to Dorothy would be perfectly legal and could be upheld in a court of law. Several eminent lawyers in Canada, including Senator Ross, the chairman of the Senate Divorce Committee, supported Simon's view. They all agreed that Marguerite had established a legal domicile in France in 1918 and that the court in Paris had had jurisdiction in the case.[1]

Gault's greatest concern was for Dorothy. If Marguerite succeeded in her contention that the Paris divorce was invalid, the social consequences would be calamitous. The most frustrating aspect of the situation was that there was nothing they could do to avert the impending publicity which might also prove disastrous to Gault's political career.

Gault replied to Marguerite that he stood by Sir John Simon's opinion and would protect his position and that of his wife, if necessary by taking the case to the Privy Council.

Nine months later, in May, 1928, headlines such as that in the

Montreal Star made the story public: 'FAMOUS GAULT CASE AGAIN TO BE AIRED IN COURT – Former Marguerite Stephens Alleges Divorce From Colonel Hamilton Gault Was Invalid and Applies to Have Marriage with Commandant Luigino Falchi Set Aside'

In Canada religious orthodoxy, tinged with Puritanism, was reflected in widespread disapproval of divorce. It was as well, for most citizens could not afford one. But because of their rarity, the whiff of scandal and the involvement of the rich and famous, divorces were newsworthy. The 'Gault case', as it was known, had another dimension which made it doubly so. Some read of it with uncomfortable interest.

Many well-heeled Canadians had obtained divorces in countries whose laws were less rigorous than those at home. Paris was the most popular location. As the papers pointed out, the Falchi case might well prove to be a test of the validity of all 'Paris divorces' in Canada.

Gault read the news in a short item in the London *Daily Mail* but fortunately the story did not arouse the same wide interest in Britain as in Canada. Some days later, he received a letter from Marguerite:

> In my letter to you last year asking that we should straighten out our mutual affairs in an inoffensive way through a Bill, I also told you that if you did not care to do this with me, I should be obliged to take action in the Courts. I regret that I have had to do this on account of the publicity which was bound to ensue, but at least I gave you the chance to do everything in a pleasanter way. . . .
>
> For almost three years, you see, I have been told that our divorce was invalid and that I am legally your wife. After the document signed by us both in Paris, when we agreed to forget all litigation, I am not even separated from you.

Almost in the same post came a letter from Falchi, whom he had never met, which threw some light on Marguerite's extraordinary action. He said that he had last seen her in 1925 when they had agreed amicably to obtain a separation in the Italian courts but she had since refused to come to Italy where the presence of both was required for a hearing in court. Over a year ago he had heard that she was suffering from 'a grave nervous disorder' following an operation. He added that, after their wedding in France, they had gone through another ceremony in Italy. If Marguerite succeeded in having their marriage annulled in Montreal, he would still be legally married to her in all countries but Canada. He wanted his freedom but Marguerite refused to cooperate.

Marguerite knows very well that it would be possible to have a quiet divorce in Europe between her and me, but she now insists for the annulment of your divorce, which, besides necessitating another divorce between her and you, will leave her free for Canada, while I shall remain her husband for every other country and for life.[2]

Falchi proposed that they should cooperate in opposing Marguerite's petition. Gault agreed. In the meantime, on his lawyer's advice, he gave up his annual trip to Canada where he was liable to be served with a writ to appear in court, in favour of a month's fishing holiday with Dorothy in Norway.

In September came further word from Marguerite. She spoke of Gault's Canadian lawyer's efforts to avoid litigation.

He has now been trying to influence Mr. Perron [Marguerite's solicitor] by saying it would ruin your political career etc. but I reminded him that ten years ago or more you did not think much of my reputation and at least, this time you have had the chance to do things nicely and you would not do it.

The case comes up between the 8th and 15th of October. You lay great stress on getting rid of Gino – you may be interested to know that it is you I am anxious to free myself from – Gino gives me no trouble whatever financially. I made him sign a document ages ago to that effect, even after my death. But in Italy they consider me an Italian and here a Canadian and being married to two men at a time is decidedly awkward and must be settled in some way.[3]

Gault saw that she had changed her ground. If her object was to get rid of him, why prosecute an action which, if successful, would unite them? He saw her motive now as being vindictive. Blake Redden, his English lawyer, suspected that Marguerite's ultimate aim was a rapprochement with Gault.

There was an obvious flaw in Marguerite's case. If her contention was correct that she was still legally married to Hamilton Gault, then the Canadian courts would have no jurisdiction. Her domicile would be that of her husband and that had long been established in England. The first task of the bench in Montreal would be to decide on that point and that they could not do until the new year.

In December Marguerite wrote a curiously ambivalent letter, part threat and part friendly gossip, to Gault from Cap Ferrat to say that she would be in Paris for some weeks at the Hotel Goya, 'in case there is anything you would like to have explained regarding my case'. She complained about the procrastination of Gault's lawyer and said that she would bring her case in England if the Montreal court decided it did not have jurisdiction. She ended with a note about mutual friends. She had been staying for some time with Ethel McGibbon[4] and had had lunch again that day 'with the dear old Duke of Connaught at his nearby villa, Les Bruyères, whose garden is exquisite – full of roses.'[5]

The threat to Gault's political career was obvious. A general election was likely to take place in June. He told his lawyers that, unless the hearing in Montreal could be delayed until October, he would leave politics at once. He only hesitated to do so because of the effect it would have on his party's chances of retaining their hold on Taunton.

Within a few days of her arrival in Paris Marguerite was taken ill in her hotel. Falchi, who was at the Italian Embassy there, reported to Gault that she had had 'one of her customary attacks' and consequently they could expect 'no reasonable attitude from her' for the time being. Two weeks later she was admitted to a hospital for nervous diseases where it was expected she would remain for at least two months. After only nine days she abruptly discharged herself and, accompanied by a doctor summoned from Canada and her sister-in-law, left the country. Before departing, she told her lawyers to abandon her plea for an annulment of her marriage to Falchi. She had another plan.

In May, 1929, Gault learned that Marguerite intended to ask the courts in Montreal to rule that she was legally domiciled in Montreal, that her divorce in Paris was invalid and to grant her a legal separation from Gault on the grounds that he had deserted her and had 'gone through a form of marriage' with Dorothy. Fortunately there was no immediate publicity but Gault was furious at what he saw as Marguerite's vindictiveness.

After the election in June, though no party had an overall majority in the Commons, Labour had the most seats and their leader, Ramsay MacDonald, became prime minister. While Gault had won Taunton with a greatly increased majority, he was not confident of limiting the damage to his political career when Marguerite's new case came to court. Even worse, Dorothy would become a blameless victim of the social consequences which in the 1930s would be dire.

Marguerite's lawyers were finding the case sufficiently complex without having to deal with her changing demands and ideas, all of

29. Gault with 'Shorty' Colquhoun at the Patricia's Regimental dinner, May, 1939.

30. Second World War: Gault commands Canadian reinforcement units. *Photo: Canadian Military Headquarters.*

31. Dorothy Gault on 'St Hilaire' at Hatch, from the painting by Alfred Munnings.

32. Second World War: Dorothy drove a Red Cross ambulance in London during the Blitz. *Photo: Karsh of Ottawa*.

33. Return to Frezenberg, 1 October, 1957. The Founder inspecting a Guard of Honour of the 1st Battalion, Princess Patricia's Canadian Light Infantry.

34. Taking the salute of the 2nd Battalion at the ceremony of Trooping the Colour, Hamilton Gault Barracks, Edmonton, Alberta, June, 1958.

35. The Hamilton Gault Museum at Hatch Court.

36. Gault's house on Mont St Hilaire, completed shortly before his death.

37. His last parade: Gault's funeral in Montreal, December, 1958. On the left Honorary Pall-Bearers, led by the Defence Minister, Major-General G.R. Pearkes, VC, move into position. On the extreme left is the Governor-General, General Georges Vanier. On the right, nearest the gun-shield, is Major-General Cameron Ware. *Canadian Army Photo*.

which contributed to delays in scheduling a hearing. During the winter she suffered a recurrence of her illness. By late February, 1930, her health had completely broken and on 25 March she died at her home in Montreal.

One of her oldest friends, Phoebe Campbell, who had known both of them since childhood said, 'Call her illness what you will, she died of a broken heart – she had never fallen out of love with Hamilton'.[6]

At first, Marguerite Falchi's death seemed to remove the threat of the damaging social and political consequences of a law-suit, but within six weeks another worrying possibility was raised by Gordon MacDougall, Gault's friend and lawyer in Montreal. Under Italian law a widowed husband was entitled to a portion of his wife's estate. If Falchi asserted his rights, Marguerite's executors would probably oppose him and might plead as their defence the nullity of the Paris divorce.

By November, 1930, there were indications that Falchi was proposing just such an action. Not only was Gault concerned for his own reputation, he was upset at the effect that this was having on Dorothy. For more than two years she had borne the threat to the legality of her marriage with no hint of criticism of him. On the contrary, she had dismissed her concern for her own position while being deeply affected by the consequences for her husband.

But Hammie was well aware of the situation in which she found herself, one which he himself shared. Dorothy was quietly but deeply religious and held strong views on the sanctity of marriage. The suggestion that the legality of her own marriage could be questioned was deeply painful to her. In Montreal, and even in Somerset, some doors were closed to her because she had married a divorced man. Now the situation was worse. Since Marguerite's legal manoeuvres became public in August,1927, she was the subject of wounding rumours and gossip. 'Living in sin' was an extreme comment.

Gault was determined to stop in its tracks any action by Falchi against George Washington Stephens, Marguerite's brother and sole executor. He told his lawyers that if Falchi pursued his claim he would be prepared to help Stephens with a considerable sum to settle out of court.

In the meantime he and Dorothy sought advice as to how best to ensure the legitimacy of their marriage. Canadian lawyers recommended that they re-marry, preferably in Canada. Others countered that this would be tantamount to admitting that their marriage was defective. Both Blake Redden, their English solicitor, and Archibald, the lawyer in Paris who had acted in the divorce case, advised against re-marriage stating that, unless directly challenged in the English courts, the French divorce and their marriage were prima facie good. Since Gault would not be directly involved in any claim by Falchi in Montreal, no matter what the decision of the courts there, it could not affect the legitimacy of their marriage.

Comforting though that was, it erected no barriers against prejudice and gossip.

In June Falchi issued a writ against Marguerite's executor claiming one third of her estate. He demanded a detailed accounting of her executor's actions and a payment of $370,000. Stephens declined Gault's offer of help and decided to fight.

The Gaults were holidaying in Cannes when news of the case broke at the end of August. The publicity could not have been worse. Under a headline, 'ROYAL DUKE IN A LAW SUIT – ITALIAN COUNT'S CLAIM', the report in the *Daily Mail* began, 'The Duke of Connaught and Mr. R.B. Bennett, the Prime Minister of Canada, are among those summoned to appear in a case which will shortly come before the courts at Montreal.' Both had been beneficiaries under Marguerite's will which now was being challenged.

There was little likelihood that either would be required to appear personally but Gault was acutely embarrassed. Both were friends and were unlikely to bear him any ill will. But to have the name of Queen Victoria's youngest son appear in this way was anathema to the King. The Lord Chamberlain's office would certainly note Gault's connection with the case and, being an M.P., would blacklist him – divorced persons were not received at Court. While not an absolute obstacle to higher political office, divorce was a considerable hurdle to overcome when being considered for honours or even a junior ministerial appointment.

Despite all the pressure which Falchi could bring to bear, the case was not heard for another four years. The Superior Court of Quebec found in his favour in 1935. An appeal by Stephens to the Court of King's Bench failed in 1937, as did another to the Supreme Court of Canada in 1938. Later that year the Lord Chancellor refused his application to appeal to the Privy Council. Falchi had won.

War intervened to bring an end to Hamilton and Dorothy Gault's immediate worries about the threat to their marriage. But to the end of their days a wisp of anxiety that the case would be revived, disturbed their otherwise happy married life.

Today the Gault divorce has taken on the qualities of a folk tale – people speak of it as one of Canada's great scandals. Yet it was not as sensational as faulty memories and prurient writers contend. It arose from the perceived infidelity of a distressed and wayward wife. Its only public significance was in the resulting 'Gault Case' which for years intrigued the Canadian legal establishment.

But it was also the root of private tragedy, of the eventual disintegration of Marguerite and of her, possibly unwitting, vengeance on Hamilton Gault.

Chapter 17

FLYING

When Gault entered Parliament he found an outlet for his physical energies in swimming and squash at the Bath Club in Dover Street. At Hatch he played tennis. Despite his artificial leg, he was remarkably agile and, having a quick eye, good ball sense and tremendous power, was a formidable opponent. What he enjoyed most was riding hell-for-leather after a pack of hounds in full cry, but here the loss of a leg was a significant handicap. Unable to grip properly with his stump and lacking the use of a stirrup, he had had a special saddle made with an ingenious arrangement of straps which enabled him to jump the ditches and hedges of the hunting field. The straps were designed to release automatically in a fall so that he would not be dragged.

Twice he fell and each time the device failed to release. Dorothy, who had no faith in it, kept close to him in the field and each time she was at his side in a flash. Calming his mare, Daffodil, she would sit on her head while others released the harness which held him fast. When for a third time Gault crashed to the ground in taking a high fence, Dorothy declared that that was enough. His riding would be confined to hacking about the estate.

Much as he disliked the idea of giving up hunting, he accepted that to continue would be foolhardy and that his wife was unrelentingly serious. At 47 he still could ride but without his left leg, polo, long treks in the bush and the full-blooded pursuit of hounds were no longer for him. Besides, he had another challenge in mind.

Perhaps prompted by the example of his old friend Agar Adamson, who in his early sixties had become an aviation enthusiast, he took up flying

They had seen much of each other since the war and Adamson was a fairly frequent visitor to Hatch. When he and his son Anthony came for four days at the end of May, 1929, Hammie took him to Stag Lane to show him the new Gipsy Moth he had just purchased. History does not reveal how he managed to obtain the registration mark G-AAGA.

Ten days later Gault took his first flying lesson with Captain R.W. Reeve, the Chief Instructor of the de Havilland Flying School.

Before airliners became as familiar as motor cars, the Gipsy Moth was the first aircraft which many people in Canada and Britain saw. By modern standards it was incredibly light, fragile and uncomfortable. A two-seater, open-cockpit biplane, it weighed only 931 pounds and could carry a maximum load, including fuel, of 719 pounds. Its 85 horsepower 'Gipsy' engine gave a maximum speed of ninety miles per hour in still air. With a full tank of 19 gallons of petrol it could fly for three hours.

The pilot occupied the front cockpit where he faced a rudimentary set of instruments. His controls, a joystick and rudder bar (Gault's had a special fitting to accommodate his left leg), were duplicated in the rear seat. There was no radio and precious few stations with whom to communicate if there had been. There were no brakes. The engine was started by a mechanic or the passenger swinging the propeller. To prevent the aircraft from mowing him down, the front wheels were blocked by chocks which someone on the ground pulled away when the pilot was satisfied that the engine was running properly.

Flying was a hazardous business and those directly concerned learned to be punctilious in their preparations for a flight. But there was still an atmosphere of happy amateurism at most airfields – visitors wandering about without restriction, the heady smells of castor oil and 'doped' fabric and the noise of revving engines.

A month after his first flight Hammie flew solo and on 15 October received his pilot's licence. On the same day he left with Reeve for a trip to Belgium, Germany, Austria, Hungary and France. After a relatively smooth trip with overnight stops at Brussels, Cologne and Nuremberg, they made for Salzburg via Munich. His log entries for the next few days tell something of the flying conditions of the day.

18th October – Slightly delayed fog. Bumpy in places crossing Bavarian plains: Visibility fair until near Munich where it became very bad owing to smoke from city. Landed at Schleissheim by mistake . . .

20th – . . . Reached Budapest in failing light and landed almost in dark. Bumpy over hills and very bumpy over Budapest. Never again if we can help it!! Glad to get down, thank you!!!

23rd – Munich-Boblingen-Strasbourg. . . . good visibility to hills south of Stuttgart where we encountered heavy smoke. Landed at Boblingen for weather report and petrol. Very bad visibility 1/2 km all the way across Black Forest & up Rhine valley to Strasbourg – had difficulty in finding aerodrome wrongly marked on map.

24th – Strasbourg to Paris. A rough trip in fine weather & good visibility. Sun and clouds made it very bumpy particularly over hills and forests. Coming into le Bourget it was very rough and bumpy. Heavy head winds delayed us by half an hour.

When Gault returned to England, he discovered that Agar Adamson had entered hospital in London for a relatively simple operation. When he saw him later he seemed to be recovering well but pneumonia developed. A week later he died. His doctors claimed that his resistance had been weakened by three hours spent in the icy waters of the Irish Sea where he had crashed a few weeks earlier.[1]

A gallant eccentric who had fought in most of the Patricias' battles, 'Old Ackety-Ack' had commanded them for longer than anyone else. He had been a faithful friend to Hammie who felt his loss deeply.

On the day that Gault resumed flying in the following March he had an abrupt reminder of its discomforts. He had left Stag Lane in good flying weather but west of Reading ran into a snow storm, 'in which we were tossed about and changed direction 90 degrees. Returned on course to get out of storm & made forced landing near Abingdon where we ascertained snow belt was 30/40 miles across. Decided to return to Reading.'

In June he took Reeve for another ten-day trip to the Continent, this time to the South of France, in order to qualify to carry Dorothy as a passenger. On the way to le Bourget he discovered an unsuspected weakness. 'Journey to me very bumpy and in consequence was very sick. Overcome by sleepiness over Abbeville & so handed over to Reeve, sleeping most of way.'

At Dijon he wired Patricia Blackader, then at school in Switzerland, to meet him at the airfield at Lausanne. There, to her delight, he had Reeve give her her first flight which fired in her a lifelong interest in aviation.

Three weeks after their return to England Gault, with Reeve as navigator, took part in the King's Cup Air Race. The course covered 750 miles from London to Bristol, Birmingham, Liverpool, Manchester, Leeds, Newcastle, returning via Hull and Leicester. The 101 entrants, owners of nearly half the private aircraft in the country,[2] were a cross-section of royalty, industry, high society, members of parliament and the aviation world. They included such star pilots as Squadron-Leader A.H. Orlebar and Flight Lieutenant H.R.D. Waghorn who broke world speed records in the forerunners of the Spitfire, Lieutenant

Caspar John R.N., a future First Sea Lord, Flight Lieutenant R.L.R. Atcherley who was to lead a fighter group in the Desert Air Force in 1944 and Captain Geoffrey de Havilland and his son, the famous test pilot who died in an attempt to push back the barriers of supersonic flight.

The Prince of Wales and Prince George both entered machines, as did Loel Guinness, Marshal of the RAF Lord Trenchard, Sir Philip Sassoon, W.L. Runciman, Lord Rothermere and J.D. Siddeley.

A system of handicaps was designed to even the chances of different types of aircraft. They were to land for refuelling at Bristol, Manchester, Newcastle and Hull. Gault's log for 5 July, 1930, tells something of the thrill and hazards of the day:

A great Field Day. Got away to a good start but lost time flying high to Bristol. Good going to Manchester with poor visibility around Birmingham. . . . Took chance at Hooton Park [near Liverpool], where we caught a couple of machines on the corner & got into Manchester with only a thimble of petrol left. Lost time by going too far south at Woodford & flew Pennines at 3,000 feet owing to poor visibility (smoke & filth from Manchester). . . . found turning point where another machine dived under us on our bank. On leg to Newcastle two Puss Moths passed us as if we had been tied to a post.

Indescribable confusion at Newcastle due to congestion – planes coming in on opposite circles & taking off on converging lines. A delightful flight the rest of the way home & not too bad a congestion at Hull where we had tea. –

Note: – Frightened out of my life & shaken to the core at Newcastle!!!

Gault did not record his placing in the race – his time was 7 hours 53 minutes.

At the beginning of October, Hammie and Reeve again flew to Belgium, Germany and Holland.

6 Oct 30. Berlin – Hanover. . . . Bad bump in landing but fortunately got down all right. In taxiing to control tower machine nearly blown over. RW jumped out & held outside wing down but was lifted a couple of feet off the ground by another heavy gust before he got the machine into the wind & under control. An extremely close shave to a wrecked machine. Came near a real bust up.

189

They returned to England through Paris where Pat Blackader was being immersed in French culture with the Cézanne family in Neuilly. Well ahead of his planned visit, he sent her a cheque with instructions to buy herself an evening dress so that they could celebrate her 17th birthday together.

During dinner at the Ritz, where he was well-known, he gave her her present – a necklace of rose quartz and crystals. While she was admiring it, the maitre d' produced another box 'from le Colonel.' It contained a beautiful ostrich feather fan, its handle of mother of pearl, the long curved feathers shaded from rose pink to white.

After dinner Hammie asked if she would like to go on to a show or to see Paris from the air. Thrilled at the prospect, she opted for the latter. At le Bourget they donned Irvin suits – heavy, fleece-lined flying jackets and trousers – helmets and goggles and took off.

It was a beautiful, clear night. Up and down the Champs Elysées they flew – over Longchamps, the Champs de Mars, around and around above the traffic on the Place de la Concorde and over Montmartre.

Returning to le Bourget, they landed by the dim glow of runway glim lamps. No activity could be seen. Hammie parked the plane by a hangar and began laboriously to heave himself from the cockpit while Pat scrambled to the ground. As she did so, she saw two armoured vehicles and a police car pass below a light on the control tower and head toward them.

Pulling off her helmet and flying clothes as the police arrived, she greeted them in her crumpled satin dress, clutching the long fan box, not at first appreciating how many flying rules they had broken.

The inspector in charge recognized Hammie immediately. 'Ah, mon Colonel, I might have known it was you. If you were anyone else, you would be under arrest! Don't ever be so foolish again.'

Pat commented, 'Hammie was charming, as ever, remarking to the inspector that only in Paris would you find such a beautiful night and such splendid sights. They adored him in Paris, not just because of the Regiment and what he did during the War which was well-known, but also for his generosity and panache.'

There were others who did not approve of the escapade. While Pat remained Gault's ward, she had been legally adopted by his sister Lillian and Percy Benson. When she returned Benson forbade her ever to fly with Gault again. She argued to no avail. Lillian reminded her of her mother's tragic death and said she must consider the awful effect it would have on Hammie if she were to be injured or killed while with him. It was an argument which Pat realized, sadly, she could not try to refute.[3]

On his return flight to England from Paris Gault flew over the wreck of the R–101, the British dirigible, near Beauvais – 'a deplorable sight', he commented in his log. It was doubly so to him for he knew several who were killed in its crash and he himself had had a ticket for an earlier flight which was cancelled.

At the time he bought G-AGAA he had not revealed to Dorothy that he proposed to take flying lessons and to pilot the machine himself. Later that year he tossed his new pilot's licence on a table in front of her and asked what she thought. With difficulty she kept control of her feelings. She tried to appear suitably impressed but privately was furious that he had not told her what he was doing. She decided on drastic action. In the next few weeks, she found frequent reasons to go to London where, secretly, she took lessons at the de Havilland school.

As they sat down to lunch on the day that Gault and Reeve returned from Europe, Dorothy dropped her own new flying licence in front of him and said, 'What do you think of that?' He was unreservedly delighted. Next year, when he had gained further experience, they would fly together.[4]

If you would keep the stream of truth running pure and clear,
Then you must dam the Beaverbrook and drain the Rothermere.
(verse in Gault's hand ca.1931)

As his political career progressed, Gault lost no opportunity to speak on the need for fostering trade and cohesion within the Empire. In the general election of May,1929, despite the Conservative party suffering a crushing defeat, he won his seat with an increased majority.

Gault had entered parliament to promote economic cooperation between the countries of the Empire through a system of preferential tariffs. From his maiden speech he had consistently advocated that cause. In doing so he became one of the better-known voices of the Imperialists, an uncoordinated grouping of believers by no means confined to Britain where, paradoxically, the public seemed careless of the advantages inherent in the Empire which bore their name. Many of the staunchest advocates of freer trade were in the dominions and colonies.

A consistent supporter of the imperial idea was Lord Beaverbrook, the publisher of the *Daily Express*, who in 1923 had encouraged Gault to stand for parliament. No political party had since espoused the cause. Although among Conservatives there were several enthusiasts, Stanley Baldwin, their leader, was lukewarm. To force his hand and to enlist public support, in July, 1929, Beaverbrook launched his 'Empire

Crusade' for completely free trade in agricultural products and manufactures between the countries of the Empire.

According to the *Express* the world was dividing into two blocs, the United States and Europe. The British were faced with three choices: subservience to America; deteriorating with Europe or becoming prosperous within an Empire made one by Free Trade between its parts.

There was an immediate and enthusiastic public response. Beaverbrook, the arch-propagandist, was not above bending the truth. On 5 August a headline on the front page of the *Express* proclaimed that Canada had joined the Crusade. 'Great Canadian Journal Speaks Out.' The paper quoted was *The Alberta Farmer*.

For weeks the campaign rolled on gathering more and more support but Baldwin would not commit the Conservatives. Beverley Baxter, the editor of the *Daily Express*, asked Gault for his 'frank opinion of Empire Free Trade as a policy to be placed before the country.'[5] Before he could reply, Beaverbrook published his 'manifesto', a pamphlet entitled 'Empire Free Trade'.

Replying to Baxter, Gault said that, from the point of view of practical politics, a Free Trade Empire was a long way off, adding that it could only be reached by proceeding step by step. On the same day he wrote to Beaverbrook,

> My dear Max,
> I am all with you in your Empire policy but you go too fast . . . a Free Trade Empire is the ideal goal worth working for and in such a policy, I believe is to be found the solution of many of our problems both at home and abroad.
> The trouble is that the English consumer is fearful of any tax on food . . . the bringing about of Free Trade within the Empire must, in the first instance, be supported by an intensive educational campaign showing that the economic benefits to be derived will outweigh fears of an increase in the cost of living.[6]

Two weeks later Gault spoke out against Empire Free Trade becoming the catspaw of party politics which would prevent it from being considered on its merits. It was naive to think that it could be achieved by simply sweeping away tariff barriers. Australia, Canada, New Zealand and South Africa had built up their secondary industries behind the protection of tariffs. The people of Canada would never allow themselves to be merely the growers of raw material for the industries of the Motherland.

We must remember in dealing with this question that England is only one of the component parts of the British Commonwealth, and that the ideal of Free Trade within the Empire can only be reached by cooperation of the Governments, both at home and abroad.[7]

In the new year Beaverbrook, frustrated by Baldwin's refusal to support his ideas, decided on direct political action. He proclaimed the formation of a 'United Empire Party' which would support Conservatives who espoused Free Trade but would field candidates of its own to oppose those which did not. Next day Lord Rothermere, proprietor of the *Daily Mail* and a chain of other papers, announced his support. A £100,000 'fighting fund' was opened into which money poured from wealthy men in Britain and Canada.[8]

Gault at once wrote to Beaverbrook deploring his action in forming the new party. '(It) can but defeat the very end at which you, and all of us who believe in a closer Empire economic unit, aim by splitting the Imperial vote in the country and so letting a possibly anti-Empire party into power.'[9]

While Beaverbrook bore an acute dislike for the leader of the Conservative party, Rothermere loathed him. Beaverbrook's answer to Gault hinted at the two newspaper magnates' hidden agenda, the destruction of Stanley Baldwin.

As you know, all I care for is Empire Free Trade and I am devoting my life to it – to the exclusion of all other problems with which the political parties are concerned.

The United Empire Party is not a political party – it is an economic party. It does not aim at splitting the anti-Socialist vote – it aims at consolidating the Imperialist vote for the purpose of achieving our object – Empire Free Trade.

The Empire Crusade was all very well until the Conservative Leader at the Coliseum, closed the door on all hope of his being able to come with us. His pledge at that meeting means that if he returns to No.10 Downing Street, he cannot, for as long as he remains Prime Minister – possibly five years – consider Empire Free Trade.

The United Empire Party will support all those who remain unpledged – be they Conservative, Liberal or Labour. It will also support Baldwin – without the Coliseum pledge.

In October, 1930, Gault's views were confirmed at the Imperial Conference in London when R.B. Bennett, now the Canadian Prime Minister, declared that free trade within the Empire was neither desirable nor possible but Canada was prepared to enter into deals with Britain on preferential tariffs. Baldwin agreed.

Later that year, when Gault condemned the Government in Parliament for its failure to halt the dumping of Russian wheat in Britain at prices below the cost of production, Beaverbrook wrote to congratulate him on his 'splendid' speech.

When, in January, Beaverbrook entered a candidate from his United Empire party to oppose the official Conservative candidate in the London borough of East Islington, Gault reckoned that he had gone not only too fast but too far. There was no more correspondence between them.

In a subsequent by-election in St George's Westminster, another Beaverbrook candidate stood 'in opposition to Mr Baldwin's leadership and policy' and was roundly defeated by Duff Cooper for the Tories. Baldwin's position was secure and Beaverbrook retired from the field. The Empire Crusade was at an end.[10]

As Britain under Ramsay MacDonald's Labour government moved further into recession in 1931, Gault attacked it for not coming to grips with the hard economic facts of life. 'We have got into a colossally bad habit of squandermania, and there can be no economic power for this or any other country that follows such a policy.'[11] He believed that Parliament should set an example and asked the Prime Minister to reduce all Ministerial and Parliamentary salaries by 10 percent. MacDonald would not comment.

When the Government chose to reduce teachers' salaries by 15%, using the argument that they could afford a cut better than other public employees, Gault claimed that they had chosen the wrong target and sought assurances that their pension rights would not be diminished. Again he got no answer.[12]

In August, 1931, the Labour government resigned over the nation's financial crisis and MacDonald accepted office as Prime Minister of a 'National Government'. In October he called a General Election which resulted in a triumph for the Conservatives and swept most Labour and Liberal members from the house.

Gault won his Taunton seat with an even larger majority, receiving 22,564 votes as opposed to 15,083 in the previous election of 1929. Hugh Niven, now commanding PPCLI in Winnipeg, wrote to congratulate him. Gault replied,

The swing of the pendulum has been colossal – too colossal in fact, for it leaves the large majority of some 7,000,000 Socialist voters without adequate representation in the House of Commons. However, with a Government returned to power unfettered . . . by the old shibboleths and dogmas, let us hope we shall be able to go forward to the laying of the foundation stone of Empire economic unity on the basis of co-operation and reciprocal trade at the forthcoming Imperial Conference.[13]

He was to be disappointed. That the Ottawa Conference a year later achieved nothing to that end can be laid at the door of the Depression. In the economic conditions of the day the British had to protect their farmers, while the dominions could grant no concessions to manufacturers in Britain without hurting their own struggling industries.

Gault's involvement with flying led naturally to it becoming one of his political concerns. His interest had begun during the War when he applied unsuccessfully to join the Royal Flying Corps. It developed, not only from his experience in England, where many regarded it as a sport for the well-off, but from what he had seen in Canada where it was becoming an essential form of transportation in inaccessible regions of great potential wealth.

While Imperial Airways were carrying passengers to the Continent and to Africa and India, domestic services in Britain were lagging far behind. Those who shared his views were keen to develop 'airmindedness' among a people whose traditional concept of foreign travel was centred on the sea.

Having become a pilot himself he began to promote his interest both at home in Somerset and in the House of Commons. His first recorded intervention in Parliament on air-related subjects arose from his disquiet over the state of the RAF in 1931. He asked Mr Fred Montague, the Under Secretary of State for Air, for a comparison of strengths of the air forces of Britain, France, Italy, U.S.A. and U.S.S.R. (under the Versailles Treaty, Germany was allowed no military aircraft). Montague conceded that, 'the relative strength of the Great Powers in the air is beginning to assume the importance attached to relative sea power both before and since the war'. It was no comfort to discover that the RAF ranked fifth.[14]

Speaking later in the debate on the Air Estimates, Gault called for the development of an air service between Northern Ireland and the industrial North of England, Amsterdam and Germany.[15]

In May, 1931, he became the first president of the Taunton and West Somerset Gliding Club and Dorothy one of its members. Within a week 79 had joined. To enable training to start, he gave it its first glider on condition that the members subscribe for another.[16]

It was not his first gift to Taunton. A year earlier he had bought land in the town and hired designers and contractors to produce two magnificent playing fields for the Borough. Each of ten or eleven acres, equipped with a cricket pitch, two football fields, three tennis courts, a bowling green and a children's playground, they were surrounded by paths and rows of elms and chestnut trees. In sheltered bays of hedging were garden seats made from the teak of HMS *Ganges,* one of the last sailing ships of the line.

Gault's motive was not unlike that which prompted him to raise his regiment in 1914. He was concerned at the paucity of recreational facilities in the community in which he lived, particularly in a time of depression. He had the means to provide a lasting remedy and a sense of obligation to do so. His lifelong interest in sport and in the physical fitness and welfare of the young lay behind his choice.

In presenting the fields to Taunton council he 'very insistently' emphasized that they should be available to all sections of the community, in particular to the 'poorest of the poor' who had few opportunities of taking part in sport.

In May, 1932, the Duke of York, the future King George VI, president of the National Playing Fields Association, came to Taunton to open them. He congratulated Gault on setting a splendid example to the nation. 'Do not forget that the playground, to a very great extent, forms and develops the characters of the boys and girls of this country.'[17]

Taunton showed its gratitude by making Gault an honorary Freeman of the Borough, the seventh in its history and the first Member of Parliament to be so honoured. It was an indication of his popularity that the honour was proposed by a Conservative , seconded by a Liberal and supported by a Labour councillor.

The symbol of the 'Freedom', an illuminated parchment scroll bordered by the Gault and Shuckburgh arms and the badge of Princess Patricia's Canadian Light Infantry, bore the ancient seal of the Borough which dated from 1180 A.D. It was contained in a silver casket of classical design, standing on an onyx base. The front panel depicted, in hand chasing and full relief, three groups of children at play in the classical period, the reverse, eleven Patricias marching on active service.

George Vanier wrote to congratulate him. Hammie replied, 'It is doubtful if it carries any privileges with it other than the schoolboy's definition that "a man has the freedom of the city when his wife goes on holiday".[18]

The Borough decreed that the playing fields would be named after Hamilton Gault, and so they were. Twenty-seven years later, after his death, Lady Patricia Ramsay unveiled plaques at each of them to tell the people of Taunton who their benefactor had been. The town had also wanted to name a principal street after Gault. He declined the honour: it became 'Hamilton Road'.

Next year he appealed to the government to increase their subsidy to flying clubs for pilot training and joined the parliamentary committee of the Royal Aero Club, an influential lobby of MPs. In May, 1933, he called for improvement in air navigational aids and suggested that towns and railway stations should have their names displayed so that they would be visible at 1,000 feet. Sir Philip Sassoon, the Secretary of State, said that since railway stations were in populated areas, the names would encourage low flying. Gault countered that, on the contrary, pilots would not have to fly so low as they do now in order to find where they were. Sassoon declined to act.

By the early 1930s private pilots in Britain had begun travelling to nearby foreign countries. Most airmen reported favourably in the press on their trips to France, Germany and Belgium, but some criticized the Italians as being grasping and uncooperative.

In May, 1933, Gault and Reeve returned to England from a flight down the west coast of Italy to Catania in Sicily, during which they formed an entirely contrary opinion. Typically Gault sought to correct what he saw as an injustice: he wrote a half-column letter to *The Times* describing the warm reception and cooperation which he had received.[19] That they published it is evidence of their readers' growing interest in flying and curiosity about foreign travel by air.[20]

In less than a year the seed planted by Gault's generous letter was to bear unexpected fruit.

Hammie was now qualified to carry his wife as second pilot or navigator and from July, 1931, their travels, wherever possible, were by air. Dorothy eventually became a sounder and more skilled pilot than he who, characteristically, was inclined to take risks when weather or other conditions stood in his way.

On one of their first flights across the Channel to Paris they landed at Berck-sur-Mer. There they were told that dense fog lay between them and le Bourget and several machines were waiting for it to clear. Hammie could see what appeared to be a break opening to the east. Against Dorothy's advice, he took off and found an opening in the murk but after a few miles the fog again closed around them.

The sensible course, which Dorothy tried in vain to persuade on him, would be to turn back to Berck, but Gault refused, saying confidently that they would be all right. Dorothy was furious at his stubborn foolhardiness as they both strained their eyes to find a break in the fog. Eventually they did and found le Bourget where theirs was the first machine to land for twelve hours. Gault was triumphant, Dorothy so exasperated she could not speak.[21]

Gault's flying for the year ended that month when he and Dorothy left to spend four months in Canada. He had scarcely resumed next spring when again, to his dismay, he found that being a good sailor was no guarantee against air-sickness.

13 Apr 33. Le Bourget – Fulvy – Chantillon – Beaune. . . . Very rough all the way. Encountered clouds increasing in density over Côte d'Or. Had to turn back . . . and made forced landing at Fulvy. Thence via Chatillon by railroad to Dijon & Beaune. So sick on 1st leg, had to hand over to R.W. half way. Sick again in pm – and this is what we call flying for pleasure!!

23 Apr 33. Cannes – Marignam – Montelimar – Lyons. . . . Flight to Montelimar very rough – Heavy head wind – down drafts over mountains – very bumpy – motors passing us on roads – sick after landing.

Flight to Lyons – better – slightly decreasing head wind – motors still passing us on road . . . (one current of air in AM shot us up 600 ft.)

Everywhere he went in Europe, he saw signs of the increasing popularity of flying as a sport, of the growth of commercial aviation and of the development of air forces, in all of which Britain seemed to be lagging behind.

Chapter 18

PUBLIC AFFAIRS

Gault was delighted when, in 1932, Hugh Niven, who had led the Patricias in the final dreadful hours of the Battle of Frezenberg, was appointed to command the Regiment. In the 1930's times were hard in Canada and the Patricias were restricted both in strength and equipment, but from Winnipeg Niven was usually optimistic in his reports.

'Our strengths here has been increased by 50 men and that is a very great thing and improves our training by 100%. . . . I have 6 Carden Lloyds [tracked machine-gun carriers] of the very latest type under Worthington, a grand fellow.'[1]

In December, 1931, he wrote, '.all the officers are buying new furs, Yukon pattern caps and gauntlets of unplucked beaver, so we shall be very smart'.

On 1 May, 1932,' We are all confined to barracks today, waiting for a May Day parade to break away from the police, but I don't think anything will happen except that the mess will make the odd shilling on liquor supplied to fed-up officers.'

Three weeks later he reported, ' Officers are all getting a ten per cent cut in pay'.

Gault was able to see for himself the effect of the Great Depression on the Regiment when he visited Winnipeg in October. Its strength was less than one third of that of a wartime battalion. Pay cuts, lack of equipment, restrictions on training, no money for maintenance of barracks and no promotion had become a way of life in the Permanent Force. With little money for training, much time was spent at sports and rifle shooting for which ample ammunition was left from wartime stocks.

The main task of the Regiment was to train the Non-Permanent Active Militia, or 'NPAM' as Canada's part-time soldiers were known. Every Patricia of the rank of corporal and above was trained as an instructor. They conducted officers' courses at universities and held schools for militiamen at centres in western Canada. The Regiment was able to maintain high standards for such instruction, for it was pitched at a junior level, but higher tactical and operational training was another matter. Lack of money and restricted strengths prevented the kind of experimentation and development of military thought which is so important to an army in peace.

Gault's visit took place before the nadir of the Regiment's fortunes. In 1933 Hugh Niven received orders to discharge twenty men as there was no money to pay them. Since he had recruited them himself, he felt obliged to find them jobs which, somehow, he managed to do.

As the Depression deepened, Hammie's concern for the welfare of Patricia veterans grew. He urged Niven to link the Patricia clubs which had been formed across the country into a national association linked to Regimental Headquarters, to generate the means and communications through which assistance could be rendered to those in need.

As its Honorary Lieutenant-Colonel Gault was the guardian of the Regiment's traditions. While many of the most important of these, the constituents of its ethos, were intangible, others, such as details of its uniforms and accoutrements, could be controversial – none more so than the 'Colours fiasco' of 1932.

A Regiment's Colours are the focus of its fighting traditions and loyalty and have a near mystical significance to the soldiers who serve under them. Before being presented, they are consecrated in a religious service, then treated with reverence and carefully guarded. Often soldiers have died in their defence.

The Patricias' Camp Colour had become just such a sacred object, but by 1920, when the Regiment became part of Canada's Permanent Force, it was too worn and frail for further service. Lady Patricia Ramsay had a reproduction of it produced by the Royal School of Art Needlework to be carried on ceremonial occasions. In 1929 the Patricia's were awarded eighteen battle honours of the First World War, with instructions that ten were to be emblazoned on their regimental colour. When asked, the Army ruled that Lady Patricia's Colour was the wrong size and its maroon background did not match the Regimental facings of French grey. It must be replaced by King's and Regimental Colours of regulation design.

Devoted as they were to the 'Ric-a-Dam-Doo', the Patricias asked for authority to carry it as a third colour on suitable occasions. Since even small alterations to the design of a colour had to be agreed by the King personally, this would require royal approval. Enlisting the help of the Duke of Connaught, Lady Patricia spoke to the King, who said that, if the proposal came to him officially, he would approve.

Gault undertook to have the new official Colours designed by Sir Gerald Woolaston, the Garter King at Arms who was also the Inspector of Regimental Colours. George Vanier (the future governor-general), then First Secretary at the Canadian High Commission in London, kept up the pressure on Gault's behalf on the designer and on defence headquarters in Ottawa.

In August designs were submitted to the Colonel-in- Chief: that for the King's Colour, based on the Union Flag, she readily approved. In the centre of the French grey Regimental Colour was embroidered her cipher, the initials 'VP' surmounted by a coronet in gold. Surrounding them was a garland of maple leaves interwoven with the Regiment's battle honours. In the top corner next the staff was embroidered a miniature of her laurel wreath in gold.

She approved but asked for an addition – 'in miniature of the cap badge with "the daisy" centre (being my poor sister's name flower)' – in other words, a marguerite – 'and also somewhere the light infantry bugle which is worn on their collar'.

Gault replied, 'I fear there will be considerable objection raised by the powers that be over the inclusion of any additional badges on the new Regimental Colour and although I have not referred to this subject before – to you or to anyone else – I hope you will not mind if the design of the cap badge used during the war is omitted from the new Colour. I would far sooner have referred to this in conversation than in writing, but am confident that you will appreciate and not misunderstand this feeling of mine in which there is no rancour'. In short he wanted no reminders of Marguerite. Lady Patricia answered that she agreed to the omission of a cap badge: 'As you suggest and I do not misunderstand your wish at all I assure you, nor will I ever refer to the fact that any reference was made to this between us, but will treat it with entire confidence.'

Hammie later proposed to Hugh Niven that the Colonel-in-Chief's cipher should replace the marguerite in the cap badge. Niven agreed and virtually the last visible reminder of Marguerite disappeared from the Regiment.[2]

In the meantime National Defence Headquarters had learned that five British regiments carried third Colours, some possibly, unofficially.

A proposal for the Patricias to carry one went forward and for some months nothing was heard. Then on 6 January, 1933, the War Office issued an instruction: 'The King has been pleased to command that a third Colour will in no circumstances be carried on parade by battalions of infantry of the line'.

Gault much regretted that the Patricias might inadvertently have caused other regiments being denied the privilege of carrying third Colours.

★

In early 1933 Gault was becoming increasingly concerned by the disturbing developments being brought about by Hitler in Germany. In a speech at Taunton he said that he had always respected the Germans' powers of concentrating their energies on whatever they were trying to do. They were now re-orienting their political forces toward a new and stronger nationalism. Whatever repercussions that might have upon the European situation as a whole, he could not but say, 'I for one would prefer to have a strong Nationalist Germany as a bulwark against Russian Bolshevism than I would have a weak Germany that was unable to withstand whatever pressure might emanate from her north-eastern boundaries'.[3]

Wary as he was of Hitler, the Communist threat from the Soviet Union seemed more immediate and menacing. It was a view many shared.

Four months later he and a group of other flying Parliamentarians toured Germany in their own aircraft, eleven in all, ostensibly as guests of the German Aero Club but with the full approval and cooperation of the German government. Dorothy was one of six women pilots included in the group.

After three days in Düsseldorf and Cologne, they visited the Junkers factory en route to Staaken airport at Berlin. There they were met by Herr Milch (the future Field Marshal and Inspector-General of the *Luftwaffe*) who welcomed them on behalf of Goering, the Reichs Air Minister.

At dinner that evening Herman Goering, smiling and affable, greeted Gault as a gallant soldier and fellow veteran, united in friendship now by the shared experience of war. In a speech he claimed that the British had been misled by their own press about conditions in Germany. During their visit, they must have seen, not an oppressed people but a German people who had become more cheerful, freer and perhaps prouder again.

Two days later, after laying a wreath at the German War Memorial in Unter den Linden, the group was received by Hitler at the Chancellery in the Wilhelmstrasse. He had not yet adopted uniform, but was dressed in traditional black jacket and striped trousers. The Reichs Chancellor did his best to charm them. That he failed is evident in a photograph of him with unsmiling British women on either side, backed by a row of his beaming henchmen.

Dorothy later claimed that the ill-fated von Papen, the Foreign Minister, was the only gentleman in that unlovely group of ministers and Nazi party officials. She said that where Hitler kissed her hand, a wart appeared which defied every known treatment: not until an old crone who lived alone in the woods behind Hatch cast a spell upon it, did it disappear!⁴

In a brief speech of welcome Hitler struck the same note as Goering. His English guests would, he said, have been able to see for themselves that terror did not dominate German life, that here a people had found itself again and a spirit prevailed which had been born of the ideals of a young German nation.

Indeed, flying over the green countryside in fine summer weather, greeted impressively at aerodromes, entertained everywhere at luncheons and dinners with generous hospitality and shown such sights as their hosts decided they would find interesting, the British group did obtain a pleasant surface impression of Germany. Carefully hidden from them was the reverse side of the picture – armament factories, military training, concentration camps.

The German Press slanted their reports of the visit to support the Nazi line. One claimed that the British had expressed particular interest in being shown the scene of the Reichstag fire. A *Times'* reporter drily commented, 'The visitors themselves were not aware of this'.

Before returning home the party visited Kiel where they were taken for a tour of the harbour by the Chief of the Baltic naval station, Vice-Admiral Albrecht⁵ on board the yacht *Nixe* and visited a pocket battleship.

Gault had learned more than his hosts intended. Group Captain Herring, the Air Attaché at the British Embassy, told him of his suspicions about the new régime's evasion of the Treaty of Versailles under which they were not allowed an air force.

At every airfield Hammie visited there were large, well-equipped flying clubs, busily training 'amateur' pilots. Gault knew how expensive it was to learn to fly: most private pilots in England possessed inherited means or had earned enough to afford the costs. In short, they were older than the young German students he saw under training, who more closely resembled the boys who had been eager to join the RFC in 1917. And at each of these clubs there were brown-shirted National Socialists, many wearing flying badges and decorations from the war, before whom the students stood to attention.

Civil aviation in Germany was growing in importance and some government subsidy of pilot training could be justified – but for these numbers?

As early as March,1933, stories about rearmament were current gossip among knowledgeable Germans who regarded them either with pride or dismay. There were rumours of underground factories and airports being built at an astonishing rate. An enormous school for pilots was to be built at Gatow, twenty miles from Berlin. Student pilots were 'crashing like flies, but there are plenty of them and they get commissioned as soon as they've finished school'. *Lufthansa* and *Luft-Sportsverband* were said to be subterfuges to cover intensive training for air warfare.[6]

Through Embassy officials and newspaper correspondents he met in Berlin, Gault had heard some of this. At Kiel among the German flying men and women he met were Wolfgang von Gronau, the pioneer trans-Atlantic aviator and several officials of *Lufthansa*. They appeared to be proud of their own substantial pilot training programme and of the progress they were making in expanding their fleet.

To Gault it was obvious that Germany was building an air force and was rearming in contravention of the Versailles treaty. He warned the government and Whitehall officials on his return to England and began, in every way he could, to promote the maintenance of the strength of the armed services and the expansion of the RAF.

While he was doing so, his own flying adventures continued. In July he took Mr Francis, his political agent, for a joy ride: 'Crashed machine in last landing due to making last of three S turns too slow into wind dropping left wheel on ground – breaking left longeron & left locking bolt.'

A month later he and Dorothy set out for Belgium: 'Came round by coast to avoid storms. . . . Off Lulworth Cove encountered heavy gusts of wind coming over cliffs & around cape, DBG nearly bumped overboard.'

In September he made a solo flight to Heston intending to navigate by following the railway. After twenty miles he ran into a storm.

> East of Westbury had to come down to get under clouds. Heavy rain almost blinded me & necessitated removal of goggles. After getting clear of this storm containing lightning, turned SE to avoid succession of storms . . . thence to Reading and Heston. Much lightning. Rainbow over Winchester.

In October Germany walked out of the International Disarmament Conference and gave notice of her intended withdrawal from the League of Nations. Gault warned his constituents of the implications for Britain.

> I should draw your attention to the passing milestones of European evolution. These have culminated in a new German

revolution aimed at the national re-establishment of their race and the re-militarisation of their people.

Let no-one here run away with the idea that I am raising the bogey of war. I do not believe that war is . . . imminent, and nothing could be more deplorable than loose war talk. Our statesmen and those of Europe are endeavouring to find a way towards further reductions in armaments and I give place to no man in my desire for peace.

Whether we like it or not, there is no doubt that Herr Hitler, like the Kaiser of old, is at the head of a great national movement, which with German thoroughness and ruthlessness proposes to carry out its policy without fear or the favour of any man. . . .

German training today, both athletic and scholastic, aims at the building up of their young manhood to what they think is the highest vocation to which they can be called. We must visualize what the situation will be in years to come so that we may resolve upon a policy to preserve our interests and maintain the peace of Europe. If the League of Nations should break down, it appears to me that there are only two alternatives – isolation or the balance of power in Europe.

Isolation was not a practical option for Britain. Her historic policy of maintaining the balance of power in Europe required singleness of purpose and clear-headed diplomacy backed by military force.

It is necessary for us to consider the various alternatives in the interests of peace. Had we possessed a more definite policy in 1914, the Great War might not have taken place.[7]

Later that month there was a re-union dinner of veterans of the Canadian Expeditionary Force in London. Speakers included Prince Arthur of Connaught, Lord Mottistone, who had commanded the Canadian Cavalry Brigade, General Sir Archibald Montgomery-Massingberd, Chief of the Imperial General Staff, Gault and Howard Ferguson, the High Commissioner for Canada. But the star was Winston Churchill whom Gault had invited to speak on the growing dangers of German militarism. He made plain his admiration for the man whom many regarded as a political renegade and introduced him as 'a man of guts'.

Most of Hammie's efforts to warn of the growing German menace and to enhance preparedness took place behind the scenes with officials and people of influence. In Parliament he did what he could to draw public attention to the disparity between Britain's strength in the air and that of other European powers. In February, 1934, in response to questioning by Gault, Sir Philip Sassoon, the Secretary of State for Air, revealed that France, Germany and Italy each had between four and five thousand qualified military and civilian air pilots, the USSR about three thousand, while Britain had but thirty-two hundred.[8] A few days later Hammie did his best to persuade a Committee reviewing the Air Estimates to increase the RAF.[9]

He was not by any means alone in pressing the Government to improve Britain's preparedness for war, but his contribution was valuable. It took all the weight of informed opinion to shift political leaders and the Treasury from their entrenched defence of the economy into recognizing the implications of the growing danger of war.

Hammie's interests spread wide. In February, 1934, the national press carried extensive accounts of his assault on England's restrictive licensing laws. In Parliament he moved the second reading of a bill to allow hotels and restaurant to serve drinks with meals until three o'clock in the afternoon and midnight, in effect to permit people to have drinks with lunch and dinner. He contended that it would help the trade, be convenient to the increasing numbers of people who ate out and for tourists from abroad who could not understand Britain's strange licensing rules. The aim should be to attract more of them. Hammie told the House that it was the luck of the draw that he should have been asked to move the Bill because he had no connection with the trade but, as an ordinary citizen and traveller, had often suffered from the inconvenience of the present rules.

The House discussed it good-humouredly with a mixture of earnestness and flippancy appropriate to the subject until Lady Astor, that eminent teetotaller, launched an impassioned attack. When she claimed that some MPs had been bribed by the drinks trade, there was real anger and uproar. She could name no names and was finally required by the Speaker to withdraw her allegation. So much time was taken over her intervention that, though the bill passed second reading, time ran out and it was not passed at that session.[10]

Gault's next foray in Parliament came in April when he recommended to the Prime Minister that the British government should promote, with other governments of the Commonwealth, the formation of a permanent secretariat to study all matters pertaining to the welfare of the Commonwealth as a whole and report to the governments concerned.

Ramsay MacDonald would not cooperate: a committee of Commonwealth representatives had considered the subject of economic consultation and cooperation recently and had not included the establishment of a such a permanent body in their recommendations. Gault's vision of its function, broader than MacDonald's, was ahead of the times: the Commonwealth Secretariat was not formed until 1965.

Next day he recommended that the Chancellor of the Exchequer introduce a simplified income tax return so that the taxpayer could submit his return direct without having to use a professional adviser. Hore-Belisha appeared willing, but Hammie's ideas came to naught: tax returns grew even more complicated.

On 5 May he drew the Dominions' Secretary's attention to improving conditions overseas, and asked that, in cooperation with the Dominions, he seek to further Commonwealth immigration. J.H. Thomas poured cold water on the idea by saying, 'No such scheme could succeed until economic conditions improve.'

Mussolini's posturing on the international stage, in particular his threat to Ethiopia in 1934, brought the activities of Mosley's British Union of Fascists into prominence. While they posed no immediate threat as a political force, to Hammie they had no place in a democracy. Using the examples of Russia, Germany and Italy, he warned that dictatorships relied for their life upon extinguishing everything which opposed them. Many people living under dictators disagreed with their governments, but their voice was never heard. 'You do not want your rights as free men and free women, in a freedom-loving civilisation, to be interfered with or possibly extinguished altogether by a dictatorship of either left or right. Our system has been tried and proved in the fire.'[11]

In July Gault bought a new aeroplane, a de Havilland Leopard Moth, faster and more comfortable than his open cockpit Gipsy with a longer range and able to carry a pilot and two passengers. Before he could fly it, he suffered an attack of septic poisoning in his one foot which immobilized him. After a week's treatment, the condition seemed to improve but then deteriorated. On 11 August he was moved to a London hospital for an operation which turned out to be much more serious than expected. It was followed by seven weeks of treatment during which time he was in considerable pain.

He returned to Hatch in October, much weakened, and his doctors ordered a lengthy rest. During the long and boring months of illness and convalescence he gave much thought to his future. He concluded that it was time for a change.

Next year would see another general election which might well coincide with the first hearing of Falchi's suit against Stephens and its challenge to the validity of his marriage. The resulting publicity could turn Gault into a liability to the Conservative Party. In any case his political future was limited: there was little likelihood now of his ever obtaining a cabinet post. And his avowed purpose in entering politics had been achieved. On 3 November,1934, he announced that he would not contest the next election.

Now that the country has repudiated the shibboleth of free trade – or, to be correct, the shibboleth of free imports – by the adoption of a scientific tariff which makes possible a greater measure of freer trade within the Empire through the medium of the reciprocal trade agreements, which have already yielded such mutually satisfactory results, I feel that I can regard the political ideals for which I have stood in public life as having been realized.[12]

Even his political opponents acknowledged that, as a constituency MP, Gault had been an unqualified success. He had worked hard and effectively for the people he represented and they liked him. As the *Somerset County Gazette* put it:

Popular as a politician, Colonel Gault is still more popular personally, thanks to his approachableness, his constant readiness to be of service to any constituents whenever possible, and his liberal benefactions in many directions. In the public sphere he set a conspicuous example of generosity by his gift to the town of the playing fields which will make his name remembered by future generations of Tauntonians; and the Borough honoured itself as well as the donor when it added him to the list of Freemen.[13]

It noted elsewhere that his warnings about the Fascists had not been fanciful; they were to contest eleven seats in next election, four in Devon.

Hammie and Dorothy decided that the best place for them to relax after the past trying months would be in a warm climate, far away from England. A distressing problem close to home made them eager to get away.

In June,1932, Hammie's ward, Patricia Blackader, at the age of 19 had married Lord Waleran, eight years her senior, a Devonshire peer who had recently returned to England from New Zealand where he had been ADC to the Governor-General. Gault believed that she was too young and asked her to postpone the wedding for a year, but she refused. The Bensons, who were her legal guardians, agreed to the marriage and launched a lavish wedding from Sheafhayne Manor where they now lived in Devon.

The marriage lasted less than two years. Patricia left Waleran and they were divorced in 1934. She then declared her intention of marrying Rex Hoyes, a New Zealand businessman. She was not prepared to listen to advice and, while Gault never closed his door on her, by the time he and Dorothy prepared to leave, a curtain had fallen between them and Pat.[14]

During his previous summer's illness Dorothy had become thoroughly familiar with the new Leopard Moth and, on their first flights together, she flew while he navigated. He piloted G-ACSI for the first time on 28 October, two days before they left England.

By gentle stages they made their way to Catania where, upon landing, they were arrested and searched for flying over a military area near Messina. For six hours they were held in the officers' mess at the airfield, during which time there was much telegraphing by the Italians to higher authority and by Hammie to the British Ambassador in Rome. Eventually they were released into the care of a worried Percival Campbell. Gault commented that the Italian officers had been most attentive and charming.

After a few days in Taormina they flew across the Mediterranean to Tunis, then via Tripoli eastward along the north African coast, stopping at Gabes, Sirte and Mersa Matruh. On the fourth day the temperature of their engine began to rise above normal and the oil pressure to fall. Dorothy, who was piloting, was not unduly concerned but on landing they reported the condition to a mechanic. Gault's log told what a narrow escape they had had.

> We only got to Cairo without our engine seizing up by the grace of God & a kindly Providence taking charge of (let us hope?) its own. Owing to a split pin having apparently been left out, the nut worked off one of the oil seal bolts with the result that oil pressure would have ceased & the engine seized up within 5 or 10 minutes. A veritable miracle we got down when we did!

After ten days in Cairo, they flew across the Sinai into Palestine, Syria and Jordan. At Beisan they lunched with Mary Crossley, a close friend and neighbour in Somerset, and her brother who was commanding a cavalry squadron of the Trans-Jordan Frontier Force. The Crossleys had lit a smoke fire to show the wind direction for Dorothy who was flying. They did not realize that the wind direction was irrelevant – at Beisan pilots always land up hill! Dorothy failed to do so and rolled on and on, stopping just short of disaster.

Next day they flew over the Sea of Galilee to Damascus where they spent a few days before flying into Jordan. At Amman, because of a 40 mph wind from the south-east, Dorothy showed her skill as a pilot by making a spectacular landing, sideslipping onto the strip. Their next stop was in the middle of the desert, 230 kilometres to the south, at Ma'an, where they explored Petra, then left next day for the three-hour flight to Cairo. Climbing to 6,000 feet, they crossed the high ridge to the west. Hammie noted that 'The view with the "Hill of Sacrifice" at Petra on our right, into the Wadi Arabi with a glimpse of the Gulf of Akaba, was one of indescribable lonely grandeur'.

Pausing only for a night at Cairo, they flew up the Nile for three weeks of relaxation and exploring the ruins at Luxor. At Balyana, to their astonishment, they were met on arrival by the Governor and the Chief of Police. Apparently in their honour, streets of villages were lined with police and a guard of honour was on parade at Abydos. Gault tried to explain to the Governor that he was not the expected visitor and eventually managed to persuade him that he should return to the airfield. Fortunately he did so before General Sir Ian Hamilton arrived.

On 30 December the Gaults left Cairo to explore the Mediterranean coast westward to Tunis. On the first day they covered what later were to be the battlefields of the desert war – Mersa Matruh, Sollum, Tobruk and Bengazi, where they spent the night. Next day at Sirte they learned that the airfield at Tripoli was under water and that a westerly gale made it impossible for them to reach Gabes. As a result they decided to remain, 'and so saw the New Year in with four Italian officers marooned in this Godforsaken place.'

Next day the situation was no better and they were forced to remain another night. That was enough for Hammie and in the morning, despite conflicting weather reports, they decided to go on. Fuel was running short when they put down at Homs, not realizing that it was a military airfield closed to civilian traffic.

As they came to a halt a truckload of police surrounded the aircraft and covered them with rifles. Brusquely a sergeant ordered them to get out, demanded their passports and documents, then marched them to a nearby hut, Hammie protesting in his inadequate Italian all the way. The door of the windowless shack slammed shut and was locked. Seated on a rickety bench in the dark, Hammie and Dorothy were distinctly alarmed.

After about an hour they were released by a wasp-waisted Italian captain with a detachment of native troops. He would tell them nothing but politely invited them to climb into the canvas-covered back of a truck with the soldiers.

The vehicle set off at speed, bumping and splashing over the pot-holed roads. Eventually it turned into a driveway, stopped, then reversed toward the formidable nail-studded door of a large stone building. The soldiers sprang to the ground and lined the space between the vehicle and the entrance. The officer asked the Gaults to alight and motioned them toward the door of what looked like a prison.

They entered a large marble hall across which a red carpet led up a wide balustraded stairway. At its foot, smiling, stood the local Commandante, Maggiore Count Maria Guarini di Castelfalciano with his staff of sixteen officers at attention behind him. He apologized for the 'informality' of the reception at the airport, explaining that civilian aircraft were not normally welcome there. The Governor-General, Marechale Italo Balbo, had already been informed that Colonel and Mrs Gault were travelling through Libya, so that when he learned that they had landed at Homs, he said that they were to be shown every courtesy. Their aircraft was, even now, being re-fuelled and, in the meantime, they were to regard the officers' mess, in which they now stood, as their home. He then introduced his staff and led them in to a champagne lunch.

As the weather was bad, we decided to remain and view the ancient Roman remains of Leptis Magna which surpass anything we've ever seen in classical beauty and decoration. On the way back, drenched to the skin as we then were by torrential down-pours, the Commandante who was short of an eye due to the war, drove us into a ditch from which we were dragged by native troops – dinner & bridge in the Mess.

In the morning, when they came to leave, they found that Balbo had ordered that they should pay for nothing, even the aircraft's fuel, but were to regard themselves as guests of Tripoli.[15]

The Gaults had met Balbo in England during one of his memorable long-distance flights, but his generosity was probably due less to that than to Hammie's enthusiastic letter to *The Times* about his tour of Italy with Reeve in 1933.[16]

In mid-January, having been delayed for a day by snow and fog at Berck, they crossed the Channel and made for Heston. On landing they were unable to see a gasometer a thousand yards away. After nearly three months in the sun, they were back in England with a vengeance.

Later that year they travelled to Austria. On the way home they took off from Basle with Graham Gadsden, Doris's husband as passenger. The field was used by gliders and, unknown to Hammie, his tail skid snagged one of their tow ropes which lay concealed in the grass. He noticed that the aircraft seemed sluggish as it climbed slowly, trailing behind it a hundred metres of steel cable, and headed into France. As he approached the airstrip at Dijon, he was intent on clearing the power line which lay across his path, not realizing that to cross it spelled almost certain disaster. On the ground a crowd of spectators with a firetruck and an ambulance, watched in horror for the inevitable crash. As the aircraft crossed the power line the tow-rope bounced upward off a hay stack, cleared the high-tension cables and Hammie touched down safely to the cheers of the crowd.

In the summer of 1937, with Mary Crossley as their guest, the Gaults flew to Salzburg in a new Vega Gull. Mary was surprised to find that it was Hammie, rather than Dorothy, a pianist, who decided what concerts they should hear and showed a considerable knowledge of music.

They returned to England from Innsbruck. Given the altitude of the field, the Vega, with full fuel tanks and three passengers with their bags, was overloaded when they took off. Hammie had passed the point of no return when he realized that she was not going to rise off the grass strip. He pushed the nose and the throttle down to get maximum speed and began to lift off through a field of corn which had encroached onto the airfield.

For a moment the machine was stalled and hit the cornstalks plus some sort of hay-pole hard, dinting the starboard wheel fairing and bumping the port wheel as she keeled over under flying speed. This however set her free and we pulled up to 800 feet above the valley where we continued on our course until we debouched onto the Bavarian Plains and flew to the north of the line of mountains to Luidan.

A few hours later their friend, Bobby Perkins, who had watched in horror and was worried that the undercarriage was damaged, received a wire at Innsbruck – 'Machine arrived intact plus cornstalks, Hammie.'

Chapter 19

THE EVENING OF AN ERA

In November, 1937, Hammie's mother, Louisa, died at Parklands, her Taunton home, at the age of 91. She had moved there in 1912 to be close to her daughter and, much loved by her family, had provided a focus for them and their celebrations ever since.

That apart, Hammie and Lillian were good friends and were frequently to be found in each others' houses. Mary Cunningham described them as, 'such a handsome pair. She had remarkable, sparkling eyes. Percy Benson was wont to organize party games. I wondered how any man, faced with those beautiful eyes, could concentrate enough to succeed in removing a matchbox from under her chin.'

Now in his mid-fifties, Gault was an imposing figure.

> When you walked down the street with Hammie you were aware that he was 'somebody' – his dynamic personality, his 'presence' was apparent to everyone who saw him. People noticed; heads turned. But behind his confident manner he was very sensitive and cared what people thought of him. Because he was divorced, he and DB were not accepted socially by some of the locals and, of course, not at Court.

Mary Cunningham [formerly Crossley] was with them when they received an invitation to a Garden Party at the Palace. His delighted reaction was 'at last we are accepted'. This was followed by deep disappointment when he realized that the invitation had been sent to them by Canada House as part of the High Commissioner's allocation, and not by the Palace.[1]

Hatch Court is not a large house by English standards but an architectural gem built in the Palladian style of Bath stone at the edge of the village of Hatch Beauchamp some five miles from Taunton. Facing south, the two-storey square building, with towers at each corner, is flanked by graceful wings which curve outward toward the rear. An arcaded piazza, which extends the width of the front, looks out on the park with its herd of fallow deer. Behind the main structure, stables, carriage shed and garage surround a flagged courtyard. To the north stand the village church and the buildings of the home farm.

The interior is spacious, elegant but not intimidating. The principal changes which Hammie brought to the house were the installation of electricity, central heating, plumbing, bathrooms and a new lead roof, raised by eighteen inches from its former level to give more space to the servants' cramped attic rooms.

Both he and Dorothy enjoyed entertaining and, when they were at home, there were frequent dinner parties and weekend guests to enjoy their hospitality. Mary Cunningham opined that it was the last house in England where, when you arrived, your car was taken away by the chauffeur[2] to be garaged for the night and when it was returned to you, it had not only been polished but filled with petrol. A store of one-gallon cans was kept for the purpose near the garage.[3]

Guests were cossetted, Dorothy being meticulous in planning for their comfort. As an example, she would have buckets of wet hay placed behind the dining room curtains to reduce the smell of cigar smoke so that the room would be fresh at breakfast time.[4]

A figure of consequence at Hatch was James Hicks who had been Hammie's coachman since 1905: in Montreal he had driven sleighs as well as the family carriages. In later years Gault regarded him more as a friend than a servant. In 1935 he died aged 72. As in business and the army, Gault ran a 'tight ship'. Butler, groom, chauffeur, gardener, woodsman, all had cash books which he regularly inspected in detail, insisting they be accurate.

Though Hammie had given up hunting, he still rode almost daily, while Dorothy had lost none of her boldness and skill as a horsewoman. In 1933 she won the point-to-point staged at nearby Jordans by the local hunt.

Into this scene from what is now another age came an eighteen-year-old Canadian girl, the daughter of Hammie's old friend Philip Mackenzie, to stay for the 1935 Christmas holidays. She was the first child born in the Patricias in 1917 when the Regiment was at Wolverghem in Belgium. To celebrate her arrival, her father constructed a drink from the only materials at hand, oranges and rum, known henceforth as a Wolverghem Cocktail. After many had been consumed, the officers wired Katherine Mackenzie, ' Congratulations. Call her Wolverghem.' She later claimed, 'I should have been a boy because I was called Percival Molson after my father's best friend who was killed shortly before I was born. . . .Hammie always called me "Wolfie".'

To her Hatch Court appeared enormous:

There was a spacious front hall with a fireplace, a wide Y-shaped staircase at one end, and a tall, singularly lugubrious and upright butler who always seemed to be in the background. There was an impressive staff in the kitchens, servants' quarters somewhere in the back of the house. . . . I slept in the room Dorothy had slept in as a child. It was in a tower and had a little fireplace and windows that looked out on the park.

My breakfast and my mail were brought to me every morning on a tray, and as we rode almost every day, my riding clothes and boots were whisked away each evening to be cleaned and brushed. I wore second-hand boots from Moss Bros. in London, a jacket, stock and bowler hat all belonging to Dorothy. My bath, and it was huge, was drawn for me at the end of the day, before we changed into evening dress for dinner.

The grounds were beautiful and Hammie had a riding ring with fences for jumping. It was there that I faced my first 'baptism of fire'. Hammie asked if I had ever jumped on a horse and I, unabashedly, lied and said 'Yes'. He put me on his Daffodil – she was very large – who took me over my first jump. I did not fall off but ended up on top of her ears. Hammie looked at me and said 'I could see the whole of England between you and the saddle!' After several lessons I was taken out with the Taunton Vale Hunt – very posh, very correct, and very thrilling. . . .

Dorothy, whose reputation as an equestrienne was unparalleled, was an excellent teacher. She kept a close watch on me. Once when I took a header going over a bank and a brook she was there to pick me up and help me to climb up on my horse again. I was Canadian, in borrowed clothes, on a borrowed horse, and in those days in England, on the hunting field, sensed that I was looked on as colonial and that I had to mind my P's and Q's.

I made many mistakes; one in particular I will never forget. We were in 'full cry' galloping like mad after the fox, over fences, across fields and streams and God knows what else when we went through a gate. The gate is held open by each rider as he/she passes through it by catching it on his/her crop and passing it on to the next rider, who in turn does the same until all 'the field' has ridden through. Last through shuts the gate. For some unknown reason I was near the front and as I shot through the gate I let it slam on the rest of the field behind me and went galloping after the hounds who were after the fox. Dorothy came up to me and told me that I had to apologize to each and every one of those people that I left apparently fuming on the wrong side of the gate. This I did, but it did not do my reputation as a visitor from Canada much good.

One day the hunt met at Hatch. A number of people came to stay in the house the night before. They brought their horses and their grooms. Breakfast was in the dining room (no trays that day). Everyone arrived on the dot in their riding habits. On the sideboard were scrambled eggs, bacon, kedgeree etc., all in silver entree dishes, on silver trays, served with silver spoons – so much silver. The lugubrious butler and the maids moved silently about looking after everyone's needs. I was a few minutes late. I had my riding pants on and Moss Bros. boots, a shirt open at the neck, no stock and no jacket (I would put those on later, I thought) and a yellow cardigan with the sleeves rolled up. A terrible faux-pas. I was gently but firmly sent upstairs to dress correctly.

Before we started out that morning, when we gathered in the court-yard at the front of the house and were up in the saddle ready to move off, the butler and the maids circulated among us and passed us glasses of sherry on silver trays.

Another unforgettable day, not because I made a mistake, but because I was given, or was told I had earned, 'the mask' or the fox's head to mark my first time in at 'the kill'. Instead of 'blooding' me, a form of initiation where a little of the fox's blood is wiped on your cheek, I was given the mask. I was told it would be taken home and Hammie would have it mounted for me, but I was so thrilled with all of this that I asked if I could ride home with it myself. . . .Home we rode, quite literally into the sunset – the huntsmen in their pink coats, the weary, slobbering hounds and one tired but happy colonial with a bloody fox's head clutched firmly in her right hand.

On New Year's Eve Dorothy, wearing a dramatic velvet cape, Hammie in white tie and Wolfie returned to Hatch after a party to find the piazza aglow with light. Laughing, they joined hands in a circle in front of the door and sang Auld Lang Syne.

There are some things in this life I will never forget – that beautiful house and the events that took place while I was staying there, above all the kindness of Hammie and Dorothy Gault – those halcyon days at Hatch.[5]

While Hammie delighted in the enjoyment of others and was always prepared to enjoy himself, he was troubled by the dark shadows cast by

SQUA·AA·A·D SHUN!

CGL·IN·CHIEF DRILLING THE "HATCH COURT VOLUNTEERS" AUGUST 1939.

A favourite 'game' during young people's parties. The Colonel drills the Hatch Court Volunteers, beating the time with serving spoons on a Regimental drum.

the seemingly endless Depression, the plight of Great War veterans and the growing threat of war.

His interest in veterans welfare dated from 1917 when he had spoken so eloquently in Montreal on the country's obligations to its returning soldiers and had advised local groups of ex-servicemen to band together to promote their interests.

The problems of reintegrating the millions of returning men into civilian life after the war, the care of the disabled, of widows and their families, were unprecedented in scale. As always, Governments tended to show little imagination and to do the minimum possible consistent with the political pressures to which they were subjected. It was a new field in which all major countries were on an equal footing as far as ideas and experience were concerned.

The early 1920s saw the formation of veterans' organizations throughout the Empire which joined together in the British Empire Service League.

By 1926 Gault was the Canadian Legion's representative on the Council of the BESL in London and, as a disabled veteran himself, was able to make a unique contribution to its work, a task he continued through the 1930s. He supported the building of the Canadian National War Memorial on Vimy Ridge and attended its unveiling by the King in 1936. While an MP, he was a champion of veterans' causes in Whitehall and Parliament.

In 1939 Gault became chairman of the London Association of Canadian Ex-Service Men. Its 100 members were the nucleus of a national association which, after the Second World War, became the Canadian Veterans Association in the United Kingdom. At the same time he was President of the 'Empire' branch of the British Legion which embraced members from the Dominions and Colonies living in Britain.

With the the threat of war in Europe growing, the Canadian and British Legions, as well as urging their governments to re-arm, helped arouse public awareness of the dangers ahead. From an attitude of almost total apathy, people began to see the armed services with new eyes.

> After the Armistice Day parade in Winnipeg in 1938, all the local papers commented on the Regiment's turn-out. This new interest marked the changing mood of the times. . . . 'soldiers had begun to matter once more.'[6]

In early 1939 a host of part-time organizations in Britain began to compete for volunteers – the Auxiliary Fire Service, ARP, the Red Cross, St John's Ambulance and, above all, the Territorial Army and the Reserves of the Navy and Air Force.

In March the British Government decided to double the strength of the Territorial Army. There were calls for a national register of volunteers who would be prepared to serve in an emergency. In Gault's view the time for reliance on volunteers had passed. No longer able to argue the case in Parliament, he set out his reasons in favour of a compulsory national register in a letter to the *Daily Telegraph*:

> In modern warfare, where the carefully planned blow of the aggressor is aimed at obtaining a decisive victory, it is essential that the nation so attacked should be able to mobilize its maximum strength at a moment's notice, either for defence or counter attack.
> The voluntary national register will have to be largely reclassified, if not entirely scrapped – thus causing confusion and delay – when at the outbreak of war, the nation attacked is brought face to face with reality and is compelled to adopt the conscriptive principle as

the best means of developing its fighting strength in both battlefield and workshop.

An England fully mobilized through the medium of a compulsory national register will give the lie to the idea prevalent in some foreign countries that she has become a third class military power.[7]

In Canada the coming of spring in 1939 brought with it signs of emergence from the Great Depression and a growing realization of the menace of Nazi Germany. There were still masses of unemployed, but times did seem to be getting better. A curious atmosphere of optimism overlaid the shadow of impending war.

The forthcoming visit of the King and Queen in the Spring of that year provided a focus for the country's patriotism and brought a resurgence of national pride. There was none of the jingoism of 1914 – few Canadians had any illusions about war. Across the country units of the Non-Permanent Active Militia were expanding, as were local naval divisions and reserve squadrons of the RCAF. Young men in their hundreds were crossing the Atlantic to join the RAF.

In August it would be 25 years since Hamilton Gault raised PPCLI, but, being the holiday season, that would be a poor month in which to celebrate the event. Instead the Regiment chose to mark their Jubilee on Frezenberg Day, the 8th of May. Moving some two weeks ahead of the King, Gault made a triumphal progress of his own to Winnipeg, Victoria, Vancouver and Edmonton to visit the Regiment and its veterans.

The Patricias were in a mood for celebration. They had survived the drab years of the Great Depression, during which their very existence had been threatened, and the time was right to remember past achievements and to honour the veterans who had made their history. His old soldiers were delighted when they learned that Hammie was to be with them, while the young were eager to meet their Founder whose deeds were legends within the Regiment.

The programme at Winnipeg reflected their enthusiasm. On Saturday, 6 May, Gault took the salute when they performed the stately ceremonial of Trooping the Colour, then presented new drums to the band. In the evening there was the Patricia Club annual dinner, on Sunday a church parade. The anniversary of Frezenberg on 8 May was marked by a holiday. That evening an officers' dinner was followed later by a party for all ranks. Next day there was an 'Assault-at-Arms', a demonstration of military skills and sports to which the public was invited. In the evening, Gault dined with the sergeants then attended a regimental concert.

It had been a smooth and impressive performance during which Hammie was only aware of one hitch. He had returned to the Fort Garry Hotel with little time to change from service uniform into mess kit, only to find no batman there to help him. He could have managed by himself but only slowly. Lieutenant Cameron Ware, his ADC, took over the unfamiliar task of fitting Horace, Hammie's wooden leg, into the skin-tight 'overalls' of the Founder's mess kit. When he presented them to Gault, who was sitting on the edge of his bed, he was horrified to realize he had it in the wrong trouser leg. Hammie's shout of laughter could be heard throughout the hotel.

In Edmonton more than 100 veterans of the Regiment, including Louis Scott who had rescued the Ric-A-Dam-Doo at Sanctuary Wood, were there to meet him. In Victoria the one company of the Regiment stationed on the West Coast paraded in scarlet full dress at a memorial service at the Cathedral. In Vancouver Gault joined seventy of his veterans at a 'smoker' and paid a farewell visit to Jim Christie, the old bear hunter turned soldier who had led the Patricias' snipers throughout the Great War and who was now dying in Shaughnessy Hospital.

A report by Alan Morley in the Vancouver *Sun* was typical of the newspaper accounts. He wrote of Hammie in the Great War:

> Canada's idolized beau sabreur ... who spent his personal fortune to raise a great regiment for service overseas – a man whose picture clipped from newspapers decorated the mirrors of thousands of bright-eyed hero-worshipping girls from coast to coast – the man for whose regiment Princess Patricia embroidered the colour with her own hands – the man who turned down a hatful of decorations he might have had – who was all that a man was supposed to be in those stirring days and who had that extra bit of colour, that final touch of gallantry which caught a nation's imagination at a time when all men were brave and gallant and colourful.

In late June, at the end of their Canadian visit, the Gaults were guests in a party of six on a fishing expedition off the Gulf of Saint Lawrence. With seven guides, they embarked at Sept Iles in what Dorothy described as a 'lugger' to sail down the north shore to the mouth of the Romaine River. Ten hours later, in a cold arctic dawn, having slept hugger mugger in the hold, they arrived at a tiny Indian settlement fifteen miles north of Anticosti Island. There they changed to a smaller boat to travel some miles up the Romaine.

Beyond the swift deep waters of a huge lagoon dotted with rocky islands, further progress was blocked by two raging rapids. They made camp among the stunted spruce of the boulder- strewn shore, confident in their host's assurance that here was the best fishing in Quebec.

For days the landscape lay grim in its grandeur under heavy grey skies and it was very cold. Hammie's host and companions were dedicated anglers. Dorothy's comments in a letter written at the time[8] give an impression of the seriousness of the expedition.

> We have cold ham every day for lunch which is eaten in silence unless you have an intelligent remark to make about FISH, which no one (even the old men) can catch. Hammie got the only decent one and we are beginning to think it was the last of the species.
>
> I am very happy as Hammie, although fishing, has kept his sense of humour and we are together all the time as I help him over the rocks and other hazards.

She ended the letter with a poem – two of its verses:

> I cast my fly upon the pool.
> 'Don't make a splash like that, you fool,'
> I knew my host would like to say,
> Instead of which he turned away and frowned. . . .
>
> Death, death is sure to come, and if the fish aren't 'taking',
> Some of these old men will make for me
> A tombstone 'neath a stark spruce tree
> And all the time I find I'm wishing
> They won't inscribe 'She died while fishing'
>
> 'But I know they will!'

Chapter 20

GAULT'S THIRD WAR

Returning to an England preparing for war, Hammie began casting about for an active role to play. At 57 he had little hope of a field appointment in the army, but, with his experience, there should be a training or staff job which he could do.

In August, 1939, with war imminent, he applied to the Canadian Army but was told that all mobilization appointments had been filled. He was bitterly disappointed. As a qualified pilot, he next applied to join the RAF. They told him that there was no vacancy which he could fill – and they requisitioned his Vega Gull.

The first impact of war on the village of Hatch Beauchamp was the arrival of a bus-load of children from the East End of London, evacuated from the capital to spare them the danger of air attacks.

Eileen Barnett, eleven, was in charge of her two younger brothers and her sister, Marie. Her mother had told her that they must try to stay together. Eileen was growing alarmed because the people who met them at the village hall seemed to be taking only one or two children. If no one wanted them, they might end up in a children's home. It was then that Marie saw a beautiful woman, more elegant than anyone she had ever seen, watching at the side of the hall. She said to Eileen, 'She has a kind face. Let's try her.'

Dorothy Gault immediately said that of course they might come with her. After gathering up all the evacuees who had not found a place, she led them out and piled them, eleven in all, into Hammie's Rolls and her Bentley and took them home.

They had seen nothing like Hatch Court, where they were quartered in what, for them, was luxury in the Clock Tower. After supper in their own dining room, very much awed and a bit frightened, they went to bed. Dorothy, lovely in evening dress, came and wished each of them good night.

A schoolteacher had been engaged and, next day, began a routine of school, wholesome meals, kindness and discipline. The children regarded Dorothy as a sort of fairy godmother, 'The Colonel' with awed affection.

Each Sunday they trooped across the park behind the Gaults to the ancient and lovely church which stands behind Hatch Court. Eileen Barnett recalled that she had been sent a sixpence by her parents. When the collection plate was passed she felt she could not afford the whole sixpence and asked for change. Hammie was standing beside her and heard. Without taking his eyes off the Hymnal, he put a shilling on the plate and quietly said, 'This is from Eileen.'

Every evening the children assembled in the hall in front of its roaring log fires. Seated on the elegant curving stairs, DB and Hammie talked to them about the day's events, then read to them before they went to bed.

At Christmas Hammie played Santa Claus. Out of the pocket money which was given them each week, the children were determined to buy presents for DB and The Colonel. At Woolworths in Taunton they each bought the same, cheap scent and an ashtray. In wrapping her presents, Marie Barnett dropped her ashtray and it broke. She was in despair until the teacher took her to the village shop where she bought Hammie a handkerchief for fourpence but remained somewhat ashamed of her present which seemed insignificant compared to those he would receive from the others.

Hammie heard of her tragedy. When he came in to see them having their Christmas tea, he was waving the handkerchief in the air. After thanking them for the beautiful ashtrays, he said, 'Look at the lovely handkerchief that I got.'

From that day to the end of her life Marie adored him.[1]

In Canada mobilization of two infantry divisions began before the end of August. When war was declared she offered one for service with the new British Expeditionary Force in France. Until it was ready for the field, the 1st Canadian Division would train in England. One of its battalions was Princess Patricia's Canadian Light Infantry.

In mid-September the High Commissioner for Canada, Vincent Massey, invited Gault to join a committee of Canadians resident in Britain to coordinate the welfare activities being organized in anticipation of the arrival of their troops in Britain.

One of the most successful of the projects, in which Hammie himself was involved, was the Beaver Club, in the old offices of the London County Council in Spring Gardens, near Trafalgar Square. With its canteens, reading room, information bureau, baths and recreation facilities, including one of the best dance floors in London, it became a haven for men of all three services.[2]

On the last day of 1939 Hammie welcomed the Patricias to England at Morval barracks on the outskirts of Aldershot. 'Shorty' Colquhoun, who had been captured whilst on reconnaissance with Gault at St Eloi in 1915, was in command. It was bitterly cold, pipes in the hutted camp were frozen and there were only small paraffin heaters to dispel the chill, a reminder to both men of the discomforts which had greeted them on Salisbury Plain in 1914.

Gault wore uniform for the first time in the War when, in February, Lady Patricia Ramsay, the Colonel-in-Chief, reviewed her regiment which she had not seen for 21 years. He felt very much on the side-lines when he learned that his old friend, Carton de Wiart, was in command of the British expedition which was being sent to Narvik to counter the German invasion of Norway. Only later did he learn that the Patricias had moved to Scotland preparatory to a direct assault on the port of Trondheim and that the expedition had been cancelled before they could sail. He was present at a Regimental Field Day, held on the polo grounds at Fleet to celebrate the 25th anniversary of Frezenberg. Two days later the Germans invaded France and the War took on a new character.

Canada's 1st Division had been destined for the BEF and 'holding units' had been established in England to house replacements for its anticipated casualties. After the débâcle in France, Canada decided to double, if not treble, its forces in Britain with a commensurate increase in the number of reinforcement holding units. These were to be formed into two groups. On 4 June, 1940, (the day the evacuation of the BEF from Dunkirk was completed) Gault was offered the command of one of these, a position for which his experience in 1917–18 uniquely fitted him. With scarcely a second thought, he leaped at the chance.

'A' Group, Canadian Holding Units, would be in the garrison town of Bordon in Hampshire, south of Aldershot, and it was there, in the second week of June, that Hammie began to realize the enormity of the task in front of him.

His units would be the temporary home of all reinforcements arriving from Canada, there to be trained for service in the field. His first task would be to organize his headquarters and the new units of the group, but at the moment there was little he could do.

On 11 June the leading units of the 1st Canadian Division had sailed from Plymouth to Brest as the vanguard of the 2nd BEF. Within four days, with French resistance collapsing, they were recalled. All the Canadian staffs in England were involved and had no time to consider base units.

To Dorothy, Hammie wrote:

I am beginning to think I've got myself back into the Army just when I ought to be getting myself out! Trust me to go tilting at windmills when the wind is blowing a gale! Tonight it's difficult to sum up this new situation. . . . I only wish you and your ruddy family (all of it) were safe out in the woods of St Hilaire . . . instead of with all of them at Hatch for the Bosches to loot!

My guess is you had better be thinking of putting the silver away.

Five days later came a letter from Harold Balfour, the Parliamentary Under Secretary of State for Air, an old friend, saying that the RAF needed pilots to ferry new aircraft and to fly air gunners and wireless operators under instruction.

Frankly I expect you're doing more interesting and responsible work than this; but if you do want to come along and join the RAF, in the humble rank of pilot officer (at any rate at first), just let me know.

Hammie raged,

If the old fool had only offered me this three weeks ago, I would have leapt at it, for it would have given me lots of flying without the responsibilities of command.

By that time he had selected his staff and was hard at work. He told Dorothy to tell everyone else to stop writing to him, for he was answering their letters until 11 and 12 every night.

The fact is I've got a hell of a lot to do and it is taking me all my time to do it, starting every morning at 0700 hrs, when I haven't been up half the night with the troops (as I have been twice this week) as a result of their fool red alert business. Why can't they let us sleep when they are dropping bombs miles and miles away, I can't think – I don't mind the bombs but I do hate having my sleep disturbed.

One piece of good news was that he had heard from 'the Campobello kids', Percival Campbell and Miles Wood, who had escaped from St. Jean de Luz 'by the skin of their teeth.'

Before they came under his command, Gault had inspected the

holding units and was not impressed. Guards were slack, soldiers untidy, in a general atmosphere of *laissez faire*. The keen edge of a professional military establishment was missing. At his first COs' conference, he spoke his mind, which jolted some comfortable officers out of their complacency. A few days later he wrote, 'Today an officer remarked, "Your guards and sentries seem to have improved in the last week." This is still a long way from what I want but 'pon my soul, I really believe they are better.'

Hammie and Dorothy's letters to each other during this time of enforced separation were frank and warmly affectionate. Both longed to be together to face the threatened dangers of increased bombing and a German invasion. On 14 July Hammie wrote that he had stopped for lunch with Dorothy's sister and her husband en route to see General McNaughton, the senior Canadian commander in Britain.

> Pearl was looking lovelier than ever and as usual roused some of the evil that seems to be deep down within me. . . . Col. Turner sent you his respects and remembrances. It really is extraordinary – no not extraordinary at all! – how you seem to have got off with all these old men who are years my junior but really don't look it. . . .
>
> If the situation doesn't blow up during the next ten days, what about your coming up for a weekend at the end of the month to Liphook where Nelson used to meet Lady H.

Two days later, Hammie's irritation boiled over.

> I've had a hell of a day, so forgive me if I'm short and abrupt. I've got 3 hours' work ahead of me tonight. I've come to the conclusion that our system is rotten and that the leadership from top to bottom is irresponsible and futile, the junior officers and NCOs not being worth a damn. Tomorrow I'm reading the riot act to COs. My God! but the regimental officers of 25 years ago did know their men and did try to teach them something while these b—f—'s seem to think they've got nothing but privileges and certainly no responsibilities.

He was soon more cheerful.

> You'll be glad to learn that while everything is by no means right, my depression of t'other day has worn off although I'm somewhat disappointed that the *Daily Express*'s prophecy of today

being Der Tag hasn't come off. Have got some 600 through their musketry in the past few days, and believe me, the music of a score of LMG's in line was good to listen to. Tomorrow I'm looking forward to inspecting a contingent over which some time in instruction has been spent, and may God damn them and curse them if they aren't up to scratch – curse this war and Hitler for keeping us apart, in body anyhow.

The contingent he referred to was a mobile column he had organized as part of the defence against invasion. After inspecting them he commented,

[They were] by no means perfect,but they did look something like soldier boys and gave evidence of having tried to turn themselves out in accordance with the book – and my orders. . . .

I'm very much afraid that Adolph has changed his mind and doesn't intend to attack – damn him! He should have done so two weeks ago and hasn't: another month and it'll be too late for him to do so this year, and next year we should be attacking him. . . .

If he'd only attack this summer we might be able to give him hell and so bring the war to a victorious and an earlier end than otherwise.

Hammie's strategic judgement may have been faulty, but he hadn't lost his fighting spirit. Having said that, on 1 August, Gault predicted that the 4th would be Der Tag. After the war, German records showed that their air offensive against Britain, designed to clear the way for invasion, was scheduled to begin on 5 August, the date later being fixed as the 10th.

During the next month the Battle of Britain was fought in the skies over the southern counties, while the Canadians, watching the vapour trails high in the blue, expected at any moment the call to action.

In the warm sunshine of Saturday afternoon, 7 September a large force of German bombers and fighters fought its way up the Thames to make the most damaging daylight attack made on London during the war, followed that night by relays of bombers, guided by the tremendous fires, which added to the devastation in the capital. Prompted by this change in tactics and a concentration of barges in the French Channel ports, the British Chiefs of Staff that night issued the code word 'Cromwell' – the order for the defending forces to stand by at immediate notice.

On Sunday Hammie wrote to Dorothy,

Just as the gunners' fortnightly dance was commencing, the mystic word came through and in a trice, *les officiers* were fading just as they did from the famous Brussels ball. Within a few minutes the machine was working. I had the time of my life and thoroughly enjoyed myself. The machine worked with creaks, but no groans, and on the whole, pretty well. Well within two hours, all was set, . . . and I free to carry on with my job of commander. By the time I'd got round my lines and got back to Area, it was past 4, and so after a visit to my own Headquarters to see that all was well, I turned in for a couple of hours sleep. Today I'm on the crest and feel almost like a fighting man once more – blast and hell! If only I could grow another leg, I'd be a brigadier at least. Though I hate to say it, I'm a damn sight better than most of the crowd I see.

During the previous June German bombers en route to targets in the West Country began being intercepted over Somerset. Several bombs and land mines fell in the vicinity of Hatch Court raising concern about the safety of the evacuees. Local authorities consulted their parents and by the middle of the month all had returned to London. A battalion of the Ulster Rifles was quartered in the park at Hatch, where they set about digging trenches and an anti-tank ditch in preparation for the expected invasion.

When the Germans switched their bomber offensive onto London, they concentrated initially on the East End where the Barnetts and the other evacuees had returned. Though Dorothy and Hammie had assured them that they might come back to them at any time, nothing was heard from their former charges.

Members of their own family were in danger. On Friday, 13 September, Dorothy's sister, Pearl Sykes, wrote from Bashurst in Sussex. She wondered if her youngest daughter, Nicky, would be safer at Hatch – they had had more than 30 bombs in their small village and immediate district and could hear German bombers overhead, en route for London, virtually all night.

I have three children sleeping on mattresses on the cloakroom floor, perfectly happily and, although the house shakes and the doors and windows rattle at least four to six times each night, they sleep peacefully through it all. If the invasion really comes, let me know if Nick would be better here or with you.

Two nights earlier the next village had been bombed and the District Nurse's house hit.

> The local warden and First Aid got her out, seriously hurt. She was moved into the village hall next door. The plane came back on its tracks and a bomb got the village hall, killing five people, including the V.A.D. . . .The District Nurse was also killed. It wiped out all the people in the village who were capable of helping. After this of course, one just lies and listens to the roar coming over, wondering if we get the next. It is very foolish and I know we will get accustomed to it.

Far from dispirited, she went on,

> We are littered with crashed Messerschmitts – six down in this immediate district. About three days ago, we had one with three Spitfires on its tail, right over the house – the roar of machine guns also – literally drowned the sound of engines – it was too exciting for words.

In the first post next morning came a cry for help from Mrs Barnett. Could her children return to Hatch? Within an hour Dorothy was on a train to London to gather up all her evacuees.

At Paddington she found a raid in progress. The first few taxi drivers she tried were unwilling to take her to the East End but eventually one agreed. Past the pathetic sight of wrecked and burning homes, they eased slowly down streets littered with debris, looking for the homes of the evacuees. At the first two houses on her list Dorothy was warmly welcomed, but at the next found nothing but a policeman and a time bomb. He frowned as she approached.

> 'This is not the place to stand talking. Don't you know what's happening? Can't you hear something?' . . . I could hear the planes, but very far away. However, then a bomb dropped so I put on my tin hat and told the Bobby I would keep him no longer.

Dorothy told her driver, with whom she had just had tea – made by his wife in their kitchen – that, as a married man, he should take the policeman's advice and take shelter. He replied, 'I never do. They won't hit me, I'm too wicked.'

The last house of call was locked. Dorothy found an open window and climbed through to find the family – man, woman, children and dogs in their Anderson shelter at the bottom of the garden.

So I finished my arrangements by howling down the hole in the ground, into which I was invited, but, having got a whiff of the insufferable fug, politely declined.

By the time she left the East End she had located all the children and had found them transportation back to Hatch, except for three whose house had been destroyed and were in the care of the London Council.

Covered in dust and dirt, she checked into the Berkeley, then went out to find a hairdresser. Being Saturday, none were open, but the hall porter at the Ritz made an appointment for her with the renowned Mr Topper,

[Who] had never done anyone but men, and all Kings and Emperors and Princes at that. However, he turned out to be an ARP first aid man and took me to his bosom, and literally clipped off all my hair, which surprisingly looks quite nice.

Another raid started as she began to walk back to the Berkeley. Suddenly planes were overhead, bombs began to fall and splinters from anti-aircraft shells rained onto the street. She ran into a strange house to take cover,

[With] a terrorized soldier and an old man and a French woman and a dog.

Nothing more happened, so after a bit I went back to a lone partridge and a half bottle of burgundy, which the maitre d', who asked me to remember him to you when I wrote, said you must taste next time. . . .Moral of this letter – ALWAYS TAKE COVER – to please me!'[3]

Hammie wrote across it, 'I certainly will.'

The bombing continued during the autumn and winter of 1940–41, though the immediate threat of invasion receded. There was much for Hammie to do in developing a sound organization for housing and training reinforcements, as well as coping with the myriad administrative tasks of a Canadian unit in Britain. For training policy, equipment and personnel administration, his reinforcement group came under Canadian Military Headquarters in London. For its accommodation, it looked to the miserly clerks of the British barrack services, for training areas and ranges to Aldershot Command, for air raid protection to the local ARP organization, for local defence in case of invasion, the local British field commander. With all this Gault could cope, but he became increasingly frustrated by the indifferent quality of the individuals with whom he had to deal.

Well-trained officers and NCOs were in critically short supply; few were assigned to the reinforcement organization. Instead Gault had a mixture of elderly militia officers and others unfit for service in the field, leavened by a few officers attached from field units. It was over twenty years since the last war had ended: those who had served in it were out-of-date. Others were inadequately trained, had never experienced the hard life of a soldier and knew little of military administration. Knowing no better, they tended to opt for the easy life, took every opportunity to get out of barracks and, in the process, served as poor examples to the young officers and soldiers entrusted to their care.

Through his own example, combined with frequent talks to his officers and constant supervision, Hammie worked tirelessly to improve this state of affairs.

From the nature of their function, the Holding Units soon came to comprise three types of officers and men: those keen to join their parent regiments, those unfit to do so, and the dross of the army whom no one wanted. Lacking the cohesion and equipment of the battalions they were designed to reinforce, Gault's units were limited in the amount of realistic training which they could conduct. In this they matched their predecessors of the First World War, a situation with which he was all too familiar.

Officers who served under him attested to the high standards which he demanded in their care of their men, his eye for detail, and his constant striving for realism in training.

As in the First World War, field commanders were loud in their complaints that their reinforcements were inadequately trained. Major-General Price Montague, the commander of Canadian base units in Britain, invited that formidable warrior, Major-General G.R. Pearkes, VC, DSO, MC, GOC of the 1st Canadian Division, to see for himself how training was conducted within the holding units.

We had some 6 hellish hours yesterday of George Randolph Pearkes raising hell about training . . .

Price told me quietly that his wife was being buried that afternoon . . . He's a funny old stick in many ways, hard as the devil in some ways, but very human and dependent on friendship and sympathy in others. I couldn't say much to him when he told me, as we were on G.R.'s tour of inspection, so wrote to him last night. . . .

Yesterday of course, with G.R. storming round, everything was about as bad to my eye as it could be. One unit which has been turning out good guards had about the worst looking lot of ragamuffins I've ever seen on duty and worse still did not know their stuff. The new New Guard which, in the distance looked much better, G.R. never glanced at. Then where a squad was doing bayonet fighting, the lads, who weren't doing the exercises too badly, hadn't had their hair cut for months and spoiled it all by looking frowsy. Thank God the last platoon in training which he inspected was in the gym: this was good, looked good and apparently favourably impressed the GOC 1st Canadian Div – can't you see it all? Old George out for trouble, storming at everybody and raising hell!

During November Dorothy was on duty in London where Hammie found her at her ambulance station shortly before her tour of duty ended.

From now on you must go slower and take better care of yourself – if not for yourself, then for me. You look tired and undernourished, so hurry up and get fat and 'fresh' looking. No wonder you're tired! . . .

Here's the address in Germany of one of our ex-Patricia officers of the last war. Will you please arrange to have a parcel sent to him for Christmas, and occasionally thereafter. If not too expensive, we might send the poor mutt one a month.

Hammie's promotion to the rank of colonel was eventually published at the end of November, 1940. There was no leave that Christmas and Dorothy's mother 'Mummy Shuck' and his niece, Anne Sykes, sent him a hamper from Fortnum & Mason.

The servants really did us proud at Christmas and Burley [his batman] had the ante room decorated with coloured streamers, subdued lights and in the corner, a Christmas tree . . . while the Mess staff dished up quite one of the best Christmas dinners of oysters, turtle soup, the smoked salmon, turkey, mince pies, cakes etc., I have ever sat down to . . . Please note the position of the saumon fumée in the menu – alas the steward (!) and chef (?) never having seen or heard of it before, and feeling that raw fish must be cooked before being served, produced the delectable food, roti, but for heavens sake don't tell Mummy Shuck or Anne. The servants had meant so well that I didn't have the heart to point out their mistake, but now you know why it is non bon to send such delicacies to the Canadian Army.

In the autumn of 1940, as a draft of reinforcements for the Patricias was preparing to leave Winnipeg for England, two young officers removed the Ric-A-Dam-Doo, the original Colour, from its place of safe keeping. Concealing it in their kit, they carried it to England, their avowed intention being that it should be carried in battle as in the First World War.

The Army did not agree. To it the young men had committed every offence from theft to conduct to the prejudice of good order and military discipline. They were given a harsh sentence which was subject to confirmation by General Montague.

They appealed to Hammie who saw the 'crime' in a different light than the officials who had dealt with it. When he asked Montague to exercise clemency, the former High Court Judge was adamant that an example must be made of the two officers.

Usually a stickler for proper channels, in this case Gault showed that he was not above using an informal approach through Dorothy.

All these damn lawyers are the same – including Price for whom I still have an affection – for the one thing they want is to make a case and show how clever they are regardless of the fact that too much legality does not always make for justice. Anyhow, when and where you get the chance to press for clemency and the expungement of the award on the grounds that these gallant young gentlemen may be giving their lives any day now for King and Country – and it would be a great gesture to show that they are forgiven by the damn fool military authorities, who have in this instance lost their humour and sense of proportion, before they are called to face their Maker — – Have you got me Steve? Anyhow it's all a bloody jumble and, if I press the matter further, I let Price down, and if I don't, I let the boys down, so I'm 'twixt the devil and the deep sea – Price being the devil and rather on the defensive high court of justice plane!

Montague was a fairly frequent visitor to Hatch where Dorothy kept open house for friends in the Canadian services and she sometimes saw him in London. Whether she was able to appeal to him is not known, but the incident shows the lengths to which Hammie would go to support his regiment.

In the following August Hammie attended a lunch given by General McNaughton for Prime Minister Mackenzie King before a Canadian Army Sports Meet.

> The PM was most affable to yours truly and reminded me of our regular Christmas cards of old – I gave him a lot of marks for the personal touch in a big DO. . . . I got the shock of my life and shuddered to the core when the PM was booed on his way out to the microphone by a section of troops. They weren't mine, thank God, and I would gladly have shot them all had I had the chance. . . . MacKenzie King stood up to it and made a damn good speech and quite frankly my opinion of him went up a whole lot as a result.

In the same letter he told Dorothy about Frank Worthington, a former Patricia, now commanding the 1st Canadian Army Tank Brigade.

> Worthington has promised to raid you as soon as he can – he's a very big noise on tanks and goes rabbit shooting with a .22 calibre tube pushed into his 2 inch tank gun. He doesn't kill many rabbits, but he says its grand sport for his gunners and makes it interesting at 30 mile per hour.

There was now a gap in his correspondence with Dorothy until April, 1942. In the interval the Canadian Army in Britain expanded considerably and with it Hammie's group of holding units. With at least three full colonels under his command he was promoted to the rank of brigadier.

Gault's headquarters had moved to a newly built camp at Witley, near Godalming in Surrey. Hammie with his staff lived at nearby Borough Farm. In the meantime Dorothy had been promoted in the Red Cross and was in charge of an ambulance unit at Taunton.

On 19 August the Canadian 2nd Division suffered terrible casualties in its disastrous raid on Dieppe. Hammie had no forewarning of the raid or of a likely need for reinforcements. It was late that day before he learned of the scale of the losses. He had learned in the First World

War how important it was to refill the ranks of a decimated battalion quickly to minimize the shock to its survivors.

He immediately went to the 2nd Division's reinforcement unit and ordered every available man to the stricken battalions. Spurred by his driving presence, the unit came suddenly to life. It was then after supper on a Wednesday, a normal working day, and a stream of men had left camp for the pubs and cinemas of nearby villages.

N.C.O.s and Military Police brought them hurrying back to camp. With a scurrying colonel of the reinforcement unit in tow, Gault visited every section of the unit to speed the process of readying the reinforcements to leave.

After midnight hundreds of men, the drafts for seven regiments, were assembled and inspected. Quietly Hammie told them of the heavy losses in their new units. He advised them to remember that their new comrades would have lost close friends, to keep their comments to themselves and to get on with their new jobs willingly and quietly. Then columns of three ton lorries carried them off in the darkness toward Sussex. The sun had not yet risen when they rendezvoused with guides from their regiments.

About three o'clock one morning in October Hammie climbed from his bed, strapped on his artificial leg and headed for the bathroom. Suddenly it gave way and he fell heavily to the corridor floor, injuring his stump. There he was found, in agony, nearly three hours later by Lieutenant Stuart Graham. While waiting for an ambulance, Graham asked his Brigadier why he had not called for help. Hammie glowered at him, 'You young fellows need your sleep!'

The stump was broken. Gault spent several weeks in Bramshott Hospital in great pain, then pneumonia developed and for a time his life was in danger. Gradually he recovered enough strength to be sent home to Hatch to convalesce but weeks went by before he could wear his artificial limb.

To be idle when there was a war on was anathema. While a new commander of the reinforcement group had been appointed, Gault hoped that he might be found another job. But at sixty the cards were against him; a medical board found him unfit for further service. Viewed dispassionately, the inevitability of his retirement from the Army could be foreseen, but for a man so mentally alert, so competent in the profession of arms and so confident in his ability to overcome physical handicaps, it was a bitter blow.

Chapter 21

SIDELINED

Hammie and Dorothy saw eye to eye on most things and she was his closest confidante. Believing that she knew how much he had suffered from his war wounds and from the frustrations of being partly disabled, of the emotional traumas caused by the death of Kathleen and by Marguerite, of the sensitivity which lay behind his robust and confident exterior, she was quick to protect him from further illness or injury. When he fell in the hunting field, she was the first at his side.

She often wrote of her fears for his health and cautioned him to take care of himself. When in December, 1941, after nearly a year and a half of crushingly hard work in command of the holding units, he had a succession of colds and was showing signs of strain, she wrote,

> Darling I'm more than worried about you being so seedy. I can't help it. It's quite natural that I should be. If you don't get down here this week, I'm coming right up to you and shall stand on the doorstep until you come home with me. I know that you're busy with reorganization, but you will do far better after a rest. I feel so far away and helpless and useless and miserable and if I can't be any more of a wife than this I am certainly going to Libya.
>
> For heaven's sake be careful now and don't get a relapse or you'll be a complete wreck and not a bit of good to anyone.

Shortly after Hammie left the army, Edwin Leather, a young officer in the Royal Canadian Horse Artillery, spent a leave at Hatch. One morning he accompanied the Gaults to Bridgwater to buy a new pony for Hammie's cart.

> As the three of us stood in a small enclosed yard, one of the animals became excited, for a few seconds out of control. I could never forget those seconds! On the one hand a bucking, kicking horse, a few feet away this huge giant of a man rooted to the ground by his wooden leg, immovable. In a flash this comparatively tiny woman leapt between him and the frightened animal to protect

his body with her own. Hammie roared with indignation at her rashness! D.B. just smiled and gave him one of those looks. It was the nearest I ever saw of that great man to tears.[1]

But sometimes Hammie, so self reliant, found Dorothy's protectiveness irritating, and he would lash out at her verbally with a, 'for God's sake woman!'

From the beginning of the war the doors of Hatch were open to friends in the Canadian Army, many of whom had served with Hammie in the First World War. But he and Dorothy (Blanche), known to army friends as 'DB', took a particular delight in inviting young officers to spend their leave with them. Many were Patricias, but they were quick to invite any young man or woman they met and liked. Often these came at short notice and it was not unusual to see Dorothy, the evening before they arrived, out with her .22 rifle looking for a rabbit to eke out the rations.

Some of their young guests found themselves in awesome company. George Corkett of the Patricias and his wife were invited for Easter, 1940, to find that the other guests were General Harry Crerar and his wife. The future commander of First Canadian Army was then the senior Canadian officer in London and had been the commandant of RMC when George was a cadet. Eileen Corkett commented,

It says something of Hammie and D.B. that we, aged 20 and 23, were made to feel so comfortable and at home amongst our elders and superiors at Hatch which on our first visit, seemed so overwhelmingly beautiful and glorious.

After Dunkirk, the Patricias were warned to join the 2nd BEF which was to re-enter France through Brest. Corkett arranged for Eileen to return to Canada and she spent a week at Hatch before sailing. En route to Falmouth the Regiment bivouacked nearby.

Late in the afternoon, there was a knock at the door and to everyone's surprise, there was George. Just before dinner, Hammie, in his magnificent parade ground voice, bellowed up the stairs 'Corky do you like champagne?' Of course we called down 'Yes' without thinking about it. Later he apologized for shouting but he didn't want to serve it if we didn't like it – but he felt the occasion should be celebrated. Later I learned that that was almost the last champagne in the cellar! For us! . . . George left in the morning.

237

In 1943 Eileen Corkett returned to England with the Canadian Red Cross. George, seconded to the Coldstream Guards in North Africa, had been wounded, returned to England and convalesced at Hatch where D.B. looked after him and changed his dressings.

By 1943 Hatch could not be run as it had been. Mills, the butler, the footman and even Rogers the parlourmaid had gone. Only the Barnetts of the eleven evacuees we'd known before were there. Hammie helped everywhere. He insisted on washing the dishes because he liked that better than drying and besides he said he was good at it. We had a good time talking and laughing as we worked. I wondered how there could be so many dishes to dry and realized that we were not well organized as he was picking up and re-washing the things I'd just dried. How he laughed! It was there that he showed me the 'butler's thumb' for polishing silver. It's amusing to remember such a man for showing how to touch up a bit of tarnish on the silver by rubbing your thumb on it![2]

Even during the war Hammie and Dorothy continued to give parties for the children of their friends. Among these were Lord and Lady Portman and their two daughters, Rosemary and Sheila, who lived at Staple Fitzpaine, some three miles from Hatch. One day in 1943 Hammie drove over to visit them in his pony trap. Sheila later wrote:

(Rosemary) had a goat called Topsy who used to come into the house where Hammie was sitting in an armchair. She would put her forefeet on his lap and nibble his moustache. On one of these occasions my sister had made a goat's milk cheese and presented it to Hammie.
This was his reply:
'Oh Topsy, dear Topsy, your cheese was divine
And Oh! How I wish that your mistress were mine.
For with Topsy & Rosemary life would be sweet,
And there'd always, yes always be plenty to eat.'[3]

Gault kept in close touch with the Patricias while they were in England and never failed to be with them on regimental occasions such as Frezenberg Day. He was always available to Shorty Colquhoun and later commanding officers who frequently sought his advice about welfare and other regimental affairs. Probably his most enjoyable link with the Regiment came with the visits of junior officers to Hatch, with some of whom he formed friendships which lasted the rest of his life.

First among these was Cameron Ware who had met him in Winnipeg in May,1939, and had come to England for training courses before the outbreak of war. Hammie not only found him congenial but sensed in him the qualities which make the ideal infantry officer. In time he came to regard him almost as the son he never had.

In the first months of 1943, while Hammie was convalescing, the Regiment trained hard for unspecified offensive operations: significantly, they spent weeks in Scotland learning the techniques of amphibious operations. In June, as far as Hammie was concerned, they disappeared. Then on 10 July came word of the Allied invasion of Sicily followed by news that the Patricias had been one of the assaulting battalions. They had had few casualties and were advancing into the interior.

Cam Ware was second-in-command when, early in the Sicilian campaign, the Patricias took part in a difficult attack which had to be postponed because their supporting tanks arrived late. Flailing about for a scapegoat, their brigade commander, Chris Vokes, unjustly fired Lieutenant-Colonel Bob Lindsay.[4] Ware succeeded him.

Gault followed the Regiment's fortunes in Sicily and Italy as closely as newspapers and heavily censored letters from his friends, particularly Ware, allowed him. While confident that they would perform well, he nonetheless was reassured by the news that they were operating with the same efficiency and élan which had been their hallmarks in the First World War.

Because of censorship, Ware could not tell him where the Regiment was operating, but, coupled with press reports, Hammie knew when they had been in the thick of such hard-fought and costly battles as the capture of Ortona and the breakthrough of the Hitler Line. Whenever he could, he helped expedite the flow of 'comforts' – the extra woollens, food delicacies and cigarettes – which eased the lot of the soldier in the line. Generous as ever, he sent gifts of cigarettes for every man each Christmas.

Ware later commented that Hammie kept track of everybody. As an example, when Rex Carey, a lieutenant, was captured on the Moro River, Hammie wrote, 'I do hope Rex Carey will turn up. I like the cut of his jib.' He referred to Carey again from time to time.[5] Ware commented, 'Carey did the usual (for a Patricia officer) – he escaped and got within the sound of our guns, but was captured again'.

But as always, Gault's main concern was the fighting prowess of the Regiment. There was little he could do to influence it from such a distance. In his lonely position of command, Ware valued Hammie's advice and reassurance. The initial Canadian drive up Italy ended in late October,1943, when they went into billets and established a divisional leave centre at Campobasso. After a few days of rest, Ware saw signs of them becoming too relaxed. He began a programme of intensive training for the Patricias. Hammie commented,

> You're damn well right in laying down to the troops that second best is no good for us. Whatever the other blokes do, we must always strive for the perfect – discipline, physical fitness, efficiency, morale – the perfect fighting machine.[6]

In March, 1944, Gault congratulated Cammie Ware on being awarded the DSO. He ended his letter with an unprecedented admission of his frustrations,

> I hope that you boys will finish things up as they should be finished before long and so enable me to regain a little of my one-time self-respect, for to tell the truth, I'm absolutely browned off nowadays with nothing to do – but, mark thee, with no complaints at all.[7]

During his political career and later, Gault had been in the habit of noting quips, sayings, morals and his own thoughts on scraps of paper which he kept for use in speeches. After he was injured in 1942 he had more time for reflection and began to record some of these in a notebook. A few are well-known quotations but most are original.

They reveal an honest man, an elitist, distressed by the behaviour of others less forthright than himself, and frustrated by his inability to play a more significant part in events. Even more, they reflect a change in the focus of the patriotism which was so central to his life.

His first maxim was set alone on the first page: 'To thine own self be true, and it must follow, as the night the day, thou canst not then be false to any man.'[8]

Another: 'It is not sufficient to live in the magnificence of past history, history must continue to be made and the splendour of the future created by present endeavour.'

The next reflected his love of nature: 'God has given man a most beautiful world in which to live. It is only man that turns it into a veritable hell.'

Military ones were pungent: 'If present day officers thought as much of fighting and killing as they do of promotion and pay, the war would be nearer its end.'

'Soldiers are not made by dressing up civilians in khaki.'

'There should be no respect for power unless it is used with wisdom and justice.'

'I will serve in any capacity where I am wanted, but will never join the lists of climbers.'

He was disenchanted with politicians: 'Long corridors of waiting, whispering, watchers wondering which way the cat will jump.'

'Socialism is the political term for mass robbery.'

'A gentleman is at a considerable disadvantage in a society ruled by thugs.'

Under the heading of 'Personal', he revealed the rankling hurt inflicted upon him by Marguerite:

'A thought arising out of the abdication of King Edward VIII: "No woman is worth a broken career or a wasted life" (from one who knows!) 10 Dec 36'

'One can go to the courts for law, but not always for justice.'

Gault was born into a family and society which was fiercely loyal to the King, to Canada, and to the British Empire of which it was a part. To him the Empire was a partnership of self-governing countries with the England from which it had grown, first among equals, at its centre. The indifference of British politicians to the Imperial idea had been brought home to him during his career in Parliament. He was now suffering the familiar disillusionment of the overseas British when they discover of what little consequence their concerns appear to be to the United Kingdom.

'This England to which I came with feelings of admiration, respect and love, and which I shall sometime leave with some admiration, a little respect, but no love.'

'I like great Britishers, not little Englanders.'

He had also come to recognize the shallowness of the lives led by many of the people he knew: 'The life of an English country gentleman is an existence for a louse, not a man.

Did he regret the career that he might have had in Canada?

'The Gaul is lost who goes to Rome.'

Having been used to such an active life, Hammie now could no longer ride or fly: driving through the Somerset lanes in a cart pulled by a fat little pony was a poor substitute. His business affairs and the management of the Hatch Court estate were in the hands of others. War-time restrictions prevented travel. He began to think longingly of the beauty and freedom of The Mountain at St Hilaire.

When he learned that if he remained in England he would be subject to the savage British income tax, it tipped the scale – he decided to return to Canada . On 25 September, 1944, he and Dorothy sailed in the *Queen Mary* for New York.

Chapter 22

HOME

Much as he loved his mountain, there was no practical possibility of Hamilton Gault living beside its lovely lake until the last winter of the war had passed, nor could he decide on the future pattern of his life until peace returned. Though less well known to the general public than he once had been, his name and reputation as a vote-getter were certainly known to the leaders of John Bracken's Progressive Conservative party. In the late spring of 1945 when a general election was called, Hammie was offered the nomination as their candidate in his choice of two ridings in Montreal.

On 24 May, 1945, he wrote to Cam Ware,

> I nearly got myself involved in this forthcoming election, but as the call came at the eleventh hour and the deputations couldn't give me the answers to any of my questions (including finance), I gave it a miss. I'm not sure whether to be sorry or glad that I'm not in the fray for I'd love to get my teeth into the meat of life again, but it's a fool idea to take on a battle before you've got your information and been able to arrange your dispositions.

The Gaults had taken a restored farmhouse on the Lake of Two Mountains – metre thick stone walls, floors of 14 inch planks, the inside walls panelled in 18th century white pine. Over the doors, cut deep into the stone, were the words, 'The Cross and Heart of Christ', above the date, 1816.

In a letter to Mary Cunningham, Hammie wrote,

> I've never had a 'close up' of a Canadian election before, but it's the most Heath Robinson affair you ever saw in your life. From everything being left to the last moment to the candidate giving perhaps three addresses – two to small audiences, driven together by curiosity or some other extraneous desire, and one over the local radio. I can't see democracy ever working except where a people take their politics seriously and are sufficiently soundly educated to

distinguish between merit and fraud. In consequence of declining to stand merely because no one could answer any of my casual questions, I've probably saved the equivalent of a few thousand pounds, for I would have been beaten in French Canadian Montreal! . . .

How I wish this idiotic country of mine was one with you in England but I fear the ideals of the Imperialists of my generation will never now be realized. The only thing now is to pull together, and this is not going to be too easy with different economic orbits, different exchanges and currencies and different races pulling this way and that. . . .

The Rivière des Prairies flows fifty yards away and the heavens and trees are full of bird life from the Canadian robin . . . and ubiquitous swallow to red wing, bobolink, meadow lark, the white-throated sparrow (a misnomer) who calls 'Poor Can-a-da, Can-a-da, Can-a-da', the golden and Baltimore orioles, the latter with its fiery orange plumage, and a host of others . . .

We're down now on the Madeleine after the wily salmon. The river is lovely, quite one of the most lovely I've ever been on, with its crystal clear pale green waters whirling down to the sea in little falls and rapids between dogwood and alder backed by spruce, cedar, maple and mountain ash, stretching up the steep sides of the high hills of the Gaspé. [We fish] from long, rakish Gaspé canoes (22 feet in length) which the canoemen pole up the rapids and carry round the falls – a lazy way of fishing which suits me down to the ground. Here and there one can wade but the wading pools are very limited. Myriads of gold and black butterflies are about and of course, the mosquito which in the Gaspé grows to the size of a humming bird and hums louder![1]

In January, 1944, the Patricias had left Italy for North-west Europe where they took part in the liberation of Holland. After the German surrender a new battalion of the Regiment was formed in Canada to fight the Japanese. Many veterans of the European campaign volunteered to join it; others stayed with the army of occupation in Germany. On 1 October the remainder arrived in Halifax where two trains took them on to Winnipeg. On the way the men were given leave passes for thirty days and told to report back at the end of it for demobilization. A huge crowd was assembled to meet them at the station. There was no attempt at formality – the battalion simply disappeared into the arms of its welcomers. Hammie met them there a month later, after their leave, to thank them and wish them well.

With the end of the war, the Patricias were reorganized as a battalion of the new Canadian Regular Army with Cameron Ware in command. He wrote to Gault about some of his problems, including the selection of officers.

Hammie commented,

I agree with Allenby when he said that of the military virtues, he placed character ahead of either brains or experience. Your second-in-command, adjutant, quartermaster and regimental sergeant major must be men of character and worth. If not, they won't be worth a damn to you and they'll be bound to let you down sooner or later.[2]

He and Dorothy spent the winter at the Ritz Carlton in Montreal. Although he had not taken part in the June,1945, election, he joined the Progressive Conservative party. At an organizational meeting of the St Lawrence – St George Division, he called for the leadership to issue a clear statement of policy, declaring that no candidate has a right to ask his constituents to sign a blank cheque. He would not support any party until he knew what it stood for,

Bluntly he told them that the result of the last election in the Division was no better than it should have been. Their party had managed the election badly – matters that should have been attended to months before were left to the eleventh hour.[3]

He was edging into public affairs. In April he was elected president of the Canadian Red Cross Society in Montreal and, later, of the Montreal branch of the Royal Empire Society.

In 1946 he told Ware that he and Dorothy were going to England in April for the wedding of their niece, Anne Sykes, after which, in May, they would move to the Mountain for the summer months to discover if they liked the prospect well enough to settle there for the remainder of their lives. The alternative would be to return to Hatch,[4]

and probably go broke under the existing regulations within two years. Of course, if I could find a job here in Canada, nothing would induce me to return to England, but as far as I can make out, the brave new world has no place in it for me.

As Ware later commented,

'He was the largest single shareholder in the Bank of Montreal, which isn't small potatoes, but apart from directorships, he really found nothing in Canada.'[5]

While in London for the Sykes wedding, Dorothy was the victim of a bizarre medical accident. To her mother she had appeared pale and singularly lacking in energy. Mrs Shuckburgh advised 'colonic irrigation,' a treatment fashionable at the time. While undergoing it, her bowel was ruptured. In agony, she was rushed to the London Clinic: on the operating table, she nearly died. More than once the doctors thought they had lost her and were amazed that she rallied.

For weeks her life remained in danger. Hammie wrote to Ware,

Of D.B.'s desperate illness I have told you. The situation remains about the same, although these past few days the mean temperature has shown a slight improvement: if this can be maintained, a second operation, we pray, will not be necessary. It has been a long vigil with D.B. putting up a gallant fight throughout. With God's mercy, and her own indomitable courage she's going to pull through alright, but the SHADOW has loomed large at times during these past two months.

When they returned to the Mountain in the autumn, they were still undecided as to where they should build their house. Only by living there for a year could they see the effect of the changing seasons on the views and angles of light. As a start they picked a site for a cottage in which they could 'camp'. It would not be ready before the spring of 1947.

During one of their frequent visits, Hammie was walking along a wilderness path when he met a stranger who, in hushed tones, told him that this was private property and he must be careful not to let *le gardien* know he was there or he would be told to leave. Hammie thanked him for the warning and they both agreed it was a beautiful place to walk.

Eventually he and DB decided that the cottage was on the ideal site for the house. It was moved and they commissioned an architect to design a stone manor house in the Quebec style.

In October, 1947, Gault flew to Calgary to see the Patricias for the first time in their new home. He was greatly impressed by what he found – a well equipped battalion of regular soldiers with good morale and a sense of purpose. He and Dorothy, with her mother, spent that winter in the warmth of Barbados.

Since Hammie's wayward ward, Patricia, married Rex Hoyes in 1935, he had had virtually no communication with her. During the war he learned that an airfield had been built at Marwell, their estate, and from mutual friends that Pat continued to live there, but he knew few details.

The airfield served as a satellite to that of a very large aircraft factory at Eastleigh, the approaches to which were difficult because of the balloon barrage around Southampton. Hangars were built at Marwell for the modification of American medium bombers and Cobra fighters for the RAF, and for the conversion of Spitfires to Seafires for the Royal Navy. It also became a test field used by several organizations under the Air Ministry. Pat, duly qualified, was its air controller until the Air Ministry promoted her to manage the airfield, which she did for three years.

By 1944 the various test and conversion activities at the field had ceased. Shortly after D Day, Air Chief Marshal Sir Arthur Tedder, Eisenhower's Deputy, and his wife invited Pat to come to Normandy to open 'Malcolm Clubs' for the airmen of the 2nd Tactical Air Force, patterned on those which Lady Tedder had formed during the North African campaign. Pat leapt at the chance. The clubs were a great success and for her efforts in North-west Europe she was awarded an MBE.

Later, after the German surrender, she moved to Cairo to supervise all the clubs in the vast Middle East Command. By 1948 her work was done and she returned to England. There, in London, she met a neighbour, Brigadier Tom McCarthy, who to her surprise turned out to be a friend of Dorothy Gault's. A warm invitation to Hatch swiftly followed.

Hammie welcomed her with the same warmth he had always shown, never referred to her marriages and was tremendously proud of her achievements. In March,1949, with his unreserved blessing, she married Tom McCarthy.[6]

Gault was now in his late 60s, a time when most men have retired from business or the professions. His sister Lillian's son, Clive Benson, had come out from England to manage his business affairs and he had accepted that it was too late for him to embark upon another career. He and Dorothy with their two Bedlingtons lived happily on the mountain from early spring to the late autumn each year, followed by winters in England and by the Mediterranean.

While most of the St Hilaire estate was wilderness, it included orchards which Hammie proceeded to develop. The project was not a success. By 1952 his losses over the previous four years amounted to $6,000 and he threatened to allow the orchards to revert to primeval forest if they failed to become profitable soon.[7]

When he came to Montreal from the mountain, Hammie made his headquarters at the Ritz. One hot day in August, he telephoned Rowan Coleman, a distinguished Patricia officer, then Registrar of McGill, to meet him there. Together they drove out to the mountain in Gault's Cadillac to look at the orchards, Hammie driving it like a steeplechaser. Bumping up a rocky track, Coleman feared that they would be hung up on a boulder and the car damaged, but Gault had a fine sense of its capabilities. They arrived at the cottage unscathed.

Standing by the lake while Dorothy was cooking supper, Hammie said 'Let's go for a swim', whereupon he peeled off his clothes to the bare buff, unstrapped his leg and plunged in. Coleman hesitated, feeling rather shy as he had not done such a thing since he was a boy, but felt he had to conform. As he followed into the lake, he was struck by the power of Gault's Australian crawl.

About 50 yards from shore Hammie bumped a beer bottle, floating in the water. He roared with rage and cursed at the miscreant who had besmirched his lake. He then reared up and threw it onto the shore. It was an awesome demonstration of physical power by a man nearing 70.[8]

Gault remained an active supporter of the Conservatives and attended their 1948 convention in Ottawa. His interest in politics was now related to policies and to returning the Party to power rather than to thoughts of office for himself. Occasionally he wrote letters to the papers, sometimes fighting a rearguard action for the idea of Empire. In May,1945, he advocated national flags for Canada and the other independent countries of the British Commonwealth, based upon the Union Jack with the heraldic arms of the country superimposed upon its centre.[9]

In December,1949, he cautioned against moves to sever the ties which bound Canada to the Empire in the name of a sovereignty which, in large measure, she already possessed. In an uncertain world, Canada had neither the military nor economic strength to stand alone. No country could join a group of others for mutual defence or economic cooperation without sacrificing some of its freedom to do as it sees fit, in effect, a portion of its sovereignty. This Canada had already done by joining NATO.

But of late the clamour for sovereignty has risen to such an extent that many are wondering where our country is heading, more particularly, when in an age of power politics we have no adequate forces for its support and maintenance, should the ties of tradition and sentiment, which have bound together the greatest civilization since the Roman Empire, be abrogated. . . .

Are we soon to be asked to drop the Crown and stand alone in a world where sovereignty without power means nothing? Such a course would be disastrous to our young nationhood which seems to stand today at the cross roads. Whither are we going? To be an isolated minor power is unthinkable and impractical.[10]

In 1951 he wrote a long closely argued letter to the *Montreal Gazette* on the dangers of inflation which was copied by many papers across the country as well as in England.[11]

But his abiding interest remained his Regiment. When he visited Calgary in 1947, he presided at the founding meeting of the PPCLI Regimental Association which brought together the Patricia Clubs which had existed since the First World War in cities across the country and in England.

A year later the Patricias were converted to a parachute battalion, charged with responsibility for operations in the Arctic. On a hot June day Hammie watched a company parachute onto the Sarcee Training Area, envying its young men their new military activity in which he could not join.[12]

With the outbreak of the Korean War in 1950 the Regiment was rapidly increased to three battalions, each of which in turn fought with distinction in that strange battleground. At its end, Gault was well satisfied that they had upheld the fighting traditions of the Regiment.

In 1953 the 2nd Patricias moved to Germany, being relieved there two years later by the 1st. In September,1956, Hammie visited them at Fort Macleod, their barracks near the village of Deilinghofen on the eastern outskirts of the Ruhr. From there, with a guard from the Regiment and a group of its veterans, he drove to Frezenberg.

On the right of the line which he had held in 1915 he planted a maple tree around which, later, a memorial was erected. Three of the 'Originals' joined him, Hugh Niven who had commanded the remnants of the Regiment on that terrible day, Colonel Pearson and Sergeant H.F. O'Connor. They found it difficult to recognize the battlefield of 1915 in the green, softly undulating Bellewaerde and Frezenberg ridges. It was easier to sense the link between the immaculate guard of honour from the Regiment and the battle-worn Patricias who fought there 42 years before.

That same year the Regimental Depot moved into a new home in Edmonton – The Hamilton Gault Barracks.

In the autumn of 1957, as Gault's new house was nearing completion, it was set afire and the interior destroyed. Gault professed to believe that it was an accident:

> I must admit that the loss to fire of the new house came as a bit of a shock, as well as a surprise to this old and ancient couple who had been deprived of a house for so many years. . . . How it happened, nobody knows, but the labour and the thought of a good many years went up in smoke and flame in a very few hours. I am particularly grieved for the workmen, superintendents, contractors, architects and all concerned who were taking so much interest and putting so much effort into the undertaking.

He showed no bitterness but simply ordered rebuilding to begin at once.[13]

In the spring of 1958 Gault flew to western Canada to be with the 1st Battalion in Esquimalt and the 2nd in Edmonton for their Frezenberg celebrations.

Some years earlier, Hammie had decided that, in the public interest, his unique 2200 acres of mountain wilderness at St. Hilaire should be preserved intact. Being so close to burgeoning Montreal, it lay under the threat of despoliation by property developers, yet for the same reason, its value as a naturalist's paradise and an area for public recreation was immense. Before he revised his will in 1957, he obtained the agreement of McGill University that they would accept his gift of the estate and would observe the conditions he imposed upon its use.

He had not been well during his visit to the Regiment and when he returned to Montreal, he learned that he had only a limited time to live. Faced with the inevitability of early death, in August, 1958, he gave the estate to the University, reserving the house and a small area for private use for the remainder of his life. In the letter accompanying the donation, he wrote:

> The mountain of St Hilaire is my most treasured possession and in offering it to McGill it is with the hope that its beauties and amenities may be preserved for all time to come, not only in the interests of the University itself, but through its corridors of learning, as a great heritage for the benefit and enjoyment of the youth of Canada.

250

Such contacts with the peace and beauty of nature should be an influence towards the better and selfless citizenship on which the future of Canada depends, and it is with this thought in mind, and in the hope that my gift may be to the glory of God and to the honour of our country, that I offer it for acceptance to McGill.

'Museums take many forms, but the finest of all surely is the conservation of a natural habitat', was but one of the reactions of the University to what elsewhere they described as this 'startling gift'. They decided to divide the property into two sections, one to be used for public recreation and a programme of nature study and conservation for schools; the other was to be left as the last stand of virgin Canadian wilderness within easy reach of Montreal, for scientific study and observation.[14]

In 1960 it became a migratory bird sanctuary and in 1978 was designated by UNESCO as Canada's first Biosphere Reserve.

Late in summer of 1958 Hammie and Dorothy moved into their new house which he now dubbed 'Gault's Folly'. In September the value to the Army of the honorary position he had held for so long in the Regiment was formally recognized when he was appointed 'Colonel of the Regiment' of Princess Patricia's Canadian Light Infantry. He wrote to Cammie Ware:

I have formally and tentatively accepted the invitation contained in the Adjutant General's letter to become the first Colonel of the Regiment . . . but only if it is the Regiment's desire that I should do so. In accepting, . . . I think I ought to tell you, in the strictest confidence, that, to use racing parlance, 'my number has gone up on the board' (cancer of the right lung) and that although the end may not be imminent, from now on, according to my doctors, it will be a 'rearguard action' as far as I am concerned. They tell me that at my age, the disease is apt to move on slowly, and that it may take a year or so, more or less, before the inevitability of life occurs. No commiserations please as it is all in the day's work and time is racing on. *Toujours prêt* has always seemed to me to be a good motto: I've sometimes thought I'd like to see the Regiment adopting it! All this of course means that I shall get less and less fit as time rolls on and that in accepting the first Colonelcy of the Patricias, it can only be for a short or intervening period until my successor – who, please God, will be you – is appointed . . .

We have formally and provisionally moved into Gault's Folly, but alas the workmen have not yet moved out and I expect it will take another couple of months before poor old D.B. gets things sorted out.[15]

In the middle of November Ware flew from Calgary to have the new Colonel of the Regiment sign a special order of the day to mark his appointment. He stayed with the Gaults in their new-found comfort on the mountain. That night it was black tie for dinner and Hammie, though much weakened, was his cheerful and ebullient self. On 22 November he wrote an enthusiastic letter to Roy Stevens, congratulating and thanking him on his third volume of the Patricia's Regimental History. It was very much in Gault's style:

> Thank God you are inclined to understatement, so that your mentions of the magnificent episodes of bravery of individual officers, NCO's and men in the battle of the Hitler Line reads like the epic it was . . . I'm still as weak as the proverbial cat in hell, but look forward to seeing you here next week.

On the 28th he died.

With the Regiment thousands of miles away in western Canada they were unable to bury their Founder and Colonel as they would have liked, though his military funeral in Montreal was impressive enough. After a service in the Gault family church, St George's, he was borne on a gun carriage behind a military band to the cemetery on Mount Royal, followed by officers of the Regiment and other military mourners who had flown in from across the country.

The Governor-General and the Minister of National Defence were honorary pall bearers. It was not made clear whether they were there in an official or a personal capacity, for Georges Vanier and George Pearkes were both old friends. Warrant officers of the Regiment bore his body into the crematorium and its buglers sounded the Last Post and the Rouse. Later Dorothy carried his ashes to England where they are buried in the ancient church beside Hatch Court.

Two of Hamilton Gault's contributions to Canada, the founding of its most famous regiment and the conservation and gift of his wilderness estate, reflect an instinct, deeply rooted within him, to preserve and protect the nation and the land from which it grew. That, through inherited wealth, he was able to satisfy it in a way that others could not, does not lessen the generosity and concern for the public good which lay behind his actions. For these he has been honoured, if inadequately, by his countrymen.

His third contribution is more difficult to quantify. For most of his life he gave himself to the service of his country and his fellow men. As a Member of Parliament in England working for the closer integration of the Empire and its defence, even as consul-general for Sweden, he believed that he was serving Canada's interests. His philanthropy, his work for ex-servicemen are part of it. All these activities were commendable but not necessarily the stuff of greatness.

But it is the gift of something less tangible that is preserved in the hearts of men: his example of what a citizen and a soldier should be. That he was selfless, brave, generous and humane, that he was imaginative and assiduous in his work, that he strove for perfection and cared for his men were but the underlying elements of his quality.

His massive integrity and towering personality raised him above other men. He could speak to students, young soldiers or the most cynical of veterans about their heritage as citizens, about the honour of the Regiment and the Army, of the military virtues of honesty, selflessness and duty, and not only would they listen but they would believe him.

As its Founder, he is revered by his Regiment: in the gift of himself, he is an exemplar for the nation.

BIBLIOGRAPHY

Unpublished Sources

At Hatch Court, Somerset, the Hamilton Gault papers
At Princess Patricia's Canadian Light Infantry Archives, Calgary, the Gault
and other contemporary files, the Ware papers
At the National Archives of Canada, Ottawa, the Adamson, Borden and
Papineau papers
At Inverey House, Scotland, Lady Patricia Ramsay's papers and photo-
graph albums
At the Riksarkivet, Stockholm, Swedish Foreign Ministry files related to
Gault and the Consulate in Montreal

Official Histories

The History of the War in South Africa 1899–1902
Duguid, Colonel A.F., *Official History of the Canadian Forces in the Great
War, 1914–19, Vol 1.*
Nicholson, Colonel G.W.L., *The Canadian Expeditionary Force, 1914–19*
Edmonds, Brigadier-General J.E., *Official History of the Great War, Military
Operations France and Belgium – 1915 Vol 1 and 1916 Vol 1*

Public Documents

At the National Archives of Canada
Parliamentary sessional paper No.35a – 1903, 2–3 Edward VII –
*Organization, Equipment, Despatch and Service of Canadian Contingents
during The War In South Africa 1899–1902* – Col. Evans final report to
the Adjutant General and the Staff Diary of 2 CMR.

War Diaries, 1915 –18
Headquarters 3rd Canadian Division
Headquarters 7th Canadian Infantry Brigade

Princess Patricia's Canadian Light Infantry
3rd Divisional Wing, Canadian Corps Reinforcement Camp
Castell Hopkins, *Canadian Annual Review of Public Affairs, 1902*

At the Public Record Office, Kew
War Diaries, 1914–18
Headquarters 27th Division
Headquarters 80th Brigade

Published Sources

Chambers, E. J., *The 5th Regiment, Royal Scots of Canada,* 1904
Chisholm, Anne and Davie, Michael, *Beaverbrook, A Life,* 1992
Dundonald, Earl of, *My Army Life,* 1926
Deutelmoser, Adolf, *The 27th Infantry Division in the World War,* 1925
Frankland, Noble, *Witness of a Century, The Life and Times of Prince Arthur Duke of Connaught,* 1993
Fraser, S.B., *McGill University, Vol. 2, 1895–1971,* 1984
Fromm, Bella, *Blood & Banquets. A Berlin Social Diary,* 1990
Frost, Sydney, *Once a Patricia,* 1988
Gwyn, Sandra, *Tapestry of War,* 1992
Hodder-Williams, Ralph, *Princess Patricia's Canadian Light Infantry, 1914–1919, Vols. 1 and 2,* 1923
Howard, Oswald, *The Montreal Diocesan Theological College,* 1963
Hubbard, R.A., *Rideau Hall,* 1977
Hutchinson, Paul P., *Canada's Black Watch,* 1962
   Five Strenuous Years
Miller, Carman, *'No Surrender' : The Battle of Hart's River,* 1991
   The Canadian Career of the Fourth Earl of Minto 1980
Pakenham, Thomas, *The Boer War,* 1979
Ricard, Abbé Ant., *Vie de Monseigneur Jean-Baptiste Gault,* 1864
Stevens, G.R., *Princess Patricia's Canadian Light Infantry, Vol 3*
   A City Goes to War, 1964
Times History of the War in South Africa, 1901–2
Williams, Jeffery, *Byng of Vimy, General and Governor-General,* 1983
   Princess Patricia's Canadian Light Infantry, 1972

NOTES

Abbreviations:

Adamson – Adamson papers in National Archives of Canada, Manuscript Group 30 – E149. Unless otherwise noted, indicates letters from Lt-Col Agar Adamson to his wife Mabel.

AHG – letter to or from Andrew Hamilton Gault contained in Gault papers

Gault – Gault papers at Hatch Court, Somerset

NARC – National Archives of Canada, Ottawa

PRO – Public Record Office, Kew

PSP 35 – Parliamentary sessional paper No.35a – 1903, 2–3 Edward VII – *Organization, Equipment, Despatch and Service of Canadian Contingents during The War In South Africa 1899–1902*

Papineau – Talbot Papineau papers in NARC, Manuscript Group 30 – E52. Unless otherwise noted, indicates letters from Talbot Papineau to his mother

RAS – Riksarkivet Stockholm, Swedish Foreign Ministry File

Ware – Ware papers in PPCLI Archives, Calgary

Chapter 1

1 Ricard, Abbé Ant., *Vie de Monseigneur Jean-Baptiste Gault*, Paris, 1864
2 Gault. Undated memo by Mathew Hamilton Gault
3 Mathew Henry Gault account supplied by Howard Marler
4 ibid
5 Biographical sketch of Mathew Hamilton Gault, Founder of the Irish Protestant Benevolent Society supplied by Dr Henry Gault
6 Mathew Henry Gault – Marler
7 Interview with Michael Hinton, biographer of A.F. Gault 12 Oct 1990.
8 Records the Montreal Cemetery Company
9 A.R. Carman in *The Canadian Magazine*, July, 1903. The Château Apartments now stand on the site of Rokeby.

10 AHG to Percival Campbell 15 Jun 06
11 Interview Mrs Doris (Benson) Gadsden 31 Jul 90

Chapter 2

1 Chambers, *The 5th Regiment, Royal Scots of Canada*, p 72
2 NARC. Memoir William Frederick Athawes NARC (MG30 E402).
3 AHG to Campbell 10 Jan 02
4 AHG to Campbell 11 Feb 02
5 ibid.
6 Chambers p 82
7 PSP 35 – Lt-Col Evans' report to Adjutant-General 16 July 1902
8 AHG to Campbell 27 Feb 02 from Kitchener's Kopje, Newcastle, Natal
9 AHG to Campbell 16 Mar 02 from Volksrust, Transvaal
10 ibid.
11 PSP 35 – Staff Diary 2 CMR.
12 PSP 35 – Staff Diary 2 CMR.

Chapter 3

1 30 July 02
2 12 Aug 02
3 14 Aug 02
4 Chambers, p 85
5 *Montreal Daily Star* 16 Mar 04
6 Hutchinson, *Five Strenuous Years*.
7 *Canada Monthly* Nov 1914
8 AHG 28 Oct 04 to Campbell at the Savoy Hotel, San Remo.
9 AHG 15 Dec. 04 to Campbell at Grand Hotel, Grasse, France.
10 AHG 27 Jun 05 to Campbell at Hyde Park Hotel, London
11 AHG 12 May 06 to Campbell, Madrid

Chapter 4

1 RAS 14 Montreal of 2 Apr 09, Gault's duties are outlined in Swedish Royal Ordinance of 1906 concerning the Consular Service
2 RAS 14 Montreal of 15 May 09, de Loynes to Ministry of Foreign Affairs, Stockholm
3 RAS 14 Montreal of 9th and 16th Jan 11
4 RAS 12 A. Hamilton Gault of 13 Nov 12

Chapter 5

1 Gault. As with his Mistassini trip Gault kept a diary of his East African Safari 1912–13 from which this and subsequent quotations in this chapter are drawn

Chapter 6

1 Gault. Letter from G. Ambrose Lee, *York Herald* 6 Jul 11.
2 do 3 Aug 11
3 do 29 Nov 11
4 'Thanks be to God'
5 The record and examination was not sent for judgement until 11 Dec 15, judgement being given on 14 Dec 15 by Mr Justice Guerin.
6 Signed photos of Duke & Duchess, a souvenir of the visit, are owned by the Stephens' granddaughter, Lady Stirling.
7 Duchess of Connaught's diary quoted in Hubbard, *Rideau Hall* p 132
8 Press reports of divorce case in Ottawa 1916.
9 Her niece, Lady Stirling, in conversation with author.

Chapter 7

1 6th Montreal Field Brigade and 72nd (Vancouver) Regiment
2 From Military Secretary
3 The association of Princess Patricia with the new regiment was formalized by an exchange of letters on 9 August. Gault wrote to her from the Rideau Club in Ottawa:

> 'I am writing to ask your Royal Highness if, in the event of a contingent of five hundred men being raised and sent forward with the least possible delay under the command of Colonel Farquhar, you would honour the regiment by allowing it to be called after you – Princess Patricia's (Canadian) Light Infantry.
>
> 'It would be the greatest incentive to us all to be permitted to carry your name to the front, and would afford the greatest pride to the regiment to feel that it had the sympathy and support of Your Royal Highness.'

To which, she replied:

> 'My parents have readily acceded to your request that the regiment so generously being raised by you should be called after me. I am pleased and proud indeed to be associated with it in this way, and to

think that your corps will bear my name; and I wish to one and all in it the greatest success in their service for the Empire.

'I need hardly say with what deep interest I shall always follow the progress of the regiment.'

4 7 Aug 14

5 Gault. In 1921, Sir Eugene Fiset, the Deputy Minister of Militia and Defence, informed Gault that his $100,000 had been deposited to the credit of the Receiver General as a lump sum; there was no detailed accounting for its expenditure. PPCLI had been equipped to the ordinary scales for CEF units. The value of clothing, arming and equipping the regiment in Canada amounted to $154,480.07. On its departure for overseas, it had returned to Ordnance, stores and equipment (mainly tentage, camp equipment, training weapons and ammunition) worth $55,436.51. The net cost of equipping the Patricias was $99,043.56. (DEOS 1358–2 of 21 Jul 20).

6 Hodder-Williams p 8

7 As a sergeant, he was killed near Tilloy on 28 Sep 18

8 Pipe Major J. Colville to Colonel Farquhar. Hodder-Williams p 8

9 Papineau. Quoted in letter from Talbot Papineau to his mother 10 Sep 14

10 Ware. Notes prepared by Lady Patricia Ramsay 27 Jul 63 for CBC broadcast

11 Gault. Guy Ogilvy to AHG 15 Sep 14

12 Marsden was the first man officially enlisted in Canada. Winner of the DCM in South Africa, he was later commissioned in the 38th Bn. CEF in England, won the MC and as a captain served with the Canadian Siberian Expeditionary Force

13 PPCLI Archives. W.H. Marsden to Major D.O. Kearns 15 Mar 62.

14 In England, these were seen by the Guards who designed similar ones of their own. In the 1939–45 war, they were adopted by all regiments and corps of the Canadian, British and other Commonwealth armies.

15 15 Sep 14.

16 Adamson 12 Oct 14.

17 AHG to Campbell 4 Nov 14 and AP, Mabel Adamson to her mother, 10 Nov 14 .

18 PPCLI Archives. W.H. Roffey to Bastedo 19 May 64.

19 War Diary PPCLI – marching out state.

20 Hutchinson, *Five Strenuous Years*, p 24.

21 PPCLI Archives. W.H. Roffey to Bastedo 19 May 64.

Chapter 8

1 PPCLI Archives, St Eloi file. To his wife, 11 Jan 15.
2 ibid
3 McKinery returned to Canada where he was promoted to command the 66th Infantry Battalion which he brought to England. It was broken up for reinforcements. He was sent to France in 1917 to command the 4th Labour Battalion. In November of that year he was awarded a DSO of dubious provenance for keeping a light railway operating under shellfire. In the Second World War he became a major-general on the staff in South Africa and was known to claim that he founded and led PPCLI in the First World War.
4 9 Feb 15
5 11 Feb 15
6 20 Feb 15
7 PPCLI Archives. Stanley Jones letter to his wife 11 Jan 15
8 PPCLI Archives. R. Richards, former Private, 'Story of the PPCLI'
9 Papineau. 3 Mar 15
10 Adamson 3 Mar 15
11 Adamson 4 Mar 15
12 Court Circular 27 Mar 15.
13 AHG to Buller 7 Apr 15
14 Wigram to AHG 8 Apr 15
15 *Montreal Gazette* 8 May 15
16 Gault. 13 Apr 15
17 Hodder-Williams p 55
18 PPCLI Archives. Pte J.E. Brice personal account 18 May 64
19 Major Gault, three Captains (Adamson, Hill and Dennison) and ten Lieutenants
20 Edmonds 1915, p 317
21 Two battles took place in 1915 on the Ridge which lies between Bellewaerde Lake and the village of Frezenberg. The first, in which Gault took part, known officially as the Battle of Frezenberg Ridge, was fought between 8 and 13 May, the second, the Battle of Bellewaerde Ridge began and ended on 24 May and marked the end of the 'Battles of Ypres 1915'
22 Hodder-Williams p 60
23 ibid p 62
24 PPCLI Archives. Niven papers
25 PPCLI Archives. Note on service in PPCLI by Pte H.G. Hetherington, later Lt Col in British Army.

26 PPCLI Archives. Niven papers -Letter to J.W. McLaren 28 May 65
27 Reproduced in *Montreal Gazette* May 1915
28 Hodder-Williams p 76
29 Adamson. 8 May 15
30 AHG Service records

Chapter 9

1 *Montreal Gazette* 8 May 15
2 Lady (Marguerite) Stirling interview with author 16 Apr 91
3 PPCLI Archives. Letter from B.F. Bainsmith 8 Sep 80
4 Adamson. 14 Jul 16
5 NARC RGIII, Vol 4705 folder 84, file 8
6 Letter Buller to AHG 13 Apr 15
7 Gault.
8 Papineau. 31 Oct 15
9 Adamson. 31 Oct 15
10 Hodder-Williams. p 88
11 ibid p 90
12 PPCLI Archives. *Tales of the Trenches 1915–1918* by P. Howard Ferguson, MM
13 Hodder-Williams. p 90 footnote
14 Stevens, *A City Goes to War*, p 32
15 Adamson. 10 Nov 15
16 Adamson. 15 Nov 15
17 Papineau. 30 Jan 16
18 PPCLI War Diary
19 Adamson 14 Feb 16. Lieut. & Paymaster G.H. Bennett Aug 1914 to 26 Jul 1915.
20 *Montreal Herald* 18 Mar 16
21 The Law Clerk of the Senate informed the author that all such records dated earlier than 1930 have been destroyed. The National Archives of Canada confirmed this. The Senate, unlike government departments, is not obliged to preserve records in NARC.
22 Montreal *Daily Star* 16 Mar 16

Chapter 10

1 To fill an urgent need for officers for Tunnelling Companies of the Royal Engineers, a British general asked a regimental parade of the

Patricias if any were qualified as mining engineers. Seventy stepped forward.

2 *London Gazette* No. 29275 of 25 Aug 15
3 Hodder-Williams p 103
4 PPCLI Archives. Sgt F.J. Kendall narrative.
5 PPCLI Archives. Unpublished manuscript, *Pawn No. 883* by Walter M. Draycot p 91
6 AHG to Campbell,17 Apr 16
7 Draycot p 92
8 Kendall narrative.
9 AHG to Campbell 23 Apr 16
10 Hodder-Williams p 106
11 Author's papers. Buller to Lady Evelyn Farquhar 23 May 16
12 Deutelmoser, Adolf, *The 27th Infantry Division in the World War 1914–18*, p 39
13 Hodder-Williams p 124
14 To the Mayor of Taunton, Somerset, 15 Feb 63
15 He turned up later commanding a corps at the battle of Cambrai, 1917.
16 PPCLI Archives. To W.E. Bastedo 17 Apr 64
17 Letter from Leslie Hamilton Gault to Henry Gault 15 Jun 16

Chapter 11

1 AHG military records and AP,13 Jun 16
2 Letter from Leslie Hamilton Gault to Henry Gault 15 Jun 16
3 Gault. 11 Jun 16
4 Gault. 24 Jun 16
5 Independent Order of the Daughters of the Empire
6 Gault contributed to the family endowment of The GORDON HOME BLACKADER MEMORIAL LIBRARY of architecture at McGill University, in his memory
7 Adamson. 14 Jul 16
8 19 Aug 16
9 dated 10 Oct 16 NARC, Borden Papers, M.G. 26, HQ (a), Volume 77, p 39659
10 Adamson. 5 Dec 16
11 5 Jan 16
12 Gault. ref letter AHG to Adamson 27 Jan 17
13 Hutchinson, pp 142–3
14 Gault. Press report and letter from Col Paul Hutchinson to DB Gault 14 Dec 58

15 Gault. Letter from W.D. Lighthall, 15 Feb 17 and draft constitution.
16 Journals of the Senate of Canada, Seventh Session, Twelfth Parliament 1917, Vol LIII.
17 Adamson. 17 Mar 17
18 Gault. 26 May 17

Chapter 12

1 PPCLI Archives. *A Memory of Hammy Gault* by P.M. Armishaw
2 Adamson. 24 Jun 17
3 PPCLI Archives. Narrative by Col. GR Stephens
4 Adamson. 26 Jun 17
5 Adamson. 14 and 30 May 17. In 1917, Princess Patricia also designed their 'bugle' collar badges and their buttons.
6 The 'Marguerite' is still to be found on the Patricias' full dress belt buckles.
7 Adamson. 4 Jul 17
8 Papineau. 5 Jul 17
9 Adamson. 8 Jul 17
10 11 Jul 17
11 Papineau. 10 Jul 17
12 PPCLI Archives. *A Runner's Memories of Tilloy*, A.M. Francis, MSM
13 Papineau. 10 Sep 17
14 Papineau. 18 Sep 17
15 Papineau. 28 Sep 17
16 PPCLI War Diary
17 Obituary in *Red Hackle*, April 1959
18 Adamson. 29 May 18
19 Adamson. 6 Jun 18
20 Adamson. From HQ 20 Div BEF. 8 Apr 18
21 *London Gazette* 30739 of 11 Jun 18
22 Adamson. 21 Jun 18
23 Adamson. 22 Jun 18
24 PPCLI Archives. *Tales of the Trenches 1915–1918* by P. Howard Ferguson, MM
25 PPCLI Archives. Eric Knight to AHG 2 Jul 39
26 Gault. Letter to Lt-Col C.M. Hore-Ruthven, GSO1 3 Cdn Div, 9 Sep 18
27 Gault. Dyer 20 Sep 18
28 Gault. quoted by Dyer 4 Dec 24

29 PPCLI Archives. Letter A.G. Pearson 1 Jul 65
30 Adamson. 16 Oct 18
31 16 Oct 18
32 Adamson. 18 Feb 19

Chapter 13

1 Hodder-Williams, p 401
2 PPCLI Archives. Bastedo papers.
3 PPCLI veterans in conversation, CBC film, *Comrades in Arms*, 4 Aug 82
4 PPCLI Archives. *Tales of the Trenches 1915–1918* by P. Howard Ferguson, MM
5 PPCLI Archives. Eric Knight to AHG 2 Jul 39
6 Nicholson, p 530
7 PPCLI Archives. Narrative by Bernard Warner
8 PPCLI Archives. Eric Knight to AHG 2 Jul 39. Knight was author of, among others, the stories of *Sam Small*, *The Flying Yorkshireman*, of *Lassie*, of *This Above All*, and of *A Short Guide to Britain*, issued to all American servicemen arriving there in the Second World War. As a colonel in the US Army, he was killed whilst en route to the Casablanca Conference in 1943.
9 Hodder-Williams p 405
10 ibid p 407
11 Ware. Niven to Ware 11 Apr 63
12 *The Border Cities Star* 11 Nov 24
13 Gault. Memorandum by Major-General J. Sutherland-Brown 26 May 19 quoted in letter of 21 Mar 47 to AHG from Col P.E. Belanger.
14 Adamson. 21 May 19
15 *London Gazette* No. 31370, 3 Jun 19

Chapter 14

1 Gault. Letter WB Ross to Gordon McDougall, 18 Mar 20
2 AHG to William Blackader 12 Nov 20. *Somerset County Gazette and West Somerset Free Press* both of 13 Nov 20. Interview Patricia McCarthy, 28 Jan 93
3 Gault. Dorothy Gault letter 13 Oct 21
4 Interview Patricia McCarthy 28 Jan 93
5 Gault. 16 Dec 21
6 Gault. 18 Dec 21

7 Gault. Harry F.B. Shuckburgh to AHG 21 Jan 22
8 Gault. Hutchinson to Dorothy Gault 14 Dec 58

Chapter 15

1 AHG to Beaverbrook 9 Mar 30
2 Henry Hopkinson Tory MP for Taunton 1950–56 never went to Rockwell Green without a police escort – Sir Edward Du Cann to author 20 Oct 93.
3 'EVE', *The Lady's Pictorial* 5 Dec 23
4 *The Times* 8 Dec 23
5 AHG from Dorothy 12 Aug 24
6 16 Nov 24
7 *Canada*, London & Montreal, 8 Nov 24
8 *Herald* 27 Jun 25

Chapter 16

1 Gault. Joint opinion – John Simon and Norman Bucknill 28 Feb 22 supported by W.F. Chipman, 11 Mar 21, N.G. Guthrie, 12 Mar 20 and Hon. W.B. Ross, 18 Mar 20
2 AHG from Falchi 22 May 28
3 Gault. Letter M. Falchi to AHG 15 Sep 28
4 Frankland p 372. The widowed Duke of Connaught admitted to Leonie Leslie, his close friend and confidante that, had she been free, he might have wished to marry Ethel McGibbon with whom he and the Duchess had been friends since they met in Montreal.
5 Gault. 27 Dec 1928
6 Conversation with author, 1973.
7 1 Sep 31

Chapter 17

1 AHG to Lt Col M.R. Ten Broeke 27 Nov 29
2 On 31 March 1930, there were 209 privately owned aircraft in Britain.
3 Interview Patricia McCarthy 29 Jan 90
4 Told to author by Dorothy Gault 1971
5 AHG from Baxter 21 Oct 29
6 AHG to Beaverbrook 31 Oct 29
7 At Taunton, reported in the *Daily Express* 12 Nov 29
8 Sir James Dunn and Andrew Holt of the Royal Bank of Canada.

9 AHG to Beaverbrook 21 Feb 30
10 Chisholm & Davie, *Beaverbrook, a Life,* pp 280–306
11 To Taunton Conservative Association 28 Feb 31
12 *Daily Herald* 18 Sep 31
13 AHG to Niven 24 Nov 31
14 *Illustrated London News* 28 Mar 31
15 *Air* April 1931
16 *Somerset County Gazette* 30 May 31
17 *The Times* 13 May 32
18 AHG to Vanier 21 May 32
19 16 May 33
20 *The Times* 16 May 33
21 Told to author by Dorothy Gault 1971

Chapter 18

1 The future 'father' of the Royal Canadian Armoured Corps
2 Gault. 4 Feb. 32
3 *Somerset County Gazette* 11 Feb 33
4 Conversation with Dorothy Gault 1971
5 *The Times* 10 Jun 33
6 From, *Blood & Banquets* p 111.
7 AHG to the Taunton Mayoral Banquet 11 Nov 33. *Taunton Courier* 15 Nov 33
8 *The Times* 1 Mar 34
9 *Somerset County Herald* 3 Mar 34
10 *The Times* 10 Feb 34
11 Speech to the Taunton Divisional Council of the Junior Imperial League 11 May reported in *The Times* 14 May 34 and the *Taunton Courier* 16 May 34
12 *Daily Telegraph* 5 Nov 34
13 *Somerset County Gazette* 10 Nov 34.
14 Interview Patricia McCarthy 21 Jan 94
15 Flying log and Interview with Patricia McCarthy 10 and 11 Mar 91
16 In 1929 Balbo was made Air Minister in the Italian government. He quickly raised their air force from mediocrity to the point where it stood comparison at the time with any other in Europe. In 1933 Mussolini who was jealous of Balbo's success and popularity, took over the Air Ministry himself and sent Balbo into splendid exile as Governor-General of Libya. In 1940, Balbo was killed at Tobruk in an air crash, Italy claiming he had fallen in action against the RAF. The British

Foreign Office denied it and rumour had it that he was shot down on orders of Mussolini.

Chapter 19

1 Interview Mary Cunningham 1 Sep 90
2 Jasper Durman was chauffeur at Hatch Court for fifty years. His father had been coachman to Dorothy Gault's uncle, WH Lloyd for 20 years.
3 Interview Mary Cunningham 1 Sep 90
4 Interview Patricia McCarthy 10/11 Mar 91
5 Mrs. F.N. Ritchie (Percival Molson Mackenzie) to author 29 Jan 92.
6 Williams, *Princess Patricia's Canadian Light Infantry* p 37
7 29 March 39
8 To her niece, Anne Sykes 26 Jun 39

Chapter 20

1 Interview Marie Barnett 9 Apr 90
2 *Observer* 7 Jan 40
3 AHG from Dorothy written on train returning to Hatch 15 Sep 40.

Chapter 21

1 Gault. Sir Edwin Leather's address at Dorothy Gault's funeral, St. Mary's Church, Taunton, 25 Nov. 72
2 Mrs. David Howes (formerly Eileen Corkett) to author15 Apr 91. George Corkett was killed in Italy in 1944.
3 Lady (Sheila) Knutsford to author 19 Jan 91
4 This sorry incident is covered in detail in Sydney Frost's excellent *Once A Patricia* p 531 et seq.
5 Ware.
6 ibid
7 ibid
8 Hamlet, Act 1, Scene 3, line 75

Chapter 22

1 2 July 45
2 Ware.
3 ibid
4 ibid

5 Ware. address to young officers PPCLI 1978
6 Interview Patricia McCarthy 28 Jan. 93
7 Letter to Ware, 6 Jan. 62
8 Interview Brigadier Rowan Coleman, 12 Oct. 90
9 *Montreal Gazette* 30 May 45
10 *Montreal Gazette* 14 Dec 49
11 19 Sep 51
12 June 1951
13 Ware. 4 Dec. 57
14 Fraser, *McGill University, Vol ii*, 1895 – 1971, p 328
15 Ware. 21 Sep 58

INDEX

Where appropriate, relationship to Hamilton Gault is indicated in brackets. Page number followed by n indicates note.